KU-211-813

School of
HEALTH
&
SOCIAL
WELFARE

K100
Understanding Health and
Social Care

Block 5
When Care Goes Wrong

[. . .]
Learning Resource Centre

ACCN NO:
00709456

SUPPLIER:
Open Univ.

CLASSMARK:
362.1 OPE

COST:

LOCATION:
Loan

DATE RECEIVED:
03/00

The Open University, Walton Hall, Milton Keynes MK7 6AA

First published 1998. Second edition 1999. Third edition 2003. Fourth edition 2004.

Copyright © 1999 The Open University

All rights reserved; no part of this publication may be reproduced, stored in a retrieval system, transmitted, or utilised in any form or by any means, electronic, mechanical, photocopying, recording or otherwise, without written permission from the publisher or a licence from the Copyright Licensing Agency Ltd. Details of such licences (for reprographic reproduction) may be obtained from the Copyright Licensing Agency Ltd of 90 Tottenham Court Road, London W1P 0LP.

Designed, edited and typeset by The Open University

Printed and bound in the United Kingdom by The Charlesworth Group, Huddersfield

ISBN 0 7492 6853 0

For information on Open University courses and study packs write to the Information Assistant, School of Health and Social Welfare, The Open University, Walton Hall, Milton Keynes MK7 6YY, phone 01908 653743, or visit www.open.ac.uk/shsw

4.1

68233/k100b5u18i4.1

K100 Course Team

Original production team

Andrew Northedge (Chair)
Jan Walmsley (Deputy Chair)
Margaret Allott (Course Manager)
Tanya Hames (Course Secretary)
Joanna Bornat
Hilary Brown
Celia Davies
Roger Gomm
Sheila Peace
Martin Robb
Deborah Cooper (VQ Centre)

Jill Alger, Julie Fletcher (Editors); Janis Gilbert (Graphic Artist); Hannah Brunt, Rob Williams (Designers); Paul Smith (Librarian); Deborah Bywater (Project Control Assistant); Ann Carter (Print Buying Controller); Pam Berry (Text Processing Services); Mike Levers (Photographer); Vic Lockwood, Alison Tucker, Kathy Wilson (BBC Producers); Maggie Guillon (Cartoonist)

Staff tutors

Lindsay Brigham
Anne Fletcher
Carole Ulanowsky

External assessor

Professor Lesley Doyal, University of Bristol.

This is the K100 core course team. Many other people also contributed to making the course and their names are given in the Introduction and Study Guide.

Revision team (2002)

Andrew Northedge (Chair)
Corinne Pennifold (Course Manager)
Christine Wild (Course Team Assistant)
James Blewett
Joanna Bornat
Hilary Brown
Sue Cusworth
Celia Davies
Marion Dunlop
Pam Foley
Tom Heller
Vijay Patel
Sheila Peace
Lucy Rai
Marion Reichart
Angela Russell
Geraldine Lee-Treweek
Danielle Turney
Jan Walmsley
Jo Warner

Hannah Brunt (Designer), Deborah Bywater (Project Control), Maggie Guillon (Cartoonist), Sarah Hack (Graphic Artist), Lucy Hendy (Compositor), Julie Fletcher, Denise Lulham (Editors)

Critical readers

Fiona Harkes, Sylvia Cavenay, Gillian Thompson, Katy Sainsbury, Eunice Lumsden, Lynne Fisher, Margaret Brown, Paula Fuller, Kate Stilliard

External reviewers

Professor Gordon Grant, University of Sheffield; Mary McColgan, University of Ulster; Nigel Porter, University of Portsmouth

External assessor

Professor Gordon Grant, University of Sheffield

Contents

Study skills by Andrew Northedge

Introduction

This block looks at some difficult issues in care work, when there may be conflicting views about what to do for the best and uncomfortable feelings to resolve. The block focuses on three main areas.

Unit 18 looks at times when caring presents real dilemmas and difficult decisions, especially in residential settings.

Unit 19 focuses more on personal relationships and on how to draw the line between ordinary upsets and conflicts and real abuses of power.

Unit 20 uses a case study where there are concerns about the mental health of a woman following the birth of her first child to explore issues of power and vulnerability in care relationships.

Unit 21 builds on these three themes and explores how to put skills for dealing with risk and abuse into practice.

Some key issues from earlier in the course will be revisited, such as boundaries and roles, accountability and taboos around intimate care. You will also look at the organisational context within which decisions are made and practice evolves. The context includes attitudes and views held in society as a whole about our bodies, about sex and sexuality, race and ethnicity, punishment and abuse. We also have to consider not only what we believe to be right but what power people have to do anything; hence we also explore aspects of the legal framework within which the caring professions operate.

The block starts by looking at difficult areas of intimate care, control and protection and at the basis on which decisions are made in these areas. It then goes on to consider what is labelled 'abuse' and what can be done to act on behalf of people who are vulnerable or unable to protect themselves. Some of the images in the block are disturbing, but then some of the work of caring is disturbing. What this material does is to put into words things which are often dealt with by being left unsaid.

Unit 18
Difficult Decisions

Prepared for the course team by Hilary Brown

Updated by Jo Warner

While you are working on Unit 18, you will need:

- Course Reader
- Offprints Book
- *The Good Study Guide*
- Audio Cassette 5, side 1, parts 1 and 2
- Wallchart

Contents

Introduction

In this unit we are going to look at a number of situations which put a strain on the idea that caring is just an extension of 'being ordinary'. These include times when people are giving intimate care and situations when *control* as well as *care* has to be exercised. In these special circumstances, since the normal rules do not apply, we have to develop a set of special rules to guide practice, thinking very carefully about these core questions:

Core questions

- How can boundaries be respected in situations where intimate care is being given?

- In what situations and with what safeguards are services entitled to apply sanctions or restrain someone to stop them harming themselves or another person?

- How can choices, rights and autonomy be balanced against the need to protect people in receipt of care who put themselves at risk of harm?

- When and how can systems become abusive?

The unit has four sections which focus on care, control, protection and institutions. The examples given are mostly based on the experiences of young people and adults with learning difficulties but they raise issues which apply equally to other people receiving care. The main thread is how to make decisions when care goes beyond normal social relationships and into uncharted waters.

One guiding principle of the unit is that people need safeguards once others start doing things to (or for) them which most people would not expect to have done. This is particularly so for people who are too dependent to act as partners in care relationships. Anyone cast in the role of a 'do-gooder' has considerable licence to overstep boundaries. Sobsey argues that disabled people sometimes have fewer rights than criminals:

> *Because caregivers are seen as helping people with disabilities, they are allowed to do things that would not otherwise be permitted. For example, people who are convicted criminals cannot be incarcerated indefinitely, are allowed to make an appeal and speak in their own defence: cannot have food, fluids or required medical care withheld; and cannot be placed on aversive behaviour management programmes or given psychoactive medications against their will because these things violate their rights. People with disabilities do not receive the same protection, however, because they are thought to be 'helped not punished' by these interventions.*

> *(Sobsey, 1994, p. 142)*

Under the guise of helping, a great deal of cajoling, guidance and controlling goes on, some of it quite appropriately – *some* of the people receiving care, at *some* points in their lives, may benefit from these things. But at other times services fail to be aware of the control they exert, and the lack of independent channels for challenging service decisions or actions leaves people who use services very vulnerable.

Crossing boundaries: a case study

The first core question is 'how can boundaries be respected in situations where intimate care is being given?' This will be explored through a fictional case study set in a residential unit for young people with learning (and some associated physical and sensory) difficulties. The story is fictional in the sense that I have made the characters up and put all the separate strands together but the setting is based on a real establishment and each incident or situation is based on a real event or on the experience of someone known to me through my work or personal life. The fact that it is presented as a story (like the Jim and Marianne case study in Unit 10) does not make it any less real, it merely provides anonymity for the people and services involved.

The first character you will meet is Marie, a new care assistant. In Unit 19 you will meet her neighbour Pat, who has a sister-in-law Bernice who works in a playgroup; in Unit 20 Jenny, Geoff and their daughter Abby take over the story.

Marie

Marie is a young white woman who has recently started work at a residential unit for young people with physical and learning disabilities run by a local charity. She trained as an NNEB nurse at her local college after leaving school but did one of her placements at a day nursery which included children with learning difficulties and really enjoyed it. She was very thrilled to get this job: it is local and she can easily get there on the bus even for the early morning shift. It doesn't pay very well but it is better than being a private nanny or babysitter and she really looked forward to getting her first proper pay packet. Marie lives at home: she has been going out with her boyfriend Barry for two years and is saving up to get engaged.

Before the interview Marie was sent a prospectus about the unit, which described how it had been set up to help young people who had left

special schools to make the transition to adult living. There was also a special needs unit for people with more severe learning difficulties. The brochure said:

> We have a commitment to treating the residents here like any other young people. We provide opportunities for them to reach adulthood by making their own choices and by treating them as normal young adults would expect to be treated.

Marie was at a bit of a disadvantage in the interview because her previous experience had been with younger children. The interviewers asked her about her training and said that it would be important to treat the young people as adults and not as children. They said they were looking for someone who could act 'more like a friend than a parent'. Marie latched on to what they were saying and said she thought she could do that because she always prided herself on treating children with respect and not in a babyish way.

The head of care also asked Marie about care plans and she was able to talk about the system used at the nursery for recording what each child liked and needed during the day, such as if they had a special diet or needed a nap at a certain time, and so on. She talked about her work with Tom, a boy with Down's syndrome in whom she had taken a special interest, and how they had been working on helping him to learn new words by noticing toys he liked to play with and getting him to ask for them.

The head of care was impressed with Marie's maturity and enthusiasm and as she had a good reference from her college and from the nursery, they offered her the job. She started on the Monday after she finished college but was invited to come up for a couple of hours on Friday evening to see round the unit and to meet her 'shift', especially Joan, who was the senior care officer who would be showing her the ropes. Joan introduced her to Richard and Rachel as she was to be keyworker for them both and would be getting to know them better than the other residents.

For the first week she was to be on day duty, which involved getting people up and ready for breakfast and then helping them into the dining-room. Understandably, she was nervous on her first day but she got there on time and worked with another member of staff to help Rachel get dressed. Rachel needed a lot of help and Marie realised as they were having breakfast that she did not know how to feed someone who needed this amount of support. She looked round for help but there was no one near who wasn't busy so she 'owned up' to Rachel, who grinned. When Marie put the food in too quickly Rachel spat it out, but gradually Marie found the right speed and relaxed and they began to get on well.

The second day began in the same way except that Marie was to get Richard up first as Rachel was having a lie in. Richard had his own room and Marie knocked and went in. Joan had said Richard was a 'total care' but Marie wasn't quite sure what that meant. She had met him briefly the day before and knew he liked to play on his computer using a probe he wore around his forehead, but she felt a bit shy of barging into his room and didn't really know where to start. She had been told that he could move from the bed to his wheelchair but would otherwise need help with dressing and toileting.

When Marie went to help Richard get up it was obvious that he had an erection. She didn't know what to do: she didn't want to embarrass him but she couldn't help blushing. She wondered if she should go out of the room or go to find Joan, but if she did find her Joan would be busy and also Marie didn't know what she would say, so she decided to stay and just turn away for a bit. Eventually she took Richard to the bathroom. By this stage she was confused as well as embarrassed. She realised that Richard was going to need help to go to the loo and saw the urinal bottles on the shelf. Since he could not use his hands she had to put his penis into the bottle and keep it there while he peed. Then she took him back to his room and helped him to wash his face and get dressed.

Marie had never seen a man's penis before: although she was going steady with Barry, they had decided to wait until they were married before they had sex, which was in keeping with their religious beliefs. She felt upset that she had not realised this would be involved in the job and when she got home she thought it best not to say anything in case Barry or her parents misunderstood. She thought Barry might tell her she should leave the job so she kept it to herself. All the other women at the centre just seemed to get on with it and she didn't want to make a fuss. When her friends asked her about her new job she talked about her trouble feeding Rachel and about her time in the art room.

If Marie had got a job in a bank or a shop she would not have been expected to take a young man of her own age to the toilet, or to see him naked. Everyone acted as if it was the most 'normal' thing in the world, but it wasn't normal in Marie's world. Over the next few months Marie came to see it as normal too: when her friend Debbie came to work at the unit after Christmas, Marie forgot to tell her what she was letting herself in for.

Section 1
Care

1.1 The strains of intimate care

As you read in Block 1, intimate care involves stepping over people's usual boundaries. It takes us out of familiar territory in terms of how we relate to each other. It necessitates *breaking* the usual rules about how to behave in order to attend to bodily functions which we normally take a lot of trouble to keep private, and this 'secrecy' extends to the work itself. A key issue in Marie's story is the assumption that this area of the work does not need to be mentioned.

Activity 1

Allow about 15 minutes

A better induction for Marie?

Consider the information you have about how Marie was introduced to the work. Then make your own notes on the following questions.

(a) What could have been done differently in the interview or during Marie's first few days?

(b) How could the subject have been brought up in a way which would have made Marie's introduction to the work easier and would have acknowledged that it was a difficult position to be in?

(b) How do you imagine Marie's inexperience and the way in which she had been introduced to care work affected Richard's experience of being cared for?

Once you have done this, jot down a short statement which the head of care could have made at the end of the interview to prepare Marie for this aspect of the work. What needs to be said? How can the subject be broached in a way which leaves it open for Marie to come back if she has any problems?

Comment

For the statement I imagined something like this:

> *You will find that the work requires you to undertake some very intimate tasks, like taking a young man to the toilet, washing parts of the body – his penis, his testicles – which most people keep private. It may worry you at first. If we appoint you, I'll make sure I'm on hand when you start work, and at the end of your shift for the first week, so that you can raise any questions you might have, and ask for advice. Managing feelings about intimate care is an important part of the job. You need to feel comfortable with it, and so do the residents, who may also feel quite sensitive about it. These young people may have disabilities, but they are also men and women, and their feelings about their bodies need to be respected.*

Now look back over Marie's story and over what you have scripted for the head of care to say to her. Did you imagine that the head of care was a woman or a man? How did this affect the way he or she spoke to Marie and what it was appropriate for him or her to say? Would it have made a difference if Marie had been an older woman do you think? Personally, I found it easier to imagine a female head of care making the statement I scripted than a male.

It might also have been different if Marie had been a young man. It is possible that if *she* was a *he*, he would not have been expected to dress or toilet a woman. As we have seen in Block 1, women are expected to know how to do care work because of their previous experience in the private sphere of the family, whereas there tends to be a different set of beliefs about men doing caring work. Sometimes this includes fears that they might be less sensitive, or even abusive. In establishments like this one, men tend to do less of the actual caring work and more administration or management. These concerns help to justify this division of labour. The 'taboo' around male carers also means that service users themselves might choose not to be cared for in intimate ways by a man.

So we can see a number of factors at work in Marie's story:

- First, there is the issue that an important part of the work she is being expected to do has been left unspoken. It is 'taken for granted', silent and invisible. In turn this has the effect that Marie does not feel able to ask for help and actively colludes in keeping the silence around it by not telling her boyfriend or family, and by not passing on her experience to her friend who later joins her in the work. Marie learns that what is expected of her is to do the work without commenting on it.

- Second, Marie doesn't know *how* to do this aspect of the work in a sensitive way, without embarrassing Richard or making him feel awkward. She has to manage this part of the work so that she can also relate to Richard as his keyworker – and she hardly knows him!

- Third, we can see that this aspect of the work has something to do with gender because the rules are different according to whether the people concerned are male or female. Because Marie is a woman it is as if she is expected to know how to do these tasks without being told: because it is 'women's work'.

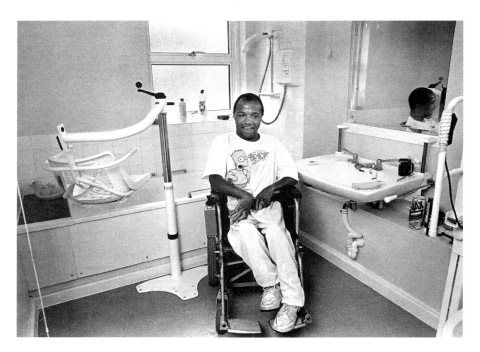

The normally private space of the bathroom becomes one in which the intimate work of caring takes place

- Lastly, we can see that the issue of intimate care cuts across the formal culture of the workplace. Marie is given information about what her job entails in a formal interview. This may have been conducted according to agreed rules designed, for example, to ensure equal opportunities. There is a job description which sets out the main requirements of the job (but which doesn't include taking people to the toilet) and a person specification (which doesn't say anything about it either). The personnel officer has not deliberately missed out these aspects of the work, but consigned them to a different space. They are part of a private sphere even within the workplace, not part of the publicly acknowledged aspects of the job. Marie does not get induction, instruction or supervision in how to do them, and they are not part of the management relationship. Especially if her manager is a man, Marie will not expect him to go into detail about how this part of her work should be performed, whereas for other parts of her job, such as how to fill in a care plan or draw up a teaching programme, he may show her what to do or assess her competence and give her feedback on how well she is doing.

It is almost as if Marie has taken on two jobs, one which is publicly acknowledged and accounted for (her professional role) and the other which takes place behind the scenes, which she has to manage privately. This sometimes causes problems as it did, for example, in Marie's third week in the job when she was told off by her manager because she was late for a meeting with Richard's social worker and speech therapist. The reason for her delay was that she was helping to clean someone up after an 'accident' in the toilet. Marie's workload is often discussed as if these private elements of it do not take up any space or time. Actually they have to take priority over the written and administrative functions but that is not openly acknowledged. Writing about nursing, Lawler (whose work you came across in Unit 4) comments that:

> *Nursing involves not only doing things which are traditionally assigned to females, and learning to do them by experience and practice, but also crossing social boundaries, breaking taboos and doing things for people which they would normally do for themselves in private if they were able.*

(Lawler, 1991, p. 30)

Key points

- Intimate care is not 'ordinary'. It presents a very unusual set of dilemmas for both the carer and the person cared for.

- Despite how 'extra-ordinary' such tasks are, care workers are often expected to be able to do this side of the work 'naturally'.

- Expectations about intimate care and caring are different for men and women staff and service users.

- Although care establishments are largely organised around the need to provide intimate care, this may not be acknowledged in the public face of the service, or reflected in its training, guidance or supervision.

1.2 Silences and concealment

Anthropologists and psychoanalysts use the term 'taboo' to describe forbidden activities, feelings or relationships. All societies seem to have particular rules and rituals to deal with bodily functions, sexuality and death, sometimes expressed in terms of hygiene or religion, and these keep them separated off from everyday life. When social rules function well they are invisible. We only notice them when we have committed a *faux pas* and caused embarrassment. Marie very quickly and correctly learnt the rules in this establishment: from the lack of acknowledgement of this aspect of the job she picked up that it was not an oversight that no one had spoken about it. It was *not to be* spoken about. In another care home down the road a friend of Marie's complained to the proprietor that one of the (male) residents tried to grab her in a sexual way. He told her quite sharply that 'if she couldn't stand the heat she should get out of the kitchen'. In other words, she was being told not to complain and that her only option, if she didn't like it, was to leave. She found she was working in an occupational subculture where only certain things are permitted to be discussed (like the auxiliaries working in Cedar Court whom you met in Unit 4).

This kind of silence tends to be produced when there are hierarchies in which tasks are delegated to some people rather than others. Dealing with intimate care tends to be a low-status task. It is often referred to as 'basic' care as opposed to the more technical tasks within nursing and the planning, educational or therapeutic tasks within residential services. In Unit 4 it was referred to as 'backstage work', following Goffman. Hughes, another sociologist, writing in 1971 coined the term 'dirty work', which is the work within any society or profession which is delegated downwards and/or concealed (Hughes, 1971). Caring for people's bodies could be regarded as the 'dirty work' of care, as well as 'backstage' work.

While nurses are taught procedures for carrying out personal care tasks, they are rarely explicitly 'taught' how to deal with the emotions these tasks occasion. Learning 'on the job' produces a kind of knowledge based on practice rather than theory which is literally difficult to put into words. This helps to keep the work and the skills it involves invisible.

1.3 Women's work

Gender and power play a role in keeping issues like this out of the public arena. One reason for women's comparative silence in our culture is that more of what they do is defined as 'private' or 'personal'. Things they talk about are often downgraded – being deemed unimportant, boring or inappropriate. When large and difficult areas of experience are left out of public discussion we need to ask why. Ignoring the experience of certain groups of people is a way of exercising power over them. It allows their points of view and their needs to slip off the agenda. Women and members of minority ethnic groups have protested against being treated in this way. But it is an experience shared by carers and users of services (Pascall, 1986, p. 30, and Brown and Smith, 1989, p. 108 make this link).

Beyond the fact that women have tasks to do which are defined as not worth discussing, is the fact that women do seem to be given roles in dealing with and containing feelings, and particularly sexual feelings. This is true in care settings and also in other work such as shop work where 'the customer is always right', or in reception where the receptionist is always welcoming and on display. Women workers often have to manage the way they present themselves and control their emotional reactions. This is particularly so in care work, when they are dealing with intimate or intrusive procedures. We introduced the idea of 'emotional labour' (Hochschild, 1983) in Unit 4, Section 6. It is hard work, partly because it is not made explicit or rewarded. In fact, you only see it is part of the expectations of the job if you stop doing it. Hochschild's work was with air hostesses, who have to put on a brave (and usually very well made up) face and be 'nice' to passengers no matter how obnoxious they are back. Similarly, carers have to be open to all the people in their care whether or not they 'like' them or find them easy to look after. If 'the customer is always right', it makes it very difficult to know when you *can* draw the line, for example in relation to sexual or racial harassment from users. If the customer is always right it is often at the expense of women workers.

1.4 Distance and closeness

A lot of emotional labour is concerned with getting the right balance between being close, friendly and warm, and maintaining a proper distance. Lawler writes about learning emotional control by sticking to a set procedure and cultivating an 'air of detachment' (1991, p. 126). In terms of care work it is never quite clear which side to err on – being too cold would be seen as unprofessional, but so is being too familiar. (Remember the dilemmas about drawing boundaries that the home carers in the Unit 3 audio cassette faced?)

Activity 2

Allow about 45 minutes

Learning to manage embarrassing situations

Now read Chapter 26 in the Reader in which Lawler discusses the way nurses learn to manage their embarrassment and the discomfort of their patients. While you are reading, jot down some notes relating each section of the chapter to your own experiences.

Here are some pointers to help you.

- The chapter starts by describing the background of the nurses Lawler interviewed in this study. If you do caring work, either in a paid or unpaid capacity, how do you think your own background has equipped you? Has it helped or made it more difficult for you to be comfortable around other people's bodies and bodily functions? If you need help with intimate care yourself, has this been made more or less embarrassing for you as a result of the way you were brought up?

- The nurses interviewed all have particular stories to tell about their *first* bed-baths, dead bodies and so on. Do you have any particularly vivid experiences like this relating to your own initial experiences of caring or being cared for?

- Have you ever been in hospital or had any intimate procedure carried out like this? Did it help you if you had a sense of the nurse following a set procedure, or would you rather they had asked you how you wanted something done, or how you would have done it yourself? If you are a carer, do you have a routine? Does it help you? Do you think it makes things less embarrassing for other people?

- If you are, or have been, a carer, have you learnt to switch off your emotions or do you sometimes find things harrowing, disgusting or unpleasant? What do you do then? Do you pretend, or do you avoid the person who needs your help? If you are on the receiving end of care, do you like your carer to keep their distance or do you prefer more of the human touch?

* Language is mentioned because that is a particular stumbling block when it comes to discussing bodily functions or sexuality. What kind of vocabulary do you feel most comfortable using at home – or at work? For example, children have their own vocabulary of 'wees' and 'poohs' while other people may use medical terminology.

Comment   You probably came up with some very personal anecdotes in response to this activity. Keep these in mind as we explore why these areas are so difficult.

In the Reader Lawler describes the context in which nurses work as a 'social vacuum'. Care workers like Marie often have even less structure. Their role is not one other people recognise. They may be called something quite vague like a 'support worker' or a 'house companion'. When they are not providing physical care they are supposed to act as a friend or equal to the person they are caring for, which means they have to switch in and out of roles and vary the distance between them as they perform different aspects of their work. They also have to maintain this very responsive personal touch even when they are responsible for looking after a group of people whose needs have to be juggled and balanced.

When people make decisions in this kind of environment there are no clear markers and after a while there is a tendency to forget what the normal rules are. One study on this subject explored how women care staff manage distance around the sexuality of men with learning difficulties. It describes:

> ... how acutely aware some women staff are of the contradictions within their role ... when it comes to performing their caring responsibilities without compounding the risk of sexual harassment from their male clients.
>
> (Thompson et al., 1997, p. 574)

Walking the tightrope between being too distant and too familiar, several women acknowledged the double messages they give out to the men they care for. For example, one woman said she wouldn't be this nice to any other man unless she was going to have a sexual relationship with him. Here we see that the expectations of her role as a carer cut across the way a woman of her age would normally expect to behave with men, leaving her, and her clients, confused. To continue Marie's story, later in the year Richard developed quite a crush on her, which she handled by telling him emphatically about her boyfriend Barry. In Thompson *et al.*'s study this was described as a common strategy and one way of re-establishing distance.

The paper by Thompson *et al.* also considers the organisational context within which much care work takes place: a predominantly female workforce with men occupying management roles. They describe the lack of support from managers and the unspoken expectation that women will *cope with* this aspect of the work, on their own. If a man service user misunderstands, the woman carer is invited to think it is her fault and something she should get right herself, not a function of the situation she has been put in. Even when the sexual behaviour of service users is seriously outside what any other women would expect to deal with at work, it is played down and not taken seriously. The authors comment on:

Women's work?

> ... the differential power which men and women staff hold within their organisations to frame behaviour such as this as a 'problem' rather than to see it subsumed as a routine part of the work.

(*Thompson* et al., *1997, p. 580*)

Steps are currently being taken to try and address some of these issues. The Training Organisation for the Personal Social Services (TOPSS) has now issued guidance for residential social care managers on the induction of new care staff in a publication entitled *The First Six Months* (TOPSS, 2002). This will enable managers to show that they are meeting the new standards that have been set for residential care by the National Care Standards Commission.

We have so far considered the issue of boundaries from the point of view of paid carers. Doing intimate things for someone you *do* know and have an ongoing relationship with can be just as difficult to manage. We saw in Unit 1 that Lynne shied away from taking on intimate care of her father. Oliver (1983) writes about the experiences of wives caring for disabled husbands. She tells how wives are expected to take on the role of carer with little help. Their presence and assumed willingness to care often lead to their husbands being discharged earlier from hospital and sent home with fewer aids or support services than a single person would have, or than a woman being cared for by her male partner. Rather than being treated as a person in her own right, 'the wife' is not able to negotiate what she will and will not do. Oliver writes of one woman who despite being:

> ... extremely distressed by the very intimate tasks she now had to do for her husband, like wiping his bottom, was told by the examining doctor [when she applied for attendance allowance] that what she was doing was 'no more than any wife should'. She broke down completely when the doctor left, and when her husband's application was turned down, forbade him to appeal, in order that she should not be put through such a humiliating ordeal again.

(*Oliver, 1983, p. 77*)

In this case embarrassment had a real financial as well as an emotional cost. Crossing boundaries is also an issue for men who take on the role of 'carer'; for example, a father might find himself coming into contact with his disabled daughter's menstruation in a way other fathers would not. Family members and care workers find themselves being asked to stretch to meet an ideal no matter how pressed they are or how unrealistic the expectations on them.

Key points

- Intimate care is seen as both 'low status' and 'women's work' (not a coincidence).

- 'Emotional labour' is more than just managing emotions. It refers to the work of maintaining at least the fiction of a close, supportive role in a relationship which is not reciprocal.

- Care workers are constantly crossing and rebuilding boundaries: hence the tension between closeness and distance in their relationships with service users.

- The lack of clear boundaries presents problems in relation to sexual behaviour as well as to intimate care.

1.5 Developing agreed ways of working

Although it may be undesirable to cut across the informality of care relationships by making unnecessary rules or regulations, intimate care is clearly one site where things can go wrong. There is a narrow margin of error. The usual social rules and inhibitions have already been broken and it is not always easy to arrive at new ones which are appropriate to the particular context within which you are caring or being cared for. Moreover, receiving or giving care arouses strong feelings which people rarely put into words.

Activity 3

Allow about 10 minutes

Help with going to the toilet

Imagine that you need help to go to the toilet. Perhaps you do receive this kind of assistance, or have done in the past. If so, you will have first-hand knowledge to draw on. Write down three things which your helper could do to ease any embarrassment or discomfort you might feel, and three things which would make the whole situation even worse. Think about who would be helping you in this situation, their gender, their relationship to you, their manner, what they say, their facial expression, and so on.

Comment

You might have included things like:

- what tone you would like them to take with you

- whether you would want them to talk while they were helping you

- whether you would like them to pretend they haven't really noticed what is going on.

Lawler's research identified the following 'scene-defining' strategies (remember Unit 4) employed by doctors and nurses when undertaking intimate care:

- They set up the caring task by making clear that the context is 'medical' rather than social or sexual.

- They use their uniform as 'a barrier'.

- They put on a deliberately matter-of-fact manner.

- They protect the person's privacy by sending other people away or drawing curtains.

- They say things which minimise the awkwardness like 'Oh, it isn't much', 'It isn't that bad', or 'It could have happened to anyone'.

- They change the style, volume and tone of their conversation to create a private atmosphere.

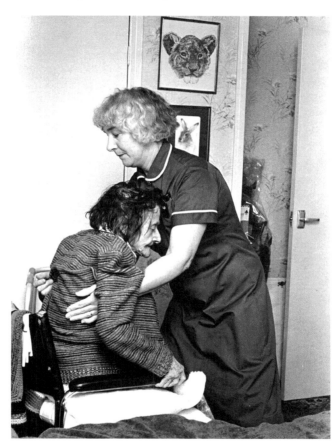

'Intimate' care?

But still nurses have to deal with their own natural reactions especially around smell, which can be particularly difficult to 'stomach'. Here they will develop ways of concentrating on the mechanics of the task, or they may take breaks by going out of the room. One of the nurses Lawler interviewed said she 'hides the horribleness from the patient' (p. 176). It is as if the worker becomes more formal to compensate for the very personal and potentially intrusive nature of the help they are giving. But this might not be appropriate if this help is being given at home or in a homelike setting.

So what can be done to help carers or people being cared for in these situations? One approach is to bring the subject of intimate care 'out of the bathroom', so to speak, and on to the job description. This has benefits for workers and management: it allows this part of the work, its difficulty and delicacy, to be acknowledged, but it also makes managers take back responsibility for how it should be done. Some services have begun to explore just what good practice would mean in these areas as an alternative to waiting until things go wrong and then saying something. For example Eric, who is a colleague of Marie's, always leaves the door open a bit when he takes service users to the toilet: anyone passing by can see that he is in there with someone. The staff are now having a discussion about whether it should be shut and, if so, locked or not. Eric says he is 'covering his back' but some people were saying that Eric is not doing his job properly. He can reasonably say that he does not know what 'properly' means until the staff group make up their minds.

Activity 4

Allow about 10 minutes

Guidelines for intimate care

Imagine you are the head of care at Marie's unit and you are asked to draw up some rules on how to give intimate care which would act as a safeguard for the residents and also for the staff. See if you can sketch out the section on bathing residents.

Comment

Did you think about the following issues in drawing up your 'practice guidance'?

- Who should give baths, what gender, and should there be one person only or two?

- Should doors be shut and locked?

- What exactly does 'bathing' involve? What needs to be washed and how?

- How will help be given? Should staff do the bathing or try to help the residents do it for themselves?

- What *don't* you expect to happen?

Key points

- Workers providing intimate care emphasise the formality of their roles to compensate for the crossing of boundaries.

- It is difficult to hold workers to account for intimate care tasks when no one has spelt out how they want these to be done.

- Agreed procedures provide one 'benchmark' for good practice which can protect service users, staff and workers.

1.6 Unofficial work cultures

The whole issue of bodily care and bodily functions tends to be driven underground and then emerges in jokes or crudeness. Picture this scene, a few months after Marie has started, when she has become more settled within the care team.

It was quite late on a Saturday night and a group of the younger staff were sitting in the staff room waiting for Jenny's boyfriend. He was going to give some of them a lift to the pub and the plan was for them to meet up with friends for a few drinks and then go for a curry. Marie was a bit late because she had been getting Richard ready for bed and he had had an 'accident' so she had to wash him and change his pyjamas. She rushed in after the others had already finished their handover meeting with the night staff. When she came in and mumbled about having to change Richard's pyjamas, Jenny started giggling and said it must have taken ages because he was so 'well hung'. Everybody laughed. If you had played back a video of the scene you would have seen that Marie froze for almost half a minute before she started laughing as well.

Activity 5   **Joking apart ...**

Allow about 10 minutes   What do you think was going through Marie's mind in that 30 seconds? Draw some thought balloons to script what she might have been saying to herself.

Comment   I think Marie might have had quite a struggle because my guess is that she disapproves of this kind of language. She may also have felt disloyal to Richard as a person she respects, and have felt uncomfortable about what could be racist undertones because Richard is black. But perhaps she also found it quite a relief to get some of her feelings out of her system before she went home. Perhaps it helped her to put work, with its peculiar rules and relationships, out of her mind so she could go back to an ordinary Saturday night out with her mates.

My first reaction to Marie and her friends was very disapproving but then I thought that maybe laughing was therapeutic. You have probably heard of 'a Freudian slip'. Although we try constantly to censor what we say, forbidden thoughts and secrets tend to leak out in the form of jokes, mistakes or slips.

Another reaction I had was to think how difficult it would have been for Marie *not* to laugh. Getting on well at work depends on going along with what other people do and fitting into the 'culture' of the place. Different workplaces develop their own jokes and jargon. Perhaps laughing about people's bodies and sexuality is one way Marie and her colleagues 'let off steam' about being exposed to the intimacy of people's bodies.

Isabel Menzies carried Freud's thinking a bit further in a classic piece of work on nursing practice called *The Functioning of Social Systems as a Defence Against Anxiety* (Menzies, 1970). She said that it was not only individuals who have an 'unconscious', but organisations and whole professions. The informal culture (the jokes, the language and also the way jobs are set up) is partly a consequence of the need to be defended from some of the things they are dealing with. For example, if you were an undertaker you couldn't get upset about every individual whose funeral you arranged. For your own sanity you'd have to distance yourself. Probably there are all kinds of 'corpse jokes' which take the sting out of the work.

A nurse I know who works on an oncology ward told me the joke about cancer being safe from 'cut-backs' in her hospital because it was a 'growth area'. Remember the nurse in Reader Chapter 26 who, with her fellow trainee, became 'hysterical with laughter' when she encountered her first death, but who then became 'sad because we hadn't witnessed anything like this before'.

Think back too to Unit 4 and Lee-Treweek's account of the 'bedroom world' at Cedar Court, where the staff made jokes about the patients' impairments which denied their feelings and needs. Was this worse than the episode in Marie's home? At least Richard was not present and aware of what was being said. Or perhaps once you start making jokes you can't draw a neat line which stops you from passing on some of the cruelty to those receiving care?

Key points

- Jokes may be used as a way of 'letting off steam' about the strains of care work.

- Aspects of the work which are not publicly acknowledged tend to get dealt with in the informal culture of the establishment or work group: open supervision or discussion may avoid this.

1.7   Establishing boundaries

Activity 6   **Managing the hidden culture**

Allow about 15 minutes   Imagine now that you are Marie's manager and you decide to call in at the unit on your way back from a day out. You often drop in unannounced to make sure everything is OK and because it is the only chance you get to talk to some of the night staff. You walk in on the joke-telling incident and hear from the corridor what has been said. What do you do?

(a)   Go in and join in the laughter.

(b)   Go in and confront the staff – if so what exactly would you say?

(c)   Turn around and pretend you didn't hear.

(d)   Decide not to challenge the staff now but to put on some staff training at a later date.

Now write a paragraph saying why you decided to tackle it this way. What went through your mind? If you decided not to intervene, think about how much worse it would have to get before you did go in and say something.

Comment   Managers clearly have a role to play in containing these aspects of the work: acknowledging difficult issues, setting agreed limits on how tasks should be approached, and helping individual staff to walk the tightrope of not being too cut off or too close to those they are working with. If Marie's manager joined in, or even initiated the joking, there would be no containment and nothing to stop things getting worse. It is up to the manager, or occasionally inspectors, to set out what is expected and then monitor whether staff keep within agreed boundaries.

Intimate care is an area in which boundaries are almost inevitably crossed but it is by no means the only area in which a spontaneous response can have unforeseen implications. We have talked a lot about the boundaries of care relationships in Units 3 and 4 and again in this unit. Now we look at a real-life attempt at establishing such boundaries. Enfield Social Services (1996) has drawn up guidelines on professional boundaries for a wide range of staff including field social workers and those working in residential care. The guidelines attempt to set markers on a range of issues in professional relationships with children and adults. In particular they cover issues about:

• not taking advantage of clients (e.g. in sexual or financial transactions)

• disclosure of personal information within professional relationships

• expressing affection in worker–client relationships.

Activity 7   **Guidance on professional boundaries**

Allow about 30 minutes   Listen to Audio Cassette 5, side 1, part 1 now. You will hear Vicky Golding, an Area Manager for Enfield Social Services, describing why her department decided to develop these guidelines and talking about some of the controversial areas in the guidelines and what it means to be 'professional'.

As you listen to the tape jot down anything you react strongly to.

 Then look through the guidelines in Offprint 24 and note down which items you agree with and which you would not want to be bound by in your own situation. If you are on the receiving end of care, think about whether you would want this kind of 'professional' relationship with your carer or if you expect them to be more open and personal with you.

Comment   The guidelines in Offprint 24 grew out of two situations in which workers had 'overstepped boundaries' by taking individual children home, but they cover the more general issue of where to set limits in professional relationships in terms of how much personal disclosure and expression of affection is ever appropriate in a professional relationship. The model of professionalism represented here is one which errs on the side of maintaining a certain distance. Did you agree with this, or would you have drawn the line at a different point?

One of the controversial areas is just how much we expect workers to reveal of themselves. The Enfield Social Services guidelines suggest that workers should not reveal much about their personal lives to their clients but this can also create difficulties. For example, Marie told Richard about her boyfriend Barry as one way of re-establishing some distance when he was interpreting their relationship on a more personal level. Another exception might be that a gay worker at Marie's unit might be able to provide a very positive role model to gay or lesbian young people if they were allowed to be open about their sexuality. Vicky Golding drew a distinction between the kind of reciprocal sharing which goes on in a self-help group where one's personal experience would be seen as an asset in the work, and the more anonymous role of a care worker or social worker. Do you agree with this distinction?

Another difficult area addressed in the guidelines is the expression of affection and touch, which would be considered quite normal for children if they were being cared for within their families; kissing and hugging, saying 'I love you' and so on were also singled out as issues in services for older people and people with learning difficulties. It might be different for service users who get affection from other relationships in their lives than for people who are isolated and otherwise deprived of any such contact. What do you think? The guidelines also address the issue of favouritism; for example, if one resident is given gifts or taken out more than others in a group care setting.

Actions are 'graded' in the guidelines so that some are forbidden altogether, such as having sex with a client, others are subject to a manager's discretion and others are up to workers to decide for themselves. Did you find this helpful? Craft and Brown (1994) highlight the importance of guidance which works to 'define the greatest possible leeway within which individual workers and teams can reach their own decisions' (p. 18) and which balance these two functions:

> ... to draw some acceptable boundary around the personal and the professional and to define the boundaries within which individual workers can respond as they think best.

> (Craft and Brown, 1994, p. 18)

If the young male care worker in Unit 3 who led Lynne to imagine he felt genuine affection for her had had access to such guidelines *before* starting work, do you think it might have prevented him from making the mistakes he did?

The open consultation which has taken place in Enfield Social Services goes to the heart of what social and care services are about. Are social workers or care staff there to replicate ordinary relationships, to compensate for a lack of them, or to provide practical help while staying in the background so that people can 'live their own lives'? We saw in Unit 3, Section 5, that disabled people want assistance without strings attached, and that 'care', despite its friendly overtones, can be more of a hindrance than a help. But some clients may rely on professional carers to provide them with affection and social contact which they do not get elsewhere. The answer is bound to vary for different people and different settings, but the process of consulting with a wide range of people and attempting to provide some clarity is an important one for clients, staff and managers.

Vicky Golding emphasised that 'professional boundaries' are important for service users who:

> *are often very vulnerable – they can be needy and boundary-less themselves and open to exploitation by a worker in a powerful position ...*

But she also points out their usefulness as a framework for managers because they:

> *clarify what is acceptable and so where a boundary has been breached, we can actually point to it and use [the guidelines] as a management tool ...*

and for workers:

> *but they are also for protecting the worker, which is really important because workers are vulnerable and don't always realise how they're leaving themselves open.*

This reflects the triangular nature of accountability which you will read more about in Block 6.

Key points

- Managers need to 'contain' difficult areas of care work.
- Boundaries are not only crossed in intimate care but in 'social' settings as well.
- Professional relationships are different from ordinary reciprocal friendships.
- Formal guidance provides a reference point which can protect service users, staff and managers.

Section 2
Control

So far in this unit we have focused on intimate care because it is one arena within which workers find themselves doing things which go well beyond normal social relationships and rules. We have seen the tension which can arise if no distinction is made between personal and professional approaches to care work and we have considered how to manage the tension between being warm/personal and distant/ professional within the same relationship. I will now examine another area of care where the usual rules just do not apply: caring relationships which include a measure of control, containment and sanctions.

At the unit where Marie works there are a number of young people who have multiple problems. Rosalie is one such young woman. She has a hearing impairment, difficulties in communicating and severe learning difficulties, and is often aggressive to staff or other residents when things get too much for her. During Marie's second week there was a staff meeting at which Rosalie was the main subject of discussion. It appeared that she had lashed out at one of the instructors and broken her nose: the instructor was now off sick and there was a lot of sympathy for her. The staff were angry and saying, 'this time things have gone too far'. Some people were angry with Rosalie but others seemed to be directing their feelings at the management. Some staff were saying they shouldn't have to work with someone like Rosalie and that this place wasn't equipped to deal with people who are as 'severe' as she is. They wanted her to be removed. The management were saying that she should be allowed to stay with some extra support put in place and they had invited a psychologist along to discuss with staff how best to respond to what she called Rosalie's 'challenging behaviour'.

Marie doesn't really know Rosalie but she felt a bit alarmed: mostly she just listened to the meeting and she noticed that Rosalie's keyworker was undecided: he thought that if Rosalie was allowed to get away with this she would just do it again, but on the other hand he had worked hard to keep her in the unit for the last six months and he didn't want to give up yet. Marie shared his ambivalence.

This situation is not unlike many which crop up in the context of children's and young people's services but in this context it appears that Rosalie's behaviour is complicated by her specific learning difficulties.

2.1 Different ways of talking about difficult behaviour

Although the staff group came together to discuss how to respond to Rosalie's behaviour, you might have noticed that they approached it from very different perspectives. As the meeting progressed they even used different words. You could say they were speaking within different 'discourses'.

Study skills: Using different discourses

When we speak to each other we have to use a shared language. But there is more to it than that. We also have to use shared ideas, knowledge, assumptions and ways of arguing; otherwise we would not be able to make sense to each other. We can sum this up as using a shared 'discourse'. Discourses spring up between all groups of people who regularly communicate with each other. There are, for example, discourses of playground talk between children. I say 'discourses' rather than 'discourse', because younger children and older children tend to talk about different kinds of things and in different ways. Also, there are varieties of 'boy talk' and 'girl talk'. Similarly, as you move between different groups of people as an adult you take part in 'street talk', 'work talk', 'hobby talk', 'close friend talk', and so on. Without noticing you adjust what you talk about, the words you use, the jokes you tell and so on, as you move from one type of discourse to another.

In a similar way there are front-line-carer discourses, medical discourses, social work discourses, management discourses, legal discourses and so on, all connected with the world of caring. These are all ways of making sense of different aspects of caring. But they are also different ways of making sense of any particular aspect of care. For example, a decision to change policy on discharging patients from hospital would be discussed quite differently within each of these discourses. The sense we make of the world depends a lot on what discourse we bring into play when we talk about it. Some discourses, such as medical discourses, are more powerful than others because the groups that use them have more power.

In a way, what you are doing by studying K100 is acquiring a new kind of discourse. You already knew a lot about care through your own experience (we all do), but by studying K100 you are gaining access to new ways of talking (and thinking) about care. You become able to make sense of care issues in new ways by taking advantage of discourses developed through academic research and writing and through professional practice. That is why writing essays is an important part of the course – and why it is important to write in your own words, while also using ideas and ways of arguing drawn from the course. You are getting practice in saying meaningful things about care using the discourses built up by experts in the field. Your aim as a student is to become fluent in a range of discourses relevant to care. Then you will be in a position to participate in debates and decision making across the field.

If you had been a fly on the wall, for the rest of the staff meeting you would have seen that these different discourses were signalled in various ways.

First, the ways in which they *described* Rosalie's behaviour were very different:

- assault
- lashed out
- challenging behaviour
- had a tantrum
- went mad.

Second, they *explained* it in different terms including:

- frustration

- trying to get her own way

- her mother has 'spoiled' her

- communication difficulties

- attention seeking.

Different ways of talking about the problem lead to different answers ...

Lastly, they had different models in mind about what kind of *response* would be appropriate.

- She shouldn't be allowed to 'get away with it'.

- We should look at giving her extra help with signing.

- She should be excluded from the unit.

- She should have counselling.

- A more detailed behavioural assessment should be done.

- She should be ignored when she behaves like this in future.

- She should be treated consistently.

- If we reward her behaviour she will do it again.

It would clearly be hard to develop a consistent approach to Rosalie's difficult behaviour if everyone has a different way of talking about it, a different view of what has caused it and a different model of how to respond. You might find it useful to think of the manager's task as helping people to communicate across the gulfs signalled by these different ways of talking and thinking about the problem.

Activity 8   **Behaviour speak**

Allow about 5 minutes   Look back over the terms people used to describe, explain and respond to Rosalie's behaviour. Circle the ones which you would be most likely to use yourself and put a line through those which you feel sure you would not have said if you had been at the meeting. Which terms and explanations would you associate with a 'professional care discourse'?

Comment   I think I might have said that she 'lashed out' but I don't know if I would have put this down to communication difficulties or to frustration. Some staff were drawing on ways of talking they had learnt through bringing up children, using the idea of a 'tantrum', reminiscent of the 'terrible twos' stage of development. Someone else had a more adult, but almost criminal interpretation by labelling the behaviour as 'an assault'. Someone else suggested that Rosalie had lost control, 'gone mad', which brings in the idea of mental illness or imbalance. In the context of professional care practice, some of these ways of explaining challenging behaviour are regarded as less appropriate than others, particularly those that suggest Rosalie's behaviour calls for some kind of punishment. In Section 4, we look at how practice based on this kind of explanation can develop into an abusive culture within a care institution.

I think that if I had to work with Rosalie I might be expressing concern about her staying at the unit unless I could see definite improvements coming as the result of an assessment or a programme. What did you think?

When the psychologist used the term 'challenging behaviour', she was drawing on a 'professional' discourse, this time derived from psychology (Emerson *et al.*, 1987). She was brought in specially: she was not there when the incident took place and does not have to deal with Rosalie on a day-to-day basis. Is her label more accurate? More useful? More respectful to Rosalie?

As a 'professional' term, 'challenging behaviour' is a relatively new label which replaced the term 'problem' or 'difficult' behaviour. Lowe and Felce (1995) discuss this kind of shift as part of 'the general movement to use more respectful, less deficiency or problem-oriented language' (p. 118). But they go on to explain that it also conveys:

> ... *something particular about how challenging behaviour should be viewed. The nature of the challenge was not a one-way affair but was a shared, or mutual, responsibility ...*

and they conclude that:

> *The change in terminology served to point up the onus on services to understand and help the individual.*

> *(Lowe and Felce, 1995, p. 118)*

It is like saying, 'it isn't Rosalie's problem, it's the service's problem'. The labels we attach to people act as markers saying, 'treat this person a bit differently' or 'watch out, you can't expect him or her to do this or that'.

2.2 Are labels ever helpful?

Many people think that changes in language to terms such as 'learning disability' from 'mental handicap', or 'challenging behaviour' from 'problem behaviour' mark a steady progress as people have become more willing to include people with disabilities into the mainstream: hence such terms are often referred to as 'inclusive language'. The impetus for some of these changes came from a group of sociologists called 'labelling theorists' who pointed out that labels could create an unhelpful self-fulfilling prophecy. But others have questioned whether there isn't also something a bit defensive and confusing about changing the words every few years, or if it doesn't sometimes play down real problems. Valerie Sinason (a psychoanalyst) sees language change as a way of shying away from difficult or painful issues. Writing about people with learning difficulties, she says:

> No human group has been forced to change its name so frequently. The sick and the poor are always with us, in physical presence and in verbal terms, but not the handicapped. What we are looking at is a process of euphemism. Euphemisms, linguistically, are words brought in to replace the verbal bedlinen when a particular word feels too raw, too near a disturbing experience.

> (Sinason, 1992, p. 40)

Do you agree with this 'bedlinen' image?

I think that labels *can* be useful if they *alert* people to special considerations, rather than *impose* differentness, and if they send respectful but accurate signals about how we should work with someone. My neighbour's son, for example, has dyslexia and found it quite a relief to have a word to explain his difficulties: on the basis of this he is now given extra help and will have extra time in his examinations. He isn't called lazy or untidy or sloppy, or any of the other judgmental terms which have been thrown his way in the past because of his perceptual problems. Sometimes making judgments on the basis of 'normality' leads us in the wrong direction. It leads us to make moral pronouncements about people and their intentions which are not justified, which in turn can lead to punitive ways of working with them.

So we might question whether Marie's managers should be saying that the staff should treat residents 'as if they are normal'. If they do so, she and her colleagues have every right to feel angry and punitive towards Rosalie for hurting her instructor. Perhaps they should instead be saying something like, 'You are doing this job because Rosalie and people like her are different; they *can't* take the same responsibility as other people of their age. You need to take some of the responsibility that they can't manage on their own'. And the same might be true of other service users, including those who tend to be more blamed than helped, such as young people who have been in trouble with the courts. That is just a different kind of challenge.

Key points

- How you understand a person's behaviour will depend on the discourse you bring into play when you speak about it.

- The term 'challenging behaviour' has been introduced to shift responsibility for managing difficult behaviour from the individual to the service.

2.3 Responding to challenging behaviour

So the 'challenging behaviour' label raises the question, 'is Rosalie *responsible* for her behaviour or not?' Should she be treated *as if* she is responsible for her behaviour and punished or held to account in some way, or should the staff take responsibility for 'managing' her behaviour to stop her harming anyone else?

Activity 9   **Responding to Rosalie's behaviour**

Allow about 10 minutes   In this activity you are going to work out a way of assessing just how responsible Rosalie is. What information would you want to have to hand in order to make up your mind?

List 10 things you would want to know more about if you were an expert being called in to help the staff respond to Rosalie.

Comment   Here are some ideas.

1   Is there a pattern to Rosalie's behaviour?

2   Do some people provoke Rosalie more than others?

3   Are there particular times of day when she behaves in this way?

4   Are there certain places which seem to trigger her outbursts?

5   Does she have any dietary needs which are not being attended to?

6   What drugs is she taking, and do they have side effects?

7   When did this type of behaviour start, or has it always been present?

8   How is the behaviour handled?

9   Is there a consistent policy for managing her?

10   Have the views of people close to her (family, friends outside the unit) been sought? If so, what did they say?

Activity 10   **Understanding challenging behaviour**

Allow about 20 minutes

Now listen to Audio Cassette 5, side 1, part 2, which features Anthea Sperlinger, a consultant clinical psychologist who works with people with learning difficulties, and Chad Botley, a manager of residential services, who both get called in to respond to this kind of situation. On the tape they discuss the approach they would take to help staff work with Rosalie. As you listen, write down some answers to these questions:

(a)   What words or phrases does Anthea Sperlinger use to explain challenging behaviour?

(b)   What do carers most often assume to be the purpose of 'challenging behaviour'?

(c)   What other explanations are there for challenging behaviour?

Comment   (a)   Anthea says that 'the starting point is that all behaviour happens because there's a reason for it ... if Rosalie was able to ask nicely ... to say whatever is going on, she wouldn't need to behave in a challenging way.'

(b)   Carers often assume that if someone with learning difficulties does something antisocial, it is because they want attention, but as Anthea Sperlinger says, there is nothing *wrong* with seeking attention and it doesn't explain all behaviour.

(c)   Anthea offers some alternative explanations which include pain, hunger, thirst, being asked to do something which is too difficult, not understanding the concept of time, being bored, possible hearing problems and lack of verbal communication.

Especially when people do not have much language we can see difficult behaviours as a way of communicating, of making things happen, or stopping things from happening. All behaviours are learnt and they usually achieve something for people. People may resort to challenging behaviour because they want you to go away or stop making demands on them. But these ideas are not only helpful in relation to people with learning difficulties: they are universal and could be applied equally to domestic violence, truancy, problem drinking, and so on.

Finding the 'function' of a behaviour, in other words what it does for the person in that particular setting or relationship, is an important first step in helping the person to change it. A psychologist like Anthea Sperlinger would usually start by asking staff to observe and record Rosalie's behaviour and to note any other times when she gets aggressive. They might use a form called an *abc* chart (or a similar assessment format), which notes what happened before an outburst (the antecedent – A), what happened during the incident (the behaviour – B) and then what happened afterwards (the consequence – C). Aggression does not always mean the same thing. For Rosalie it may be the only way she knows of saying 'stop' or controlling what happens around her: for someone else it might be the way they get staff to take notice of them or to take them to their room.

Once an assessment has focused on what the behaviour is *for*, staff can figure out how to deal with it. Anthea uses the phrase 'very vigilant and good detectives' to describe the staff's role, which requires them to stand back from the immediate situation and not react personally. In this case, if we had a video camera and could look back over the incident with the instructor, we would see that she had just asked Rosalie to sort some cards, something which was too difficult for her, so she lashed out because she couldn't do the task she had been set. This is not 'attention-seeking' behaviour, but is called in technical terms 'demand avoidance'. If Rosalie is taught a new sign for saying 'stop and go away', and as long as all the staff know that when she uses it they must act accordingly, she may not need to be aggressive in the future. At the moment the staff are not alert to Rosalie's attempts to signal when she wants to bring activities to an end: they don't all use Makaton (a signing system specifically for people with learning difficulties) or receive training in communication skills, so they also need to learn some new behaviours!

If you start from the point of view that a person's behaviour does have a function, you can try to avoid the stresses which lead to difficulties: to present activities which are right for them, and to provide enough and the right kind of support. It means that you don't just shrug your shoulders and keep out of the way of someone like Rosalie, or blame and punish her. Instead, you recognise that she isn't *choosing* not to learn or to behave badly: she just can't operate at this level of difficulty.

Key points

- Negative labels can create a vicious circle or self-fulfilling prophecy.

- Accurate labels draw attention to 'differences' which may help you to explain or interpret someone's actions or behaviour.

- Managing difficult behaviour relies on working out its *function*; in other words what it achieved for that person in that particular setting or situation.

2.4 Safeguards in behaviour programmes

Behaviour programmes should seek to build on a person's ways of controlling their environment. Punishment of any kind is not ethically acceptable in community care services even if it could be shown to work. Instead, behaviour programmes focus on building skills and helping people to develop alternatives which work for them. But planning in detail how to react to someone is a far cry from most everyday relationships, which is why we are considering it in this unit – it could even be seen as quite manipulative or controlling.

Should anyone consciously shape the behaviour of others by rewarding some behaviours and communication and not others? Are we all shaping people's behaviours anyway even if we haven't thought about it and it just happens in a haphazard way? Does it make a difference that we are dealing with people like Rosalie who have difficulty learning from the jumble of responses they usually come up against? Because we have moved beyond 'normal' social expectations we need a new set of rules.

Chad Botley, whom you heard on the audio cassette, stresses the need for staff to have a clear set of values and access to multidisciplinary input when dealing with difficult behaviour. He also identified the risk as that 'staff might tip over and respond physically instead of verbally in difficult or aggressive situations' and he also emphasised that structures should be available to 'provide a framework within which staff can feel safe to express their views and concerns'.

Activity 11 **Rules for managing difficult behaviour**

Allow about 15 minutes Imagine you are a member of staff who is being asked to respond to Rosalie in a particular way which has been set out in a written behaviour programme. See if you can come up with a list of rules that you would feel comfortable with, to guide you and your colleagues.

Comment   My rules would include:

- The behaviour we are trying to 'treat' should be something which Rosalie could change, not something like fits which are always going to be out of her control.

- We should be helping her to manage things better for herself in future, not just taking something away from her.

- We should be aiming to help her do things she wants to do and opening up opportunities for her.

- We should find a way of working with her which keeps us and other residents safe.

- We shouldn't do anything against the law.

- We shouldn't damage her or hurt her. For example, I would not be willing to hit her, although I would hold her down to stop her hurting someone else if I had been shown how to do this properly.

- We shouldn't give her medication just to make life easier for us.

- We should have a properly qualified psychologist to help us work out what is best and then discuss the programme together so we all know how to put it into practice.

Staff need clear and agreed guidelines

Some agencies have developed codes of practice to formalise rules such as these. However, even where proper programmes are in place emergencies may arise. These often call for a quick response to cool someone down or to remove others from harm. Excessive force might easily be applied in such situations unless staff are given help in anticipating and dealing with emergencies. They may be frightened or at risk themselves. This is an area of practice which needs particular attention in guidelines and is often dealt with under the title of 'control and restraint' or 'physical interventions'. As a general principle 'reasonable' force in such situations involves the *minimum* needed to calm the person down. A model national policy (Harris *et al.*, 1996) advocates the notion of a 'gradient of control' whereby:

> *... when staff respond with [any] physical intervention, they follow a predetermined sequence which begins with the application of the least restrictive options and gradually increases the level of restriction. The sequence is terminated as soon as control is established over the person's behaviour.*

> *(Harris* et al.*, 1996, p. 35)*

Key points

- Behaviour programmes should aim to expand a person's skills and opportunities, not restrict them.

- People need safeguards if any sanctions are being applied to them by staff.

- Behaviour programmes are one area of practice which requires proper professional input and monitoring.

- Services should lay down codes of good practice in relation to challenging behaviour for all staff and detailed guidance in relation to individuals, especially if working with them safely might involve any physical intervention or restraint such as their being locked in or held down.

Section 3
Protection

Section 2 explored how far it is acceptable to 'control' or attempt to change someone's behaviour. In Rosalie's case you were looking at the need to intervene to stop her hurting other people. Now you will be considering a rather drastic intervention, electronic tagging, which has been suggested as one way to protect a particular young man, Tony, from harming himself. Electronic tagging has been controversial and is usually associated with young offenders or with people who are on bail after being arrested for a criminal offence. More recently, tagging has been advocated as a means by which sex offenders can be monitored on release from prison. Tagging therefore has strong negative associations in terms of its links with the prevention of offending behaviour. However, it is also sometimes used in services for vulnerable people to help protect them from harm. For example, tagging has been used in services for older people who 'wander' on the grounds that if they can be stopped from actually leaving their establishment, with all the risks that might entail, they can enjoy more freedom within the home and grounds. But tagging raises important civil liberties issues and is seen as a particularly intrusive form of surveillance. The Alzheimer's Society is one organisation that has called for further research into how tagging might be used ethically, both to help protect older people from harm and maximise their freedom. This same need to balance rights and risks can be applied to the situation facing Tony and his parents.

3.1 Assessing risk

Tony's case has been adapted from a situation reported in my local newspaper (a few details have been changed to protect his anonymity). Imagine Marie reading the paper when she gets home from work and zooming in on the issues because they echo challenges in her own work.

NORTHERN ECHO
by our very own correspondent
Tag our Tony, say parents

'Tag our son' plead the parents of autistic Tony Smith who are at the end of their tether trying to cope. They believe electronic tagging is the only way to stop their 23-year-old boy from vanishing in future and possibly even killing himself. In his second disappearing act within three months Tony spent two nights sleeping in below freezing temperatures before he was found.

'He can't help it, he's obsessed with lorries' his distraught mum said. 'He hears voices telling him to do things and one day he is going to come to harm just because someone tells him to do something daft. There's no way we can keep him under lock and key and I have other kids to look after ... it costs the police thousands to find him and bring him back.'

Tony has the mental age of a nine year old, and disappeared on Sunday with £5 in his pocket after going to get a paper. He was found cold and bedraggled on Thursday, 50 miles away, after a massive search operation

Mr and Mrs Smith are due to meet police and social services chiefs today to discuss the tagging idea. 'The only alternative might be to lock him up and we don't want that,' said his dad.

Electronic tags are used by police to keep track of people on bail waiting for court appearances. Tony has done nothing wrong but could this be the right answer?

Activity 12   **Protecting Tony's interests**

Allow about 5 minutes   You will see that Tony's story is reported from his parents' point of view. Tony might not agree that this is the best solution to his difficulties.

Any decision of this gravity would have to be made in a formal meeting or case conference such as the one Mr and Mrs Smith are due to have with police and social services. Is there anyone else you would invite to that meeting and how could you ensure that Tony's interests were properly represented and protected in the discussion? Should Tony be there himself?

Comment   I think that it would be good for Tony to be there for at least part of the meeting. It would be good too if he had an advocate to work with him to bolster his confidence and ability to speak for himself, and if necessary to speak for him. I think I might also want an independent professional such as a psychologist there to make sure that everyone is working on the basis of accurate information.

Advocacy was introduced in Unit 10, in the context of volunteers or professional health or care workers acting as advocates for Jim and Marianne. Using Tony's story, you can explore the possible role of an advocate where a difficult decision involves weighing up rights and risks.

Activity 13   **Pros and cons of tagging Tony**

Allow about 10 minutes   Imagine you are at the case conference as Tony's advocate, with Tony's parents, social services and the police. You are there to put Tony's case in relation to the tagging idea. What arguments do you expect will be put for and against tagging? Jot down three pros and three cons.

Comment   **For**

- Tagging might stop Tony getting run over or lost.

- Tagging is better than locking Tony up.

- Tagging wouldn't be that noticeable, whereas calling out the police to find him might make people think he has done something wrong.

Against

- No one has asked Tony's opinion or assessed just how much risk he is in.

- Tony is 23. Despite his mental age, he should be treated as an adult unless there are very clear reasons not to, and that includes allowing him to come and go as he wishes.

- Tagging is a contravention of Tony's human rights.

A range of views are likely to be expressed during the meeting. For example, Tony's parents are clearly at the end of their tether and tagging might help to alleviate some of the strain of watching out for him all the time. The police are not too happy about the time and expense involved in bringing Tony back and the social services might also be glad if a way can be found to avoid emergencies like this in the future.

It is always a balancing act when you are considering restricting a person's freedom in order to stop them putting themselves at risk. It is one of those occasions when pragmatism seems to conflict with principle. On the face of it, the idea of tagging Tony looks harmless enough and could bring major benefits. But remember what Sobsey says: it conflicts with some very fundamental civil liberties. What justification can there be for limiting the freedom of a 23-year-old man in this way? And if Tony can be tagged, what is there to stop *any* parent asking the police to tag their wayward son?

What kind of assessment is necessary to inform this decision? Clearly the degree of risk involved has to be assessed, as does Tony's ability to understand his predicament and make his own decisions. Also, a range of possible options needs to be reviewed. The assessment process following this meeting is likely to focus on three questions:

How serious is the risk that Tony will leave home again and if he does what is the likelihood that he will come to harm while he is away? His parents have said that he hears voices and might do something dangerous if told to by someone else. Risk assessments may be phrased in terms of the *extent* of possible harm and the *likelihood* that it might happen. So you get different kinds of risk. There are situations which are 'minor accidents waiting to happen', like cutting your finger on the kitchen knife (which most of us do every now and then), and there are those where the damage would be devastating but is unlikely to occur, such as a nuclear accident. If the outcome of this assessment is that the risk to Tony is both life-threatening *and* very likely then action is certainly necessary.

What do we know about Tony and his capacity to make his own decisions and protect himself from harm? Tony has not done anything against the law and he cannot have his freedom removed, even for a good reason, unless he falls within the framework of the Mental Health Act 1983 which allows authorities such as health or social services or the police to intervene. After all, leaving home is a normal thing for a 23-year-old to do. But we would also want to look at Tony's situation in a more holistic way, at his relationships with his family, his current contact with services, his entitlement to benefits, his daily and weekly routine, and so on. These might be as important as Tony's 'ability' in assessing the situation and deciding what to do for the best.

What is the best intervention to address these concerns – that is, the solution which is least intrusive or stigmatising in the eyes of others? Tony's parents have seized on the idea of tagging as a magic solution in the way that ill people will seek out instant cures; but there may be other ways of protecting Tony which are not so extreme.

Another question which might be addressed in the meeting is 'why now?' because, as in many other situations, risk has been an ongoing feature in Tony's life. Sometimes when the anxiety gets too high someone will force the issue (as Tony's parents have by going to the local paper) but many vulnerable people face considerable risk and many parents and staff contain anxiety on a daily basis. Once the risk has been formally notified to management then action has to be taken to prevent it and protect the individual concerned. It is no wonder then, when services are so pressed, that they may shy away from explicit acknowledgement of risk in lots of circumstances. Once a decision has been made in the context of risk it will need to be monitored and reviewed regularly: this process is known as 'risk management'.

One of the problems inherent in this kind of situation is that there is no obviously right answer so people can be forgiven for hesitating to make any decision at all. But doing nothing may be the worst option, even if it is the path of least resistance. Do you think doing nothing is an option in Tony's situation?

Key points

- Sometimes restrictions *do* need to be applied to prevent someone from harming themselves.

- Advocacy specifically for the service user concerned can help to make sure their interests are paramount in any such decisions.

- Risk assessment should focus on the situation, the individual and the range of possible solutions, and anticipate risks rather than let things happen.

- When considering interventions which limit freedom formal safeguards should be used to guarantee civil liberties.

- Sometimes doing nothing is not a viable option.

3.2 About autism

One piece of information that needs to be considered in detail is that Tony has a label – he has autism. This is not going to provide the key to the whole problem, but it is a place to start. Autism is a very specific kind of development disorder which in many individuals is associated with learning disabilities and mental health problems. It may be that you work with people who have other specific difficulties, for example Downs syndrome or dementia. This section of the unit might guide you in seeking out information which helps you to be more aware of their needs.

Disability activists have argued very strongly against a 'medical model' of disability – one which looks for the roots of problems in an individual's impairment rather than in their social circumstances and the position of disabled people in society at large. When you look closer you can often see that problems which seemed to be 'caused' by a particular condition arise in the context of a wide range of factors including poverty, discrimination, isolation, lack of transport, inappropriate housing and lack of service provision. So problems experienced by Tony are not inevitably a direct consequence of autism. Nevertheless, it is worth understanding what is meant by this label to get a clear picture of how it affects him and the decisions he can make for himself.

Autism

Autism is a permanent condition arising in childhood, leading to a range of impairments of varying severity. These include difficulties in:

- social interaction

- social communication

- imagination.

It is also characterised by repetitive or obsessive behaviour 'as shown by stereotyped play patterns, abnormal preoccupations or resistance to change.' (Harris *et al.*, 1996, p. 6).

These impairments are associated with learning disabilities in a significant proportion of people with autism. However, others are of average or above average intelligence, although they experience similar difficulties in relating to other people. One manifestation of such a condition is called Asperger's syndrome.

According to a booklet published by the Autistic Society, because autism affects the way people make contact with others, a child or adult may appear 'aloof or indifferent' and talk *at* rather than *with* others. They may not understand or pick up on facial expressions, gestures or tone of voice. They may understand and use language very literally, not in a social way. Some autistic people have peculiar abilities alongside these impairments (for example in music, drawing or arithmetic like the character played by Dustin Hoffman in the film *Rainman*).

The condition was first identified in 1943 by an American psychiatrist called Kanner and is a very complex disorder which is still being unravelled. Many authorities believe the difficulties are caused by an underlying neurological mechanism. While most children learn relatively easily and spontaneously, autistic children have to have things really spelt out and signposted for them. They need to be taught in a very structured way and have the *consequences* of what they do very specifically pointed out to them. It has been suggested that just as dyslexia is sometimes a form of 'word blindness' or 'number blindness', autism is a form of 'mind blindness'. Baron-Cohen, a researcher who has taught autistic children, says they:

> ... *appeared singularly oblivious to what others were* **thinking** *– it did not seem to occur to them that others might think them odd, or funny or that others might* **think** *anything at all. The other thing that struck me was that their behaviour and speech seemed to be largely lacking in any* **self-reflection**.

(Baron-Cohen, 1992, p. 9)

Dustin Hoffman in 'Rainman'

Activity 14   **Does autism make a difference?**

Allow about 5 minutes   You remember that we were looking at this information to help us decide if there were extenuating circumstances which might influence the decision that would be taken at Tony's case conference. Quickly reread the box on autism and jot down any points you think you would want to explore in the context of the risks Tony faces.

Comment   I noted, for example, that Tony might be unaware that a stranger offering him a lift might have malicious intentions. I also wondered about his road safety skills and whether these could be improved by the kind of structured teaching described above. But I was left wondering about how much he understood of the risks he faced and/or how he could learn to keep himself safe ... the information about autism in general could not answer these points with particular reference to Tony.

Understanding a condition such as autism can help us avoid situations where parents or individuals are blamed for unusual behaviour patterns. This returns us to the issue of labelling. Uta Frith, an expert on autism, challenges the notion that a label is necessarily negative. It may lead to people being treated with more understanding.

> *To me it is a very false idea of kindness not to acknowledge that someone, through no fault but nature's, suffers from a biological disorder. Surely, to recognise that some people have a disorder means to recognise that they have a right to an allowance being made for their handicap? This is at least a first step towards a kinder treatment.*

(Frith, 1992, p. 19)

Key points

- Sometimes you need to find out details about a particular condition or impairment so that you can plan an appropriate level of support or intervention.

- Autism is thought to be caused by an underlying neurological mechanism which leads to specific learning disabilities and problems in making sense of the environment: these may co-exist with islands of brilliance.

- Structured routines and teaching opportunities can help children and adults with autism to learn a wide range of skills.

- Autism as a 'condition' should be taken into account in assessing the risks faced by someone like Tony, but on a very individual basis and within the context of a more holistic assessment.

3.3 Capacity

We have seen that Tony decides to leave home every now and then. If any intervention is to be set in motion to stop him, a crucial factor in the assessment and decision making is to examine whether he has 'capacity'. This is a legal term which is shorthand for his ability to understand risk and make decisions for himself. This assessment will be made primarily by a psychologist and there are two ways in which it may be made (Murphy and Clare, 1995).

- First, it might be made on the basis of an existing diagnosis which identifies an individual as one of a group who are considered to have a shared lack of capacity. For example, all people with severe learning disabilities are deemed not to be able to consent to sexual acts under the terms of the 1956 Sexual Offences Act. This is also called a 'status' test (Law Commission, 1995, p. 32, para. 3.2).

- Alternatively, a more individual and specific functional approach could be taken. This involves assessment of the particular skills or knowledge needed in relation to a specific issue. As the Law Commission puts it: whether the individual is able 'at the time when a particular decision has to be made, to understand its nature and effects' (1995, p. 33, para. 3.5).

Activity 15   **A functional assessment**

Allow about 10 minutes   How would you go about conducting a functional assessment of whether Tony has 'capacity' in relation to his decision to leave home for brief periods of time? (Assume you can consult with those professionals currently working with him.) I've suggested a *functional* assessment at this stage because I'd feel very uncomfortable about arguing for a blanket decision saying that *all* people with learning difficulties, or *all* autistic people, are a risk to themselves when they go out and should be tagged. I want this assessment to be very much geared to Tony and his individual abilities and situation.

Write a list of five areas you would want to explore in your assessment.

Comment   My list would include:

- his safety crossing roads

- his sense of direction and local knowledge

- his ability to use public transport

- his behaviour towards others

- his ability to perceive risk in the behaviour of others towards him.

Often such decisions are made informally within services in the context of staff meetings or individual planning meetings. A more formal way is to officially recognise a person's lack of 'capacity' and need for help. For example, their affairs could be administered through the civil court if they are acknowledged to be unable to manage their own finances. In extreme cases they might come within the terms of the 1983 Mental Health Act because they have a mental disorder, in which case they can be taken into hospital for assessment or treatment. Decisions under the Act are made by one or two doctors (usually psychiatrists) with input from an Approved Social Worker who has had additional training in mental health. Most people with learning difficulties do not fall within the stricter definition of mental impairment which could lead to them being detained or 'sectioned', but Tony might be an exception.

In practice, the kinds of interventions required by Richard, Rosalie and Tony are likely to be set in motion by an informal group of workers and managers who think they have the best interests of their clients at heart rather than by a formal/legal assessment process. What you have been looking at are some of the frameworks you can use to check this out.

Key points

- 'Capacity' is a legal term. Where it is judged that someone is not able to manage their affairs on account of mental impairment or incapacity, the courts can make special provision for that person.

- 'Functional capacity' is the term for a person's ability to take a particular decision for themselves.

- Lack of capacity may be formally acknowledged under the Mental Health Act 1983 and other civil legislation.

- Often services make professional judgments about capacity as it affects people in everyday matters. This has the benefit of being informal but it may mean that people are not able to challenge the service's decisions.

3.4 The least intrusive intervention

We began to examine the underlying principles in Tony's case by separating out three basic issues. You have looked at assessment of risk and assessment of Tony's ability to take decisions on his own behalf. Now you are going to consider the last question, the intervention being proposed – tagging – to see if it conforms to principles enshrined in the Mental Health Act 1983, and also in the *No Secrets* guidance from the government on protecting vulnerable adults, which we refer to in the section that follows. We might also need to consider if Tony's human rights are being abused according to the Human Rights Act 1998, for instance by unnecessarily restricting his liberty. The key question is whether this is the 'least restrictive' or the 'least intrusive' procedure. Professional ethics might also raise questions about stigmatising Tony. However, the most important issue is whether the same degree of safety could be provided by a lower-level, more ordinary kind of measure. Any deliberation should put the proposed intervention on trial rather than putting Tony under the spotlight.

Activity 16 | **Is tagging the right intervention?**

Allow about 5 minutes | Now do a quick review of whether you think tagging is an appropriate strategy. Is it the 'least restrictive alternative' or can you think of better ways of keeping Tony safe?

Comment | What have you decided? I thought about alternatives such as:

- a teaching programme to help him find his way around

- work on road safety or public transport training

- providing him with a mobile phone to make it easier for him to ring home

- pointing out to him places he could go for help if he got lost, such as the bus depot or the police station.

I did not rule tagging out completely but came round to the idea that there were less drastic measures to try first.

I also thought that respite care might be appropriate. Tony's behaviour was not only due to autism. The request for tagging was *tied* to his parents' anxiety and could be read as a signal of their 'overload'.

Landmark places

Even though this case might have to lead to a formal intervention, there are many circumstances in which the same principles need to be applied more informally to risk assessment and individual care planning. It is important to ensure that protection is not used as a rationale for unnecessarily restricting someone's opportunities or infringing their civil liberties.

Key points

- Interventions should be the least intrusive and stigmatising possible.

- Under the Mental Health Act 1983 people are entitled to the 'least restrictive' treatments and living arrangements.

- More ordinary alternatives can often be found if situations are assessed in detail and creative support made available.

Section 4
Institutional abuse

You have now worked in detail through two cases where the risks associated with an individual's behaviour had to be managed either, as in Rosalie's case, to protect others from harm, or, as in Tony's, to ensure his own safety. Where such decisions are not subject to the kind of detailed and personalised scrutiny we have worked through they can mistakenly be allowed to justify a whole regime in which restrictive practices and restraints go unquestioned. Within the broad category 'institutional abuse' (similar, as you will notice, to 'institutional racism', which you read about in Unit 11) Gil (1982) distinguishes between abuses that can happen at different levels:

> *'Programme abuse' occurs when programmes of care within an institution are abusive or neglectful. There are two examples of this type of abuse given in the sections below, including the 'Pin-down' inquiry into children's services. Gil contrasts this type of abuse with another type, which is outside the control of individuals and which he calls 'system abuse' as defined here in relation to children's services:*

> *'System abuse' is ... not perpetrated by any single person or programme, but by the immense and complicated child care system, stretched beyond its limits and incapable of guaranteeing safety to all children in care. (p. 11)*

4.1 A service which broke the rules

Contrast the way Marie's unit and the psychologist dealt with Rosalie with the way Mr and Mrs D, who managed a residential home for people with learning difficulties, treated people in their care. (Unlike the story about Marie and Rosalie, this is a real case which was considered at a public tribunal. The details are taken from evidence given at the hearing.) A young man called Darren had his glasses removed as a punishment. Another resident called Tom was hosed down outside whenever he had epileptic fits. These breaches of good practice eventually led to this home being closed under the Registered Homes Act and details of the regime there were spelt out in the tribunal's findings.

The chair of the tribunal challenged the owner about the way Tom had been treated suggesting that the owner had no 'understanding whatsoever of [his] vulnerability' and that 'it was wrong to deal with him in a punitive way'. The owner replied, 'It depends what you mean', and when asked 'Are you suggesting he was deliberately being difficult, acting out of spite?' she replied, 'They can be, yes'. This switch from 'he' in the question to 'they' in the answer suggests that the owner had made a blanket decision about people with learning difficulties rather than a careful assessment of Tom's particular abilities, needs or intentions. She put a gloss on her actions by using the notion that she was 'redirecting his activity', when clearly practices such as sending him outside in the cold for over an hour were designed to punish. The owners did not appear to understand that epileptic fits cannot be brought on at will: they just happen as a result of electric impulses in the brain. Not only were the punishments cruel but there was no point to them as Tom could not 'learn' to control his fits or to have them at a time when they were less inconvenient.

Abuse disclosures denied

Powys County Council is seeking to close a private home for adults with severe learning difficulties following allegations that residents were physically abused.

The owners of the home, Golfa View in Mid Wales, have denied the allegations and are appealing against de-registration at a registered homes tribunal next month.

A ten-month police investigation into the allegations has been dropped following advice from the Crown Prosecution Service that there was no case for further action.

Allegations of physical assault of residents and sexual harassment of staff at the home were made in anonymous phone calls to *Community Care* last week.

The allegations claimed:

- A young epileptic man was hosed down with cold water.
- An elderly incontinent woman received the same treatment.
- A boy who scratched himself had his hands tied behind his back.

(*Community Care*, 28 January 1993)

Nursing home boss jailed for abuse

Fat controller's horror home

We began this unit with a quote from Sobsey in which he said that do-gooders can overstep the mark to the extent that people with learning difficulties end up with less protection and fewer safeguards than convicted prisoners. This is where it is important to remind ourselves again about the civil liberties of service users. There are now two new pieces of guidance and legislation which seek to ensure that the rights of service users such as Tom are protected. A document called *No Secrets: Guidance on Developing and Implementing Multi-disciplinary Policies and Procedures to Protect Vulnerable Adults from Abuse (2000)*, provides guidance on how health and social care services should work together to identify and prevent abuse taking place.

The Human Rights Act 1998 provides another form of protection for people who are vulnerable, in that some of its articles can be applied to the treatment of people in care homes or who receive other NHS and social care services. Article 3 of the Act, for instance, is concerned with 'the prohibition of inhuman or degrading treatment'.

An approach which begins with rights, the sort you considered in relation to Lynne in Unit 3, reminds everyone that it is *never* permissible to deprive people of ordinary things like watching television or food and drink as part of a 'programme'. Untrained staff may sometimes be asked to work within, or accept, set ways of responding to a particular individual without the information or training to check that it makes sense. They may be muddled by fancy language or specialist advice. For staff in such unenviable positions, it is useful to remember that if a professional of any kind gives advice about practice they should always be able to explain *why* they are recommending it and what benefit it will bring to the person concerned. Staff, however junior or untrained, have a duty to ask for such an explanation.

Before we move on, look back at the rules you set out for the staff implementing Rosalie's programme (Activity 11). Would your rules have prevented the things Mr and Mrs D did to Darren and Tom? If not, how might they be amended?

Key points

- There is no point in punishing someone for something they cannot change.

- Civil rights cannot be set aside just because someone displays challenging behaviour.

- The jargon of behaviour programmes can be misapplied to justify regimes where control is given higher priority than development and where individual well-being is being put at risk.

4.2 Why do residential homes sometimes fail their clients?

One place where issues of control and protection went wrong over a very long period was the children's home which became the focus of the 'Pin-down' scandal. In this home issues of control came to dominate the regime and a policy of 'grounding' and 'time out' was used without any proper safeguards or external monitoring. Eventually this led to an extensive independent inquiry which documented the regime and its management in detail.

Activity 17

Towards an understanding of the corruption of care

Allow about 30 minutes

Read Chapter 24 in the Reader by Wardhaugh and Wilding. The authors draw out eight factors which they felt had played a part in creating and sustaining this pattern of control and repression. You will see that the authors use some frameworks you have already read about, such as Goffman's analysis of institutions. (You may recognise some of his ideas resurfacing in this analysis.) As you read, make a list of the eight 'propositions' with a one or two line explanation to help you remember the main ideas under each heading.

Comment

My notes looked like this:

1   Neutralisation of normal moral concerns – depersonalised residents have to 'obey', stop feeling pity for others' suffering – used Pin-down to break their will.

2   Power and powerlessness – staff feel powerless and have little influence over the way the place is run but they have power over the residents.

3   Particular groups at risk – people who are not valued or are stereotyped are most at risk when managers just want to 'keep the lid on' the place.

4   Managers do not set clear aims nor do outside people like professionals or lay people.

5   Enclosed, inward-looking places.

6   Staff unsupervised and no formal accountability.

7   People do not feel they can challenge professionals or those above them in the hierarchy.

8   Some client groups are seen as less than human, adults seen as children, and so on.

As you read about Pin-down, did it remind you of what you read in Blocks 2 and 4 about Goffman's idea of the 'total institution'? Although Wardaugh and Wilding make only passing reference to Goffman, and their approach does have some interesting differences of emphasis, they are clearly thinking along fairly similar lines. They too point to the effects of:

- a regime being cut off from the outside world

- the senior management being cut off from the action at lower levels, and

- those being 'cared for' being treated in a depersonalised way as 'inmates' rather than as individual people, so that eventually they take on the 'institutional perspective' and stop feeling pity for others.

However, in this case it was clearly more than simply patients being ground down by the impersonal daily routine of batch living, as Goffman describes. It was more a deliberate regime of domination and control.

Condensing these suggestions even further I came up with four key issues which might signal a service which is not providing the kind of safeguards I talked about at the beginning of the unit. These are:

1   difficult clients who are not valued and whose human status is not recognised

2   direct care staff who cannot influence, challenge or complain

3   managers who do not provide supervision or take responsibility

4   a home which is isolated from the outside world and professional debates.

Clearly there are problems at each of these levels. If they are arranged in reverse order they bring to mind a waterfall in that each level blames and dumps the responsibility on to the level below. Read them in reverse and you will see what I mean:

- isolated from outside world and professional debates

- managers do not provide supervision or take responsibility

- direct care staff cannot influence, challenge or complain

- difficult clients who are not valued and whose human status is not recognised.

The Staffordshire pin-down scandal

Date	Event
October 1989	A solicitor obtains a High Court injunction to stop the use of pin-down in a number of homes, allegedly practised since 1983
March–April 1990	A routine SSI inspection of child protection services in the county did not consider any allegations; its conclusions that the SSD failed to follow agreed procedures are not published until October
June 1990	A World in Action programme alleges that 100 young people have been subject to pin-down; the council says it will commission an independent review of the 'discontinued' use of pin-down
July–August 1990	Meanwhile, the SSI investigates four homes at the request of the Secretary of State; it reports in September
August 1990	The independent inquiry into pin-down begins, under Barbara Kahan and Allan Levy; Levy refers the Fundwell allegations to the district auditor
September 1990	Two SSI reports criticising management and staff in four homes are discussed by the council; SSD director Barry O'Neill proposed a special child care project team
October 1990	The Levy inquiry widens its scope to take in allegations that a convicted paedophile took children on outings from one or more homes, including those where pin-down was allegedly practised; a police report on various allegations goes to the Crown Prosecution Service, which later decides to take no action
December 1990	SSD director Barry O'Neill takes early retirement due to ill health; the Levy inquiry, after sitting for 75 days and hearing 153 witnesses, is not able to report until May but the council refuses to indemnify it against possible legal action
May 1991	Christine Walby becomes new SSD director, from Solihull; an SSI inspector, David Bartle, acts as a child care consultant to the authority on a three-year contract
30 May	The full report is launched; Levy, Kahan and the council hold press conferences; at least 50 young people are said to be seeking damages from the council

(*Community Care*, 24 June 1991)

'Care' regime that relied on humiliation

Inquiry condemns pin-down method of isolation and confrontation as wholly negative and entirely unacceptable.

'Another week of solitary confinement for X has had some rather peculiar effects. He is talking to himself a great deal and we have had tears several times during the course of the week. Sleeping in staff report incidents of him talking in his sleep.'

Thus the log book of a children's home in Stoke-on-Trent records matter-of-factly the appalling reality of a regime which for almost six years cast a shadow over the lives of hundreds of youngsters in residential care in Staffordshire. The regime was called 'pin-down'.

An independent inquiry report on the affair published yesterday pulls no punches. The regime was, it says, fundamentally dependent on isolation, humiliation and confrontation. It was wholly negative and entirely unacceptable.

(*Guardian*, 31 May 1991)

'I was crawling up the wall. I couldn't cope'

Fear of silence haunts 16-year-old kept in solitary confinement.

There were two rooms specifically for pin-down, two rooms on one corridor. There was one where they had a big window that faced the road so you could see everybody going past. But the one I was in just faced an old couple's flat, the kitchen.'

(*Guardian*, 31 May 1991)

The Staffordshire Pin-down scandal

Solidarity and not isolation

4.3 System abuse

The paper you have just read opens out our discussion of abuse. We began with a focus on the interpersonal – on things going bad between a carer and the person they are caring for. Now we have moved on to broader social issues – to inequality which leads to some people being *de*valued, and to systems which lead to low paid work and poor management. Decisions taken at a distance from the immediate environment can also have a devastating effect on individuals and their experience of receiving care.

Richard, the young man for whom Marie was keyworker, for example, had a 'history' of being moved from one placement to another. After several foster placements he ended up in a residential school many miles from his home town. This had the effect of loosening his ties with his family. His mother was poor and found it difficult to travel with her other children to visit him. Gradually they lost touch. And as we have seen he was placed in a large residential unit which did not have many black staff or any support for his cultural identity.

Gil (1982) calls this kind of abuse 'system abuse' because it happens as a result of actions and decisions which are structural and beyond the remit of a single individual. So we need to look beyond the behaviour of individual staff, or of a single establishment, to the values and organisation of the wider system. Within children's services, Gil defines this kind of abuse as:

> *... any system, programme, policy, procedure or individual interaction with a child [or adult] in placement that abuses, neglects, or is detrimental to the child's health, safety, or emotional and physical well-being, or in any way exploits or violates the child's basic rights.*

> *(cited in Westcott, 1991, p. 9)*

How a blind eye was turned to kicks, punches and torments

Three convicted after reign of terror at care home

Ashworth patient may have died from drug dosage, inquiry told

Patient 'beaten every day'

Elderly 'suffer in private homes'

Key points

- Institutional abuse can happen at the level of the 'programme' of care or of the wider 'system'.

- Abuse can come about because of a failure to provide adequate or appropriate support as well as through punitive, restrictive or stigmatising forms of care.

- Abuse may arise not only because of individual carers or settings but also because of wider societal problems and inequalities: this is sometimes called 'system abuse'.

Conclusion

In this unit you have looked at areas of care which cross normal social boundaries and at how this leaves individuals to manage painful dilemmas within settings which sometimes mirror society's devaluation of people needing care and those who work with them. We have considered how difficult it is to maintain professional boundaries when performing intimate tasks and we have seen how staff can become restrictive or punitive in the face of risk or difficult behaviour. We have also seen that openly debating these issues can help to take the sting out of them and that agreed and negotiated guidelines can help staff to face difficult situations and provide safeguards for service users.

Now let's look again at the core questions for this unit together with some key points relating to each.

How can boundaries be respected in situations where intimate care is being given?

- Caring relationships often cross the boundaries set by 'normal social rules' and once these have been breached it is hard to know where the new lines should be set.

- Intimate care involves 'dirty work' which, because it is a taboo subject, is often shrouded in silence and not acknowledged within the official structures and documents of an organisation; it is also often left to women.

- Intimate care stirs up difficult feelings which are usually censored but still affect the way people care for each other and the unofficial culture of the establishment.

How can choices, rights and autonomy be balanced against the need to protect people in receipt of care who put themselves at risk of harm?

- Often the philosophy of services is muddled about when they will treat people on the basis of 'normality' and when on the basis of 'special need'.

- People should be allowed to make their own mistakes unless they lack 'capacity' to make a particular decision for themselves or are at significant risk.

In what situations and with what safeguards are people entitled to use physical power to control or restrain someone to stop them harming themselves or another person?

- Control sometimes has to be part of the caring relationship but only if safeguards are in place to ensure that any intervention is in someone's best interests or will prevent him or her from harming others.

- There are legal principles to consult when making decisions on when and how to control someone's behaviour.

When and how can systems become abusive?

- Sometimes establishments become distorted or controlling, especially if there is a lack of guidance, training and support for staff, or inadequate resources to support informal carers.

- Pressures within care relationships and settings often reflect wider social problems such as the isolation or poverty of people who rely on services, and wider inequalities on the basis of race, gender or class.

References

Baron-Cohen, S. (1992) 'The theory of mind hypothesis of autism: history and prospects of the idea', *The Psychologist*, Vol. 5, pp. 9–12.

Brown, H. and Smith, H. (1989) 'Whose "ordinary life" is it anyway?', *Disability, Handicap and Society*, Vol. 4, No. 2, pp. 105–19.

Craft, A. and Brown, H. (1994) 'Personal relationships and sexuality: the staff role', in Craft, A. (ed.) *Practice Issues in Sexuality and Learning Disabilities*, Routledge, London, pp. 10–22.

Department of Health (2000) 'No Secrets: Guidance on developing and implementing multi-agency policies and procedures to protect vulnerable adults from abuse', TSO, London.

Emerson, E., Barratt, S., Bell, C., Cummings, R., Hughs, H., McCool, C., Toogood, A. and Mansell, J. (1987) *The Special Development Team: Developing Services for People with Severe Learning Disabilities and Challenging Behaviours*, Centre for the Applied Psychology of Social Care, University of Kent at Canterbury.

Enfield Social Services (1996) *Guidelines on Professional Boundaries*, London Borough of Enfield, London.

Frith, U. (1992) 'Cognitive development and cognitive deficit', *The Psychologist*, Vol. 5, pp. 13–19.

Gil, E. (1982) 'Institutional abuse of children in out-of-home care', in Hanson, R. (ed.) *Institutional Abuse of Children and Youth*, The Haworth Press, N. Yorkshire.

Harris, J., Allen, D., Cornick, M., Jefferson, A. and Mills, R. (1996) *Physical Interventions: A Policy Framework*, BILD, Kidderminster.

Hochschild, A. (1983) *The Managed Heart*, University of California Press, Berkeley.

Hughes, E. (1971) 'Good people and dirty work', in *The Sociological Eye: Selected Papers*, Aldine Atherton, Chicago.

Law Commission (1995) *Mental Incapacity Law*, Cm 231, HMSO, London.

Lawler, J. (1991) *Behind the Screens: Nursing Somology and the Problem of the Body*, Churchill Livingstone, Melbourne.

Lowe, K. and Felce, D. (1995) 'The definition of challenging behaviour in practice', *British Journal of Learning Disabilities*, Vol. 23, pp. 118–23.

Menzies, I. (1970) *The Functioning of Social Systems as a Defence Against Anxiety*, Tavistock, London.

Murphy, G.H. and Clare, I.C.H. (1995) 'Adults' capacity to make decisions affecting the person: psychologists' contribution', in Bull, R. and Carson, D. (eds) *Handbook of Psychology in Legal Contexts*, J. Wiley & Sons, Chichester, pp. 97–128.

Oliver, J. (1983) 'The caring wife', in Finch, J. and Groves, D. (eds) *A Labour of Love: Women, Work and Caring*, Routledge & Kegan Paul, London, pp. 72–89.

Pascall, G. (1986) *Social Policy: A Feminist Analysis*, Tavistock, London.

Sinason, V. (1992) *Mental Handicap and the Human Condition*, Free Association Books, London.

Sobsey, D. (1994) *Violence and Abuse in the Lives of People with Disabilities*, Brookes, Baltimore.

Thompson, D., Clare, I. and Brown, H. (1997) 'Not such an "ordinary" relationship: the role of women support staff in relation to men with learning disabilities who have difficult sexual behaviour', *Disability and Society*, Vol. 12, No. 4, pp. 573–92.

The Training Organisation for the Personal Social Services TOPSS (2002) *The First Six Months – A Registered Manager's Guide to Induction and Foundation Standards in Social Care*, TOPSS England/Care and Health.

Westcott, H. (1991) *Institutional Abuse of Children: From Research to Policy*, NSPCC, London.

Acknowledgements

Grateful acknowledgement is made to the following sources for permission to use material in this unit:

Text

'Abuse disclosures denied', *Community Care*, 28 January 1993. Published by permission of the editor of *Community Care*; Richmond, T. (1997) 'Tag our Tony, say parents', *Milton Keynes Citizen*. Adapted by permission; Marchant, C. (1991) 'Challenging conduct', *Community Care*, 24 June 1991. Published by permission of the editor of *Community Care*; Brindle, D. (1991) 'Care regime that relied on humiliation', *Guardian*, 31 May 1991. © Guardian Newspapers Ltd 1991.

Illustrations

Pp. 10, 14, 19 (bottom), 21, 49: Brenda Prince/Format; pp. 11, 19 (top): Sally and Richard Greenhill; p. 36: Courtesy of Kent County Council Social Services; p. 42: The Ronald Grant Archive; p. 52: News Team International/photo: Joel Chant.

Thanks are due to Peter McGill of the Tizard Centre for contributing to the section on autism.

Unit 19
Drawing the Line

Prepared for the course team by Hilary Brown
Updated by Jo Warner

While you are working on Unit 19, you will need:
- Course Reader
- Offprints Book
- Audio Cassette 5, side 1, parts 3 and 4
- Media Notes
- Wallchart

Contents

Introduction

You have seen throughout this course that caring is not just an ordinary relationship where common sense is a good enough guide. For example, Unit 3 discussed the need for home care assistants to establish boundaries in their relationships and Units 8 and 9 looked at the importance of care planning. In Unit 18 you explored some particularly difficult areas, including:

- intimate care, control and protection as areas which present particular challenges for those who care and those who are 'cared for'

- the dynamics of residential care and how these could go wrong

- why workers and family carers might find intimate care issues threatening because they move an otherwise 'social' relationship into uncharted waters

- the risks to civil liberties and integrity which people being cared for face in their daily interactions

- the idea of agreed guidance as one way of bringing difficult issues out into the open and strengthening professional boundaries where confusion about roles could slip over into abuse.

This unit explores these issues further. It is designed to help you draw the line between the occasional (some might say inevitable) 'ups and downs' of ordinary relationships and those real abuses of power which have to be challenged in the interests of both children and adults. In Unit 18 we reviewed the issues from inside the caring relationship. In this unit the focus is on making those judgments in more ordinary settings, in families and communities. We explore when, and in what circumstances, public 'authorities' intervene by crossing the thresholds of people's private lives.

This time you are on the outside looking in, because one important function of social and health care professionals is to step in when ordinary, unregulated, private relationships break down or go too far. So although there are some echoes of the issues you looked at in the last unit, in this one we come at them from a different angle.

You will be looking at what is meant by the term 'abuse', how decisions are made in situations where abuse is alleged or suspected, and at what point intervention should be initiated. The unit covers abuse as it affects both children and adults and deals with different forms of abuse and abusing. The material is not meant to be either voyeuristic or uncomfortable for the sake of it. It is designed to help you face up to abuse in the lives of people who use caring services and in your own life, and to search out the options and make changes. The core questions are listed overleaf.

Core questions

- How is 'abuse' defined?
- What are the different legal and professional contexts for child and adult protection?
- What criteria can be used for judging the seriousness of different kinds of abuse and abusing?
- Why does abuse happen and what pressures can lead to abusive behaviour?
- What part do gender, race, age and poverty play in the dynamics of abusive relationships?

Section 1
A health warning

The issues we shall be considering are distressing and shocking. It is a natural response to want to distance ourselves from them by thinking 'this couldn't happen in my family or my service or my neighbourhood'. But of course abuse does happen to ordinary people, in ordinary homes, day centres and schools. That is why everyone needs to think through the issues, to be prepared and to be well informed.

There are several reasons why you might find this subject particularly disturbing and it is worthwhile thinking about these to help you put support in place before you start, particularly if you anticipate the unit touching on painful memories or issues in your current situation.

1.1 You may have missed the signs

You may know individuals who, with the wisdom of hindsight, you now realise were being abused. You may regret that you did not recognise their distress or respond to things they were trying to tell you. Twenty years ago I worked with a young woman with learning difficulties who had been admitted to a group home. Her mother had died many years before and she had not had contact with services. She had been living alone with her father, who had rejected any help he had been offered and until recently, when he had been incapacitated by a stroke, he preferred to 'keep Diane busy at home'. Diane was emotionally withdrawn and her behaviour was challenging. The fashionable term in use at that time was that she was 'non-compliant'. It was easier to wrap up her distress and aggression as being something to do with her learning disability rather than with anything else that may have happened to her. We all found her difficult: she wouldn't wash or look after herself, and it was frustrating for us in that she wouldn't join in activities or pull her weight in the house. Diane also had a vaginal infection which the GP said was the worst she had ever seen. Looking back, there were signs and signals that were consistent with the fact that she had been sexually abused prior to moving to the group home but at the time it did not cross anyone's mind.

It is hard to judge practice in the past by today's standards: new awarenesses allow us to see things in a different light. It is important to acknowledge that we all make mistakes, and rather than cover them over by denial or by trivialising them, to see them as opportunities to learn for the future.

1.2 You may have been abusive yourself

Another reason for looking back with regret is if you have witnessed bad practice which you either did not recognise as such, or did not feel strong enough to challenge. In the next unit you will be listening to an experienced worker who was drawn into a culture of violence in a children's home and who describes the difficulties he experienced in knowing what to do about it. Worse still, you might have done something which you now consider to have been abusive. It may be that you feel you have sometimes reached the end of your tether, perhaps at work with a client, or at home with a partner, or with your children. It is important to keep incidents in proportion but also to challenge patterns in which violence, whether verbal or physical, becomes a way of resolving issues or releasing tension.

1.3 You may have been abused

Studying this unit may bring back memories for you, or bring things to the surface which you have tried to keep buried. You may remember incidents which you have pushed to the back of your mind.

At a recent training day David Lewis suddenly found himself remembering that he had been sexually molested when he was about 13. He had been going home from swimming around the back of the park and an older boy had pushed him into the railings and made him have oral sex. David hadn't wanted to show anyone how afraid he had been: he didn't tell anyone at the time and he hadn't told anyone since. But learning about sexual abuse for his job as a manager of a day centre had brought it all back. The sudden onset of this buried memory made David quite anxious as he lives in a small community and he wouldn't want anyone to tell his wife.

Nearly three out of five women aged 16–21 and over a quarter of men in the same age group have experienced unwanted sexual attention according to one survey (Kelly *et al.*, 1991), and 4 per cent of young women and 2 per cent of young men have been more seriously sexually abused, so David is not alone in having to face these memories.

1.4 You may be in an abusive relationship now

Abuse may not necessarily be in the past. You may find this unit especially difficult if you are currently being abused in a relationship at home or at work. The examples and exercises may make you question whether you can or should be standing up for yourself more. You may have accepted violence or intimidation as inevitable, but come to see them as an infringement of your rights and dignity. You may need to get support or information from beyond your usual social network to help you leave a violent relationship, find an alternative service, or move on from a job which puts you at risk or is making you feel unhappy or unsafe. You may not want things to continue the way they are but you may be afraid to challenge them, or feel that you have no options.

Estimates vary about the prevalence of domestic violence but it is thought to occur in between 10 and 30 per cent of heterosexual relationships (Holder *et al.*, 1994) and in a half of cases in which a woman is being abused at least one child is being abused also. Men can also be on the receiving end of such abuse although this does not happen as frequently. Thinking through the issues in this unit may help you to clarify what you have a right to in your own relationships and your options for getting support and keeping safe.

Activity 1   **Caring for yourself**

Take as long as you need   Think carefully if there are any reasons why this unit might be particularly painful or challenging for you. Jot down on a piece of paper any times when:
(a) you have felt abused by someone yourself
(b) you have been concerned about someone else's behaviour
(c) you have felt afterwards that your own relationships or practice have verged on being bullying or abusive.

Is there someone you can talk to about these times?

Are there lessons you have learnt?

Do you think you need help to keep you safe or to help you think clearly about the issues as they come up at home, in your work or in the context of your caring relationships and responsibilities?

Comment   You might want to talk to your tutor, to a counsellor or to a helpline or service which specialises in responding to people who are troubled about different kinds of abuse.

Key points

- Stepping in to prevent abuse is an important function of social and health care professionals.

- Considering abuse can trigger painful memories or feelings.

- If the material in this unit is likely to be painful for you, think now about where you can look for support.

Section 2
Different forms of abuse

To begin the unit I return to our fictionalised case study. In Unit 18 you met Marie who had just embarked on her career as a carer. Her next-door neighbour is Pat, an ordinary member of the public. As in Marie's story, a number of themes and threads have been woven together from real life. Even if they seem a bit fantastical, Pat's problems are those faced by many people at some time in their lives, although perhaps not all on one day!

Pat

Pat is Marie's next-door neighbour. She has had a rough week and has gone to visit her sister-in-law Bernice for a break. She explains over a cup of coffee how it all started and how it made her think.

'Well ... it was wet last Thursday and I hate November: the wind was really cold and I hate how it gets dark even though it is only 4 pm. I left work in a real hurry because I just had to get the shopping in. You know what it's like when you are out of cereal and there is no bread for anyone's sandwiches in the morning. I left the papers I was sorting for old Mitchell in a terrible mess and I still couldn't find the letter from Bates Limited that he kept asking for all morning. He had a real go at me about it and shouted at me right there in the front office with all the other girls listening in. If only I could have unearthed it before I left I could have relaxed and left work behind me for the evening. The more I think about it now I am sure that I gave it to him anyway. Last time he got really mad about something he had taken it out of my file himself and two weeks later he came and just dropped it in my in-tray without any word of explanation or apology. Perhaps I could find another job, although there isn't much around at the moment and the new mortgage we have just taken out makes it very difficult. We can't afford to take any risks ... well you can't these days can you? I still don't know where I could have filed Bates's letter ...

'When I got to the supermarket they were out of sandwich spread. It's always the way ... when things go wrong at work they usually go wrong at home as well. I knew Jesse would be cross and refuse to take anything proper to school ... if he can't have sandwich spread he won't have anything except a bag of crisps. I got in a right state wondering if I had time to go to the corner shop on my way home but you never know if they will have any there. If Superight don't have it probably the corner shop won't have it either so I knew he would just have to stew in his own juice. Then there I was at the checkout and what a queue! Jason Jones was on the till and although he's a nice lad he really isn't very quick, I don't know why they hired him. The woman in front ... she had a really nice emerald green jacket ... well she was taking ages unloading her trolley with the 'help' of her toddler. Well, I saw it coming really. Of course, the little girl wanted a chocolate egg: they were all wrapped up in shiny paper with little Father Christmases on top with darling little white fluffy beards. It was all so predictable looking back on it. 'Want one,' she said, but Mum says 'no'. 'Want one,' she said again. Mum said 'no' again, this time a bit louder. I just started to say 'I know how you feel, I've been there myself when mine were younger,' and I could tell the woman was getting tired and frazzled. And then suddenly, before I could get my mouth open, sort of out of nowhere, Mum lifted her out of the trolley and slapped her on the side of her thigh so hard the noise seemed to echo around the whole store. The little girl didn't scream, she just seemed to slump into the trolley seat in this sudden awful hush as everyone looked round. And I thought she seemed so shocked and small.

'I couldn't bear it … I thought "Oh God! Did I ever do that? Surely I wouldn't have ever hit mine so hard". I didn't know if I should say something … for an awful moment I thought she was going to do it again because all of a sudden the little girl let out a scream of rage and pain and her Mum was shouting at her, telling her to shut up and threatening to hit her again 'properly' when she got home. Somehow she got her bill paid and her shopping loaded up and they went off into the dark evening. Well, it really upset me. Should I have said anything? Or done anything? Should I have called social services? Oh of course not, it happens all the time … she was just having a hard time. Do you mind if I have another chocolate biscuit? Young single mum I expect and it wouldn't help to be spying on her or reporting her to the authorities … she's probably doing her best and anyway the little girl was whingeing. If it had been me with my kids on a bad day I might have done the same … But all the way home I kept thinking of the little girl's shocked expression, and I kept thinking, "is she tucked up in bed with it all forgotten and forgiven now or is she being hit again, and what if I read tomorrow in the paper that a child has been found dead?"

'I know I was getting it all out of proportion and after all who am I to preach, because just as I left the checkout myself I suddenly remembered I'd forgotten to drop mother's prescription in at the chemist's. If I concentrated on my own responsibilities instead of criticising everyone else I might get on better. So I decided to drop it off at Boots and then call in on my way home and give it to her … if she runs out of pills she gets such bad heartburn and I didn't want that on my conscience. I did have a lucky break because I found a parking space and there was no queue. So, five minutes later, with the pills in my pocket I screeched up outside the flat. The lights were on but they seemed to take ages to come to the door.

'Dad was grumbling as soon as he opened the door. "Alright, alright, alright, Pat, I've only got one pair of bloody hands. She's gone and done it again … wet herself … just as I was getting dinner. I told her if she keeps doing it she'll have to go into a home … it's no good, she does it just to get at me and I've had it up to here." I tried to apologise to Dad and calm him down a bit. "I just popped round to drop off her pills. You sound like you've had a bad day but you mustn't blame her, it isn't her fault." "It's alright for you, you don't have to wash the sheets or get up when she does it in the night … it's just for attention, she does it just to get me going." "I'm sure she doesn't really, Dad. I'll take the sheets if you like. How has her stomach been?" "Ask her your bloody self," he said angrily. Well I did and she wouldn't say but I could see she had been uncomfortable all day. I keep trying not to notice things are getting impossible, but Dad can't really manage much longer on his own, and I don't know if a home is the answer. It'll cost a mint, they will end up selling the flat and although I know it's not right to even think about it, we had been counting on getting some of the capital from that flat for the kids. Oh I feel ashamed even talking about it, but Jesse wants to go to college so much and it's the only way we could afford to help him, but if it all goes on residential care we'll have to think again.

'And then Dad was going on about my aunt. "Your Aunty Gill was round again yesterday ... says her Derek has gone and got himself a girlfriend in that home for mongols he lives in and that they are thinking of getting engaged ... well I ask you, I haven't got much time for all that fancy talk." (I know he shouldn't have used old-fashioned words like that but it wasn't worth another scene about it.) "She said she doesn't know where to go next with that lad. One minute she's going to have him home and the next she wants him locked away somewhere in the country. Your Mum was taken really bad in the night ... that pain of hers really took hold. It's no wonder we're all so grouchy."

'So I ended up grovelling and offering to do all sorts of things which I haven't really got time for ... "Oh Dad I'm sorry about the pills, but I've got them now. I'll come round on Saturday to give you a break. I'm sorry I am in a rush now ... I just can't get everything done today, it's been one of those days." Well I just had to get back to do the dinner. So I got back late and started cooking dinner and it was all really getting on top of me. Jesse went right into the sandwich spread treatment and when Allan got in, I didn't let him get his coat off before I started on about my boss and the supermarket and my mum and what I should have done. "Well, one person's abuse is another one's discipline," he says. "My mum and dad were strict but it didn't do us any harm, at least we knew where we were. But I've got no time for teachers ... they were a sadistic bunch ... they used to have us line up to break a cane over our backsides. That's just the way it was in those days ... still I wouldn't want it to be like that for our lads. Although maybe if we were a bit tougher we wouldn't have someone sulking upstairs who can't tell the difference between no sandwich spread and the outbreak of World War III."

'Well, all evening the incident in the supermarket was going round in my head, and I was feeling terrible about Mum and Dad and how they can't really manage on their own for much longer. I really envy Allan and you your confidence. He is so easy with your parents but there's always been an edge with mine. My Dad was always having a go at my brother and he laid into him sometimes. It's no wonder he cleared off to Scotland and hardly ever gets in touch now. And when he used to spank me, well there was something a bit sexual about it that makes the hairs stand up on the back of my neck even to think about it ... so anyway I persuaded Allan to go for a drink ... to take me out of myself.

'Well, you'll never believe what happened ... we went up to the Anchor and we were talking about all this stuff and when we were on our way home, the rain had set in and it was bitter cold ... but it was sensible to walk so as not to drink and drive, but with such a bitter wind and all, and we almost literally bumped into the couple who were sitting next to us in the pub right up the High Street near the bus shelter, bickering all evening they were and although I'm not one to mind arguments, the way they were going at each other in public just isn't right ... he starts yelling at her that she is a no-good slag and then he started to hit her. Well, you know how Allan hates rows, he didn't even stop to think but stepped right in between them. The bloke takes one look at him and lands the punch he was aiming at his girlfriend right on Allan, calling him a "black bastard"

> into the bargain. You'd think she'd be grateful or sorry, but no, she just turns round and shouted at both of us, "Get lost and mind your own business!" Fortunately someone called the police and an ambulance because there was blood everywhere. That's how come we ended up in casualty...'
>
> 'More coffee?'

2.1 What does the word 'abuse' mean to you?

It was certainly a bad Thursday. How seriously do you view the events Pat describes?

Activity 2

Allow about 10 minutes

Responding to the case study

Read through the list below and note your reactions to the questions.

(a)   Is Pat being bullied by her boss?

(b)   Should the mum in the supermarket have slapped her daughter?

(c)   Should Pat have said something to the woman or was she right to mind her own business?

(d)   Should Pat's dad call his nephew a 'mongol'?

(e)   How does Pat's mum feel when her husband says she'll have to go into a home?

(f)   Does Pat's mum wet herself deliberately?

(g)   Did Pat neglect her mum by forgetting her medicine?

(h)   Should money come into the decision about whether Pat's mum goes into a home?

(i)   Why does Allan feel OK about his parents' discipline but not his teachers'?

(j)   Why might Pat's brother feel differently from Allan?

(k)   Should girls be hit the same as boys?

(l)   Is Pat just making it up about being spanked?

(m)   Is the fight between the couple from the pub a private matter?

Comment

As you might have guessed, there are no right answers to these questions, but keep your comments to hand so that you can review them to see whether you have changed your views as you work through the unit.

Did you use the word 'abuse' to describe any of these incidents, memories or relationships, or do you think it is too heavy handed? You might feel that 'abuse' is not strong enough to describe the punch which landed on Allan, which could be counted as an assault. But if that punch had landed on the man's girlfriend, as was originally intended, would it have been called 'assault' or 'abuse'? And if hitting men and women is usually seen as either abuse or assault, why isn't hitting children?

Williams (1993), who has done research with people with learning difficulties about their understanding and experiences of crime, thinks the word 'abuse' is too loosely used to be useful. He sees the term as a kind of ghetto word which only applies to certain groups of people and which minimises the seriousness of what can be violent, exploitative and often criminal acts. His view is that this is because the status (or lack of it) of people with learning difficulties allows crimes against them to be trivialised or played down. (Eastman, 1993, argues the same in relation to older people.) Using a universal term like 'abuse' is helpful in that it challenges us to ask why we apply different standards to people in particular settings or relationships. Below are three examples of different standards:

1   Is it less serious for a service user to be hit by another service user with 'challenging behaviour' than for you or me to be hit at home or at work? These are similar actions, but carried out in different circumstances. They would almost certainly lead to different sanctions and interventions.

2   I would not choose to live with a man who had a previous history of sexual offending. Yet if I were a woman in residential care I might well find myself in this position without either my knowledge or assent.

3   If I were the victim of an assault I would not wish to continue to live or spend time alongside the person who had harmed me. If I were using services, I might have no option.

Certainly, the word 'abuse' tends to be used in relation to less powerful groups of people – as in child abuse, elder abuse, abuse of vulnerable adults, spouse abuse, racial abuse. But does the term 'abuse' add anything to our understanding of these situations?

Abuse takes place within unequal relationships

There is often an unequal relationship involved in abuse within which one person (ab)uses their greater power:

Policeman jailed for stealing pensioner's cash

A policeman who befriended a lonely 79-year-old spinster then abused her trust by stealing £7,800 was jailed for 18 months yesterday.

(*Daily Telegraph*, 1 May 1997)

Turning into a nightmare

The case of a desperate woman who went to a charity for help, only for her trust to be abused

When Pat Bentley needed help for her tranquilliser addiction, she placed her trust in a centre run by a well-known charity. That trust was repaid with sexual exploitation by her counsellor.

(*Guardian*, 21 May 1997)

UNSPEAKABLE ACTS

Awareness is growing that disabled people are extremely vulnerable to physical and sexual abuse and often unable to tell others of their experiences.

(*Nursing Times*, 19 February 1992)

Carer who stole from school founder, 97, faces jail after judge condemns 'meanest' of crimes

Nurse's £33,000 betrayal of trust

A carer was convicted yesterday of taking more than £33,000 savings from the founder of a prestigious preparatory school during the two years before she died at the age of 97.

(*Daily Telegraph*, 1 May 1997)

- authority in the case of parents or teachers
- economic power in the case of Pat's boss, Mr Mitchell
- physical strength in the case of men who beat their wives or girlfriends (or parents who hit children).

In the *No Secrets* (2000) guidance issued by the government to agencies on responding to the abuse of vulnerable adults, which I referred to in Unit 18, abuse is defined as follows:

> *Abuse is a violation of an individual's human and civil rights by any other person or persons. (p. 9)*

However, such a definition is too broad to be really useful in understanding and, more importantly, identifying where abuse may be taking place. The guidance provides this more detailed statement to support the definition:

> *Abuse may consist of a single act or repeated acts. It may be physical, verbal or psychological, it may be an act of neglect or an omission to act, or it may occur when a vulnerable person is persuaded to enter into a financial or sexual transaction to which he or she has not consented, or cannot consent. Abuse can occur in any relationship and may result in significant harm to, or exploitation of, the person subjected to it. (p. 9)*

2.2 Categories of abuse

Legal frameworks and policy documents issued by the Department of Health, social services and other related agencies tend to categorise acts of abuse in slightly different ways. However, a consensus is emerging in the field of *adult abuse* to log cases under these headings:

- **physical abuse**, including hitting, slapping, pushing, kicking, misuse of medication, restraint, or inappropriate sanctions

- **sexual abuse**, including rape and sexual assault or sexual acts to which the vulnerable adult has not consented, or could not consent or was pressured into consenting

- **psychological abuse**, including emotional abuse, threats of harm or abandonment, deprivation of contact, humiliation, blaming, controlling, intimidation, coercion, harassment, verbal abuse, isolation or withdrawal from services or supportive networks

- **financial or material abuse**, including theft, fraud, exploitation, pressure in connection with wills, property or inheritance or financial transactions, or the misuse or misappropriation of property, possessions or benefits

- **neglect and acts of omission**, including ignoring medical or physical care needs, failure to provide access to appropriate health, social care or educational services, the withholding of the necessities of life, such as medication, adequate nutrition and heating and

- **discriminatory abuse**, including racist, sexist, that based on a person's disability, and other forms of harassment, slurs or similar treatment.

Any or all of these types of abuse may be perpetrated as the result of deliberate intent, negligence or ignorance.

(*No Secrets*, 2000)

Old people drugged to keep them quiet

Elderly people living in nursing and residential homes are being routinely prescribed sedative drugs to keep them quiet, says a damning report.

(Community Care, 15--21 May 1997)

Child abuse is categorised in a similar way, with the exception of financial abuse. (The omission of a financial abuse category reflects the fact that children usually lack independent possessions. This bypasses some highly political issues. A child who goes without food because his or her parent has no money will be deemed to be the victim of parental neglect rather than poverty.)

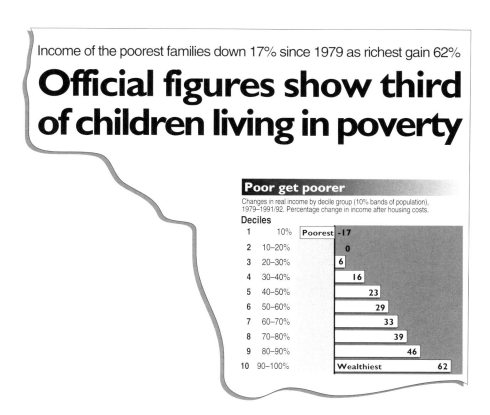

Income of the poorest families down 17% since 1979 as richest gain 62%

Official figures show third of children living in poverty

Poor get poorer

Changes in real income by decile group (10% bands of population), 1979–1991/92. Percentage change in income after housing costs.

Deciles			
1	10%	Poorest	-17
2	10–20%		0
3	20–30%		6
4	30–40%		16
5	40–50%		23
6	50–60%		29
7	60–70%		33
8	70–80%		39
9	80–90%		46
10	90–100%	Wealthiest	62

(Guardian, 15 July 1994)

Children may be abused in a family, or an institution, or in a community setting, by those known to them or, more rarely, by a stranger:

- **physical abuse** *may involve hitting, shaking, throwing, poisoning, burning or scalding, drowning, suffocating, or otherwise causing physical harm to a child*

- **emotional abuse** *is the persistent emotional ill treatment of a child such as to cause severe and persistent adverse effects on the child's emotional development*

- **sexual abuse** *involves forcing or enticing a child or young person to take part in sexual activities, whether or not the child is aware of what is happening*

- **neglect** *is the persistent failure to meet a child's basic physical and/or psychological needs, likely to result in the serious impairment of the child's health or development.*

(Department of Health, 1999)

Discriminatory abuse, which is referred to in the categories of adult abuse given earlier, is also an important area which should also be considered in relation to the abuse of children.

Now we are going to return to Pat's experiences to check how useful these labels and categories are in real life.

Activity 3   Identifying different forms of abuse

Allow about 10 minutes   Go back through the list of questions in Activity 2. This time, instead of jotting down your own quick reactions, note whether you think the incidents and relationships could be interpreted as abuse (either child or adult). If so, do they fit into the categories listed below? List each case under the appropriate heading. Where they don't seem to fit, make a brief note.

(a)   Physical

(b)   Sexual

(c)   Psychological

(d)   Financial

(e)   Neglect

(f)   Discriminatory

Comment   I listed:

Physical

- the little girl in the supermarket

- Allan abused by his teachers

- Allan by the man from the pub

- Pat's brother by her father

- possibly Pat by her father but I didn't know whether to put this down as sexual instead (or maybe both physical and sexual).

Psychological (which I thought was mostly verbal)

- Mr Mitchell, Pat's boss, shouting and maybe bullying if he is deliberately out to get at her

- Pat's father towards her mother because she had been left wet and uncomfortable.

Neglect

- perhaps when Pat forgot her mother's medicine

- when Pat's mother was left wet and uncomfortable.

Discriminatory

- Allan by the man from the pub

- Pat's father calling Derek a 'mongol'

- the man in the pub towards his girlfriend.

Trying to fit things into categories

I didn't like the fact that the decision about whether Pat's mother should go into a home was influenced by the finances of Pat's family and her son's wish to go to college, although I could quite see how this would come about. If this had been a firm decision I might have put it down as 'financial abuse', but it was just a thought and I didn't think Pat would act against her mother's interests if things got worse at home.

I also questioned whether I should put Allan down as having been physically abused by his parent(s). Although he seemed to have defined it as discipline, it struck me as odd that I might categorise Pat's brother as having been physically abused and not Allan, even though they may have experienced the same things.

Although I thought Pat neglected her mother on this occasion by forgetting the medicine, I also had questions about this. Would you use 'abuse' to describe Pat's failure to get her mother's medication? Because you know Pat didn't *mean* to forget her mother's pills, would you let her off the hook? If we say that Pat was neglectful, how do we feel about her brother, who doesn't visit at all? We have already seen that there are pressures and expectations which might lead Pat, as her parents' only daughter, to become their main carer, even though she has plenty of family responsibilities and financial pressures in her own life.

Did you come up with any other 'types' of abuse or problems in fitting these incidents or events to the headings?

Some of these questions will be revisited later in the unit. At this point, however, the last item in the comment, about Pat's 'neglect', demands further consideration. If we are going to make a judgment about someone who is doing a lot but making mistakes or overlooking things, what is our view of people who opt out altogether? Stevenson, whose research into abuse spans over 25 years, says in a report comparing responses to abuse of children with that of older people:

> ... *we are some way from being able to devise preventive strategies for elder abuse because ... there is quite a high degree of moral confusion about the status of adult relationships.*

> *(Stevenson, 1996, p. 23)*

In other words, it is hard to say what 'duty' Pat (or her brother) has to her mother in these circumstances and this makes it harder to judge her actions or her failures. A similar issue arises in the context of residential care, where abusive acts are more likely to be committed by direct care staff and at times when more senior staff have gone off duty (see Sundram, 1984). If you are left on duty alone without adequate support to meet the needs of all the people nominally in your care, who is the one doing the neglecting – you, or those who have failed to staff the service adequately? This is the sort of question you will address when accountability is discussed in Block 6. It is certainly a question to ask in cases such as the 'bedroom abuse' described in Lee-Treweek in the Reader (Chapter 25).

These sorts of issues also raise the crucial question of who has the **power** to define abuse. For example, should Allan's definition of his parents' treatment of him as 'discipline' still stand even if you are quite certain that you would categorise it as 'physical abuse'? This controversial issue of parental punishment of children is explored in much greater depth in Section 3.

Limitations to these categories

There are advantages to agreeing a single system of labels. If every area uses a different scheme it is not possible to monitor practice and make comparisons across different agencies. However, there are problems in thinking about abuse in the way I have outlined. It focuses attention rather narrowly on a certain type of act and this may simplify our thinking too much. It can obscure the complex dynamics which exist in abusive relationships and so lead us to see abuse as a single act rather than as an ongoing process – one which often includes some elements of a 'cover-up', or of cycles of abusing followed by promises that it won't happen again. Also, in practice the types often overlap. I found it hard to decide which categories some of the behaviours described in the case study belonged in. In particular, I found it hard to decide what belonged in the discriminatory abuse category and not in any of the others. I decided that many of the things which happened belonged in more than one category. For instance, the man from the pub racially abused Allan but also physically abused him by punching him. Allan may well have experienced this event as psychologically abusive as well.

In a recent study of cases of adult abuse reported in two authorities over one year, multiple abuses were documented in at least a fifth of cases (Brown and Stein, 1998). For example, a member of staff might use physical violence, or the threat of it, to coerce an adult with learning difficulties to engage in, or maintain secrecy about, a sexual act and it is hard to see how such an act could fail to cause psychological harm. This kind of overlap has been documented in relation to child protection cases as well (see Farmer and Owen, 1995); and similarly with domestic violence, which is described as involving:

> ... *a variable combination of physical, emotional, sexual and psychological abuse within a relationship context. The violence can be actual, threatened or attempted, and is usually committed by adult men against adult women with whom they are, or have been, in a relationship. As a crime of interpersonal violence it is about the use of humiliation, threats and/or force to maintain power and control over the victim and other members of the household.*
>
> *(Holder et al., 1994, p. 5)*

This kind of pervasive abuse within a relationship does not fit neatly into any of the boxes, but spans all of them. Moreover, as we saw in Unit 18, when abuse takes place within a service it may be important to be alert to the nature of the whole regime or wider system, rather than a single act or the behaviour of an individual abuser.

2.3 Evaluating seriousness

Whatever words are used, the term 'abuse' has many different dimensions. Defining abuse isn't only a matter of categorising acts into types as you did in Activity 3, but is also about judging when something is serious enough to warrant action. We will be considering this at length in relation to physical abuse of children and sexual abuse of adults with learning difficulties. The Children Act 1989 adds the notion of seriousness into definitions of abuse by stipulating that for action to be taken the child must be at risk of 'significant' harm. (In Scotland, 'significant' harm relates to emergency action, such as child protection orders, rather than day-to-day child protection work.) A measure of seriousness might be how far any abuse constitutes a criminal act, but even that is interpreted 'flexibly' by individual practitioners and police officers; also at an institutional level by the Criminal Prosecution Service, which uses a 'public interest' criterion as one factor in deciding whether or not to prosecute particular cases. The *No Secrets* (2000) guidance on the abuse of vulnerable adults makes the following statement about assessing seriousness:

What degree of abuse justifies intervention? In determining how serious or extensive abuse must be to justify intervention a useful starting point can be found in Who decides? *Building on the concept of 'significant harm' introduced in the Children Act, the Law Commission suggested that:*
"'harm' should be taken to include not only ill treatment (including sexual abuse and forms of ill treatment which are not physical), but also the impairment of, or an avoidable deterioration in, physical or mental health; and the impairment of physical, intellectual, emotional, social or behavioural development'."

(No Secrets, 2000, p. 12)

When we use the word 'abuse' we are essentially making a value judgment. We are saying that an act, or series of acts, in a relationship is intolerable. It is often a judgment made from the outside by a third party or agency and one which is liable to change over time, and in different contexts, cultures and settings. We make judgments in individual cases against the background of prevailing economic and cultural attitudes and we have to act on these judgments in the light of public consensus about how we should relate to each other.

ARE YOU IN AN ABUSIVE RELATIONSHIP?

Signs of abuse

● Your boyfriend constantly puts you down and tells you you're ugly/stupid/no good in bed.

● You believe him and feel grateful that he suffers you.

● He hits you. But he's so sorry afterwards you let him get away with it, and even cover up for him.

● He says he'll change – but he never does.

What to do if you think you are in an abusive relationship

● Recognise the problem. If he's violent there's nothing you can do to help. It's up to him to change. Even if you have a rocky relationship, that doesn't excuse his use of violence.

● Tell a friend, or member of your family about him. Opening up will be a relief, and it's good to get another perspective.

● Get practical advice – try one of the organisations we've suggested [in the margin]. They'll help with practical matters, too, such as a place to take refuge if you're living with him.

● Take a deep breath and walk out. Don't wait until the next time he hits you. You might end up seriously hurt. …

● Don't go rushing back to him, even if your feelings for one another are still there. Wait a few months and get some counselling. If you really want to make a go of it, make sure he realises he has a problem and has done something about it.

Women's Aid National Helpline: 0345 023468 (Mon–Fri, 10am–5pm).

REFUGE: 0181 995 4430. A 24-hour crisis line that can help you find a safe place to stay and offers legal advice and counselling.

Police stations now have domestic violence or vulnerable persons units. Call your local station for details.

(19 Magazine, 8–13 December 1996)

Activity 4   **Evaluating seriousness**

Allow about 20 minutes   When concerns are voiced about abuse practitioners have to weigh up one factor against another to decide whether a particular situation warrants intervention. In this activity you are going to look at some of the factors to be taken into account to arrive at these judgments.

Consider each of the incidents listed. Put a (1) by the one you consider the most serious and then rank the others down to (9), the least worrying.

(a)   Boss shouts at woman in front of other workers for losing something.

(b)   Mother slaps little girl hard on leg in supermarket.

(c)   Teacher canes whole class of boys on backside.

(d)   Daughter forgets frail older mother's medicine, causing her pain.

(e)   Husband threatens wife with going into a home when she wets herself.

(f)   Man calls his girlfriend a 'slag' in public.

(g)   Father slaps teenage son for not doing his schoolwork (Allan and Pat's brother).

(h)   Father hits daughter on bottom over his knee.

(i)   One man punches another in the face outside the pub.

Now look at your list and think about how you made your judgments. Did you base them on the harm which had actually been done to the victim (in which case Pat's forgetting to get the medicine had caused as much discomfort as the young mother's slapping her child in the supermarket)? Did you take into account the intentions of the person who was responsible for the abuse or the nature of their relationship? For each of the criteria below, take a different coloured pencil and note down a new set of numbers, ranking the incidents in a new order. Notice which ones change place when you consider the incidents from a different point of view.

Criteria:

•   how harmful the act was

•   how harmful it was in the short term and in the longer term

•   whether it was done on purpose or by accident.

Do you think there are other important criteria besides these three? Write them down.

Comment   You might like to compare your criteria with the list developed by Brown and Stein to assist staff in evaluating seriousness:

•   How vulnerable is the victim?

•   How extensive is the abuse? For example, if financial abuse, how much money? If physical abuse, what damage has been done?

•   Was it a one-off incident or part of a long-standing or repeated pattern?

•   What impact is it having on the vulnerable person's well-being?

•   Are other people being damaged or threatened by it ... for example children or other family members, other residents in residential care or onlookers?

- What were the intentions of the alleged abuser ... has it been done deliberately ... was it planned ... is there any evidence that the person actively targeted this person or other vulnerable people?

- Is what has happened against the law ... can legal action be taken, or other formal steps such as disciplinary action or a formal complaint or action under the Registered Homes Act?

- Will it happen again to this vulnerable person if action is not taken? Sexual abuse, for example, is very likely to be repeated.

- Might it happen again to other vulnerable people at risk ... for example other service users/residents, children or other adults in the household?

(Adapted from Brown and Stein, 1998)

I doubt if you got all these, but hope you found at least some common ground.

In the guidance developed by Brown and Stein, workers were asked to separate out issues of *evidence* from issues of *seriousness*. It is often difficult to get clear *evidence* about what may be going on but this should not be taken as a signal that the situation is not potentially serious.

Key points

- Evaluating the seriousness of abuse is complex.

- Factors to take into account include the extent of the harm caused, the context and the perpetrator's intent.

- Future risk is also a key issue in deciding whether action is called for.

2.4 Context as part of definition

We have seen that you can place a potentially abusive act in a category and within that you can place each act on a continuum of severity in terms of the harm it causes. So, for example, you might decide that an injury which caused bruising was slightly less serious than one which led to abrasions, broken bones or permanent tissue damage. But that wouldn't be the end of the story, would it? Did you rank the assault on Allan as more or less serious than the incident with the little girl? While the severity of the act itself makes a difference, so do the intentions of the perpetrator, the power differential and the vulnerability of the victim. Different situations are 'constructed' or interpreted differently depending on the relationship between the people concerned; for example whether they are parent and child or husband and wife. The context has to be taken into account to judge whether any specific incident separately or cumulatively crosses a threshold of acceptability. For example, you might decide that the incident in the supermarket is not in itself bad enough to warrant taking action but you might want to check if this kind of thing has happened before; if it has it would be possible for something quite minor to tip the balance and make you take action.

Thinking about these issues will almost certainly lead you to reflect on your own upbringing and your beliefs about how to raise children or what constitutes a happy marriage/partnership. You might also reflect on your attitude to whether the 'state' or caring services such as health or social services have any remit or responsibility to step in. You may think these issues are private and no one's business but your own. On the other hand, you may think the government should protect children or vulnerable adults, regulate punishment in school or at home, and legislate against fights in public and private places. You may have different views about what is right in schools or at home, between neglect in a person's own flat or in residential care (confusingly also called 'a home'), about a fight involving strangers and one involving a couple. As you complete this section, reflect for a moment on whether you tend to make different judgments about the same behaviours depending on whether they take place in the public or the private sphere.

Key points

- The word 'abuse' is not very accurate and so there is often disagreement about what constitutes abuse.

- Abusive acts can be categorised, for example as physical, sexual, psychological, financial or discriminatory and placed on a continuum of seriousness.

- Different types of abuse often occur within the same abusive relationship.

- The same act may be treated differently according to whether it took place in public or private.

Section 3
Child protection: a worked example

When we left Bernice she was washing up the coffee cups after her discussion with Pat. Since that conversation she has felt quite upset because, although she didn't tell Pat at the time, she knows the mother in the emerald green jacket. The young woman is called Sue and she brings her daughter to the playgroup which Bernice runs. She is not a single mother, as Pat had assumed, but lives with her partner, her daughter's father. Bernice has been worried for some time about the way Sue disciplines her daughter – it isn't that she is 'firm', it is more that she is erratic. She seems to take little notice of her daughter's play and to ignore her when she comes up to show off her pictures, then will suddenly butt in harshly when a more gentle reminder might work just as well.

While Pat was pondering her duties as a citizen and how uncomfortable she would have been 'reporting' the incident she witnessed, Bernice has clear duties as a professional child-care worker and knows that she should report the matter to social services if she is in any doubt. However, her 'common sense' tells her that lots of children are smacked occasionally, apparently without long-term harm. She knows that families go through bad patches but their kids turn out OK in the end. Also, she wonders what would happen if she *did* report it. Would Sue just stop coming? Is she exaggerating the matter and should she allow what she has been told 'off the record' by Pat to influence her judgment?

One evening Bernice sat down absent-mindedly and wrote the following list. These were the questions she turned over in her mind:

- Is this physical abuse or does it not count because it's her mum smacking her?

- Is it bad enough for me to report it?

- How 'normal' is it? At the moment I think it is quite extreme but does this happen in all families?

- How long has it been going on and how often does it happen? I've seen four instances that I can think of and Pat has seen one. Is Sue just going through a bad time?

- Does she make up for it in other ways? Perhaps she has good points as a mother as well.

- How could this kind of discipline affect the little girl in the long run?

- What would social services do and would it make it worse? Perhaps we should offer Sue more days at playgroup instead of labelling her as a problem.

These concerns are very typical. An overview of recent research compiled by the Dartington Social Research Unit (as part of an initiative by the government to redirect the emphasis from investigation to support in child protection matters) points to these kinds of considerations which professionals weigh up when making judgments about when to intervene:

- *moral/legal concerns ... is it wrong?*
- *pragmatic concerns ... can we help or will we make it worse?*
- *concerns about outcome ... how much damage will this do in the longer run?*

(Dartington Social Research Unit, 1995, p. 17)

These sum up Bernice's concerns. Bernice knew she would have to make up her mind whether to speak to a social worker or not, and decided to go to the library on Saturday morning to see if she could find any books or articles which would help her to clarify her thoughts.

Key points

- Anyone working with children has a clear duty to report concerns about child protection issues.

- In deciding whether to intervene workers make a judgment about whether particular ways of behaving are 'right' or 'wrong'.

- Knowing what will happen in the longer term may be part of the equation.

- Workers also consider whether their intervention could help or may make things worse.

3.1 The debate about smacking

It is clear from the story above that there are many different beliefs about what is acceptable behaviour, especially within the family. As a society our attitudes towards children are inconsistent. On the one hand, we have a complex child protection system within which to operate (which we don't have for vulnerable adults), but at the same time children are the only group not included within the general legal framework relating to assault. The police were called to the scene when Allan was punched in the nose by the man from the pub but no one called the police to the little girl in the supermarket. Parents are, and until recently teachers were, 'allowed' or 'legitimated' to use physical force to control children's behaviour. In many circles such behaviour is approved of and political and church leaders are not afraid to own up to 'smacking' their children.

At the time of writing teachers in state schools in the UK are not allowed to use corporal punishment, but teachers in independent schools are, although this is shortly to be tested before the European Court.

Blair admits smacking his children – and feeling remorse
Alice Thomson Political Reporter

Tony Blair, who has always claimed to be 'tough on crime and tough on the causes of crime', has been applying the same principles at home.

The Labour leader admitted yesterday that he smacked his children and believed corporal punishment was an appropriate tool to help to maintain discipline. The admission to *Parent Magazine* has delighted Right-wing Tories who are thrilled that the Labour leader has joined a select band of parliamentary smackers, including Virginia Bottomley and Baroness Thatcher ...

(The Times, 6 June 1996)

How common is smacking?

As Allan said, 'one person's abuse is another person's discipline'. Many people think that smacking children is acceptable in certain circumstances, perhaps depending on:

*   the relationship of the people involved

*   whether they would see the hitting as 'deserved'

*   how they would view the rights or role of the person doing the hitting to discipline or control the person on the receiving end.

A MORI poll commissioned by the NSPCC in 2002 of nearly 1,600 parents in the UK with dependent children reported the figures given in Table 1.

Table 1   MORI poll

Parents who physically punished their children	55%
Parents who say that physical punishment is the wrong way to discipline children	57%
Those who physically punish their children, but said it is wrong	44%
Those who physically punish their children, and say 'sorry' for their behaviour afterwards	69%
Parents who were physically punished as children, who now physically punish their own children	70%
Parents who were not physically punished as children who now physically punish their own children	20%

You can see from this table that parents are pretty confused about smacking. The NSPCC is among those who believe it is the government's responsibility to take the lead and make hitting children a thing of the past. This issue is, as I write (in June 2002), being debated by the Scottish Parliament, which is considering proposals to ban the smacking of children under three and to outlaw the use of implements to hit a child of any age. During the Scottish parliamentary debate, Save the Children commissioned a survey of some 1,300 children across Scotland to gauge their opinions of smacking – the first time children had been consulted on this matter. Ninety-four per cent of children believed there were other ways of disciplining children such as withholding pocket money, making them perform chores, or preventing them seeing their friends. Three quarters of them said that it was absolutely wrong for an adult to hit a child. Asked about how they felt after they had been smacked they used words such as terrified, disliked, lonely, sick and ashamed.

Study skills: Reading tables and other figures

Have you developed the habit of stopping to absorb figures rather than skipping over them? You should have found these quite easy after all the practice you have had. Just to test yourself:

*   Did you notice that some parents who have said that it is wrong to hit children also say that they do physically punish their children? What might this mean to the wider debate around smacking?

*   What else might you read into these figures?

Here are my answers:

- Some children's agencies argue that this kind of evidence of parents' muddled attitudes and behaviour shows that parents need and want alternatives to hitting their children; other ways to discipline children without hitting out.

- There are other points you might read into the figures, such as that if some parents are apologising to their children after smacking them, then those parents are experiencing some emotional pain too. You might also have noticed that, unsurprisingly, parents who were not hit as children are less likely to smack their own children.

Do you feel you are getting pretty good at drawing sense out of figures now?

Key points

- Smacking young children is accepted by most people as a reasonable form of discipline.

- Smacking can range from a light slap to hitting with an object, such as a hairbrush or belt.

- Smacking is widespread.

Is smacking a form of child abuse?

The first reading Bernice really got her teeth into was a debate about smacking which looked at the arguments for and against routine smacking of children within their families. This is reproduced in Offprint 25 which is taken from an American book, *Debating Children's Lives*, edited by Mason and Gambill (1994, pp. 195–223).

In the preface the editors explain the advantages they see in presenting issues in a debate format. They say it allows readers to see both sides of an issue clearly. But they also warn of the risk that the ideas may become polarised, so that people feel they can only take an extreme view.

Study skills: Engaging with academic debates

When you study at university level you enter a world of debates. Academic knowledge advances through the clash of different ideas. People deliberately present their positions in an 'extreme' form, so that the logical differences between ideas stand out clearly. Then they search for evidence and lines of analysis which will tilt the balance towards one theory and against another. But the debate only works in this 'constructive', knowledge-building way because it is conducted in an orderly fashion according to established rules. The idea is that you read other people's arguments carefully and respond to them point by point, through logical analysis. You are supposed to present your own case 'objectively', keeping your personality, values and preferences to one side. Ideas are meant to be judged on their own merits, regardless of their practical implications, and independently of who puts them forward.

Outside the academic world, in society at large, there are also many debates. But these are not necessarily conducted in a disciplined way. You 'win' the argument by capturing popular support or getting the backing of powerful people. Appealing to emotions, playing on people's loyalties, shouting loudly and denigrating your opponent are all part of the game, as are compromising and 'fudging the issues' to reach a resolution.

You need to develop skill in following an academic debate, as writers on different sides weave together arguments and evidence to support their particular points of view. You also need to be able to detect when they are *not* following the rules of academic argument – sneaking in emotional appeals, fudged arguments, and so on. The debate you are about to read is an excellent opportunity, both to see how academic writers battle for their own ideas, and to notice when the rules of academic debate are being broken.

I chose this offprint material for three reasons.

- It sets out some strong arguments for and against the use of physical punishment.

- It shows you some of the kinds of evidence which are used.

- It gives an idea of the role of academic debate in relation to public debate and the development of social policy.

Activity 5   Is smacking by parents abuse?

Allow about 10 minutes

Before you start to read Offprint 25 I want you to do some homework! I want you to monitor your own views on the topic as we work through the debate to see if you shift at all having read some of the arguments. The question under debate in Offprint 25 is:

'Should the use of corporal punishment by parents be considered child abuse?'

A note of caution: they use the term 'anti' to mean 'against smacking', not against the question. Also they use the term 'naysayers', i.e. those who say no to hitting children but not to the question as it is expressed here. If you answer yes, you would be against smacking; if you answer no you would be in favour of it. Before you read the offprint, register your own 'gut instinct' position. Don't agonise – just tick the point which most nearly represents your view.

Yes, corporal punishment is abuse	Yes, but I have some reservations	I don't know or can't make up my mind	No, but I have some reservations	No, corporal punishment isn't abuse

Comment   Have your response at hand as you work through this section. As you consider the points raised by different contributors, use the same headings to monitor if and how your views change. You'll be reminded to do this after each activity in this section.

Defining terms

It is possible that you found Activity 5 difficult because we haven't defined our terms. A crucial aspect of this debate is its standing in law. 'Reasonable physical chastisement' remains within the law so can something that is legal be considered abuse? And what exactly do we mean by 'reasonable physical chastisement'? So before going any further, consider what *you* meant by 'reasonable physical chastisement'? What image came into your mind? If you agreed with 'it', what were you in favour of and if you disagreed, what were you disagreeing with? You will see that the contributors to Offprint 25 all agree that some forms of physical punishment are definitely abusive, for example if it is out of control or involves hitting with an object such as a belt or stick. Their debate is about 'mild spanking' and Larzelere defines this as 'a maximum of two slaps on the buttocks with an open hand'. Straus defines corporal punishment as the 'use of physical force with the intention of causing a child to experience pain but not injury'.

Activity 6   **Reviewing your position**

Allow about 5 minutes.   So now where do you stand? In the light of the definition of corporal punishment as 'causing a child to experience pain but not injury', tick the box which represents your views now.

Yes, even ordinary corporal punishment is abuse	Yes, but I have some reservations	I don't know or can't make up my mind	No, but I have some reservations	No, ordinary corporal punishment isn't abuse

Comment   Have you shifted? If so, this makes the point that often in a debate it isn't the actual evidence that is being weighed up but the initial emotional response to the words which are being used. Part of the debate is about agreeing what the words mean, a bit like an army agreeing 'terms of engagement'.

Study skills: Understanding the importance of frames of reference

An academic argument involves making a sequence of connected points within a frame of reference. (When you write a TMA the title provides the main frame of reference.) A debate between different arguments can only take place if all sides are prepared to work within a common frame of reference (i.e. what the debate is 'all about', including the meanings of key words). In practice, a lot of the art of debating is trying to drag the frame of reference in your direction to give your arguments a better chance. Already we can glimpse this here. Terms like 'mild spanking' and 'two slaps on the buttocks' set up a frame of reference where punishment is an orderly, controlled, benign action; whereas using 'physical force' to cause 'pain' sets a frame in which punishment involves a strong person intimidating a weak one.

Do you remember the discussion about the 'construction of social reality', in Unit 4, Section 4.1? Here again we have physical reality – the slap – giving rise to different constructions of social reality – mild spanking or physical assault. Which way the debate goes in the public realm has a lot to do with which of these constructions dominates. As you will read later in an extract from the Dartington Report, 'Society continually reconstructs definitions of maltreatment which sanction intervention' (Dartington Social Research Unit, 1995, p. 15).

The debate

Now it is time to get to grips with the debate. The first contribution is by Murray Straus, who identifies himself as a researcher and sociologist; we do not know if he is a parent himself.

Activity 7   **Reading Murray Straus**

Allow about 30 minutes   This activity is in three parts.

(a) Straus is arguing that corporal punishment *should* be considered as child abuse. Before you read, try to anticipate the questions he might be answering and jot them down.

(b) When you have done that, read and make notes on his arguments (pages 97–103 of the Offprints Book).

(c) Then make some notes on what evidence he uses to support his arguments.

Comment   (a) Anticipating the questions

I thought Straus might be asking:
- Does physical punishment work?
- Does it do damage – in the short or the longer term?

Did you think of any other questions? If so, you could use these as headings to help you make notes as you read. I also wondered what kind of evidence he would produce to persuade us – he could just say 'well, I think it is wrong', or he could try to prove whether people who are physically punished go on to do this or suffer from that, using proper research studies. I put another heading for evidence so that I could make a note of the kind of information he uses to support his ideas.

(b) Notes on his arguments

These are my notes:

He starts by asking if the risks are greater than alternative methods of discipline. Then he asks:
Does it work?

- Nearly everyone does it.
- It is no better than alternatives such as explaining, or removing the child.

Does it do damage?
- Incurs risk of psychological damage.
- Increases likelihood of juvenile delinquency and assaults on others.
- Teaches child to hit more.
- Increases spouse abuse.
- Increases likelihood that person will abuse own children.
- Increases likelihood of drink problems, suicide risk and depression.

(c) What kind of evidence does he produce?
- Provides analysis of over 2,000 families.
- Doesn't provide anything on how effective it is; only on the longer-term risks.
- Doesn't say when or why parents do it.

Has he persuaded you to change your mind? Mark your position on the five-point scale again to show where you stand now.

Yes, ordinary corporal punishment is abuse	Yes, but I have some reservations	I don't know or can't make up my mind	No, but I have some reservations	No, ordinary corporal punishment isn't abuse

Study skills: Reading graphs

In the offprint you have seen a number of graphs. Look back at Figure 1.

The people being studied in Figure 1 were divided into two broad groups according to whether or not there was violence between their parents. Each group was then divided into eight groups according to how many times their parents physically punished them during their teen years. You can see the eight groupings marked along the bottom of the diagram, ranging from 'None' to '30+'. Then for each of the 16 groups (two lots of eight) the proportion of men involved in wife assault was worked out. This is shown as a 'probability' figure. The scale shows probabilities ranging from 0.6 at the high end to 0.1 at the low end. (The highest probability figure you can have is 1.0, which means that the thing you are concerned with is absolutely certain to happen; the lowest is 0, which means that there is no likelihood at all that it will happen.)

So let's look at the bottom dot on the left. We can see from the label on the sloping line that this is a group whose parents were not violent to each other. Looking down to the horizontal axis we see 'None', so they were also never hit by their parents in their teens. Looking to the left we see that for the men in this group the probability of their being involved in wife assault was between .1

and .2 (say about .14). This is a lowish probability (about a 14 per cent chance). The next dot to the right is the group who were hit once by their parents in their teens. As you can see, their probability of being involved in wife assault was a bit higher (say .16). Moving up to the other end of the line, we see that those who had been hit 30 times or more had about a .3 probability of being involved in wife assault (30 per cent). Since the dots rise steadily up the line, it is obvious that the more times boys were hit in their teens the more likely they are to be involved in wife assault when they grow up. In other words, there is a strong 'correlation' between the two.

You can read the other line in exactly the same way. This is the group who experienced violence between their parents. At the left end of the line you can see that even those who were never hit by their parents in their teens have around a 30 per cent likelihood of being involved in wife assault, rising to around 50 per cent for those who were hit a lot by their parents. We can see that both violence between parents and being hit frequently by their parents in their teens were directly related to men being involved in wife assault later in life.

The other graphs are all of the same kind. If you read the labels and again start at the bottom dot on the left, you will be able to work out what they are telling you.

Correlations and causation

The fact that there is a strong correlation between the frequency of being hit by parents as a teenager and later involvement in wife assault does not prove that one *causes* the other. For example, you might argue that people are born with personalities ranging from very mild and compliant to very confrontational and aggressive. In that case the milder, more compliant people might be less likely to arouse their parents to hit them *and* also less likely to be involved in wife assault, and the confrontational, aggressive ones might be more likely to be hit by parents and be involved in wife assault. So the fact that being hit more often by parents goes with being more likely to be involved in wife assault may be because *both* are 'caused' by *something else* (e.g. inborn personality). This is not an argument in favour of personality as an explanation, just a demonstration that correlation *never* proves causation. When two measures correlate, you can never say that one 'causes' the other. (The higher the harbour boats rise, the smaller the beach gets, but it isn't the boats rising that causes the beach to get smaller.) All you can say is that the two vary together.

Next you are going to read a contribution by Robert Larzelere, who also identifies himself as a social scientist and researcher; again he does not say if he is a parent. I am going to use the same headings to make notes on his arguments. I expect him to focus more on whether punishment works in the immediate setting but we will see ...

Activity 8   **Reading Robert Larzelere**

Allow about 20 minutes   Now read and make notes on Robert Larzelere's contribution on pages 103–107 of Offprint 25, using the headings from the previous activity.

Comment   Does it work?

- Larzelere says it works to back up a 'time out' (i.e. sending a child to his or her room) approach.

- In combination with reasoning, it reduces fighting and disobedience.

- It increases the effectiveness of reasoning alone next time – I suppose by making a child more likely to 'listen'.

- But he is talking about smacking 2–6 year-olds, not teenagers as Straus does.

Does it do damage?

- No, he says it fits into authoritative parenting, which is good.

- He notes increased risk of aggression but says it is minimal.

- He says banning it would do damage and cites Sweden, where banning spanking led to increased reports of child abuse; he thinks parents who can't smack are more likely to lose control.

- He says it is culturally insensitive to ban it.

What kind of evidence does he produce?

- Lots of studies but doesn't really explain them; mostly evidence for it working rather than about long-term effects.

Bernice picked up on the point about cultural diversity because it raised issues for her: coming from an African-Caribbean background she has often been aware that she and Allan have different views about discipline and strictness and feel differently from Pat about family matters. In the past she had put this down to individual difference but she resolved to look into it further.

So where do you stand now? Has this part of the offprint caused you to shift again, perhaps back towards the 'no' position and more accepting of mild spanking of children and/or teenagers? Mark your position on the five-point scale.

Yes, ordinary corporal punishment is abuse	Yes, but I have some reservations	I don't know or can't make up my mind	No, but I have some reservations	No, ordinary corporal punishment isn't abuse

Finally, there is a contribution by John Rosemond – he is a psychologist and runs a centre for 'affirmative parenting', and he tells us he is a parent himself.

Activity 9   **Reading John Rosemond**

Allow about 20 minutes   Now read and make notes on the last contribution (pages 107–110), using
     the same headings again.

Comment   Does it work?

- Rosemond says usually it is used ineffectively, that it should be used not as a back-up but as a prelude to some other action, that smacking should be 'a first resort'.

Does it do damage?

- Says not.

What kind of evidence does he produce?

- He calls those he disagrees with 'pseudo-intellectual, politically correct megalomaniacs' and says they have 'swollen egos'.

- He dismisses 'all' the research studies, saying they 'stink'.

- He uses his own children as an example.

Now where are you?

Yes, ordinary corporal punishment is abuse	Yes, but I have some reservations	I don't know or can't make up my mind	No, but I have some reservations	No, ordinary corporal punishment isn't abuse

Look back over your position at various stages of the debate – did you come to these readings with a fairly firm view or an open mind? Have you been persuaded to change your mind by their arguments or to think about new issues? What new information or ideas have they introduced?

3.2 Science and values

The readings left Bernice unsettled. She had several concerns.

First, the contributors took for granted that there is agreement about how we want children to behave: for example, Larzelere says that he is aiming at compliance where another person might value independence of thought or spontaneity more highly.

Second, they were not all talking about the same thing. Straus was mostly talking about hitting teenagers whereas Larzelere was talking about children from two to six. Larzelere advocated smacking as a last resort and Rosemond as a first.

Third, the authors confused the issue by bringing their own attitudes towards and versions of 'science' into the debate. Rosemond turned it into a personal attack on people who disagree with spanking and claimed it was a matter of personal responsibility rather than social policy.

Fourth, the evidence cited is variable. Straus used a sample of 2,000 families, whereas Rosemond generalised from his own experience with his own two children (from whom we do not hear). Later in the original paper Straus responded to Rosemond by stating the case for science. He says:

> The difference between scientists ... and 'zealots' ... is that scientists test their assumptions and are willing to let the findings of scientific tests have the last word. My research was designed to give the assumption that all spanking is abusive a chance to be either supported or disproved.

(Mason and Gambill, 1994, p. 221)

Study skills: Not playing by the rules

As you were reading the offprint, did you recognise that Rosemond breaks the rules of academic debate and instead adopts the tone of a general public debate? Far from taking the other side's arguments seriously and analysing them point by point, he call his opponents names, sweeps aside their research with a dismissive gesture, and tries to draw us into identifying with his own parental relationship with his children. Although Straus and Larzelere disagree with each other, they are prepared to talk within the same academic frame of reference. Rosemond is not interested in playing that game. He knows that the winner of an academic debate still has to win support within wider public debate if they want to influence policy. So he opts out of the academic debate and goes straight for the public/political game.

The status of science

Incidentally, the word 'science' is bandied about here. Science is one particular kind of academic discourse which tends to carry high status in public debates. If you say an argument is 'academic' that unfortunately tends to be interpreted as meaning 'irrelevant', whereas if you say it is 'scientific' it is likely to be taken seriously. Science is supposed to be concerned with carrying out experiments to test theories. However, in the social 'sciences' it is often not possible to carry out experiments. Instead, they tend to rely on detailed and systematic data gathering. So when displaying its 'scientific' side, social science tends to present graphs and tables of numbers, as Straus does here. Larzelere quotes numbers too, from a range of different studies. These figures are used by both to try to swing the academic debate their way, but they are also being displayed here to lend credibility to claims of being 'scientific'. Straus makes clear that he thinks scientific arguments are more open-minded and fair. However, there are times when scientific arguments are worryingly narrow, as for example with Bowlby's account of the baby-bound mother (Unit 1), and eugenicists' proposals to restrict certain people's rights to have children (Unit 16). Science has a very important role to play in debates about policies, but it should never be assumed to deliver simply 'the truth'.

The quality of the evidence is not the only issue. There is another debate going on here about whether the state has any right to interfere in the way people treat each other. In this case it is about parents and children but it could also be stated in relation to men and women or carers and their elderly relatives. Setting rules in the private sphere can be characterised as an encroachment on the freedom of individuals in their homes and personal relationships. In this case it would limit the freedom of parents to act as they think fit. But the limits it would set are on the more powerful partner in these exchanges: on the parents not the children, the potentially violent spouse, the carer not the cared for. You could argue that by limiting the freedom of these people you can extend the freedom of the less powerful person.

So at the end of the debate where do you stand now?

Yes, I think ordinary corporal punishment is child abuse	Yes, but I have some reservations	I don't know or can't make up my mind	No, but I have some reservations	No, I do not think ordinary corporal punishment is child abuse

Before leaving the debate let's review the way this exchange has been managed by the three contributors. Their debate focused on three main areas:

1   Whether corporal punishment works in terms of controlling behaviour in an immediate sense (making children more 'compliant' and obedient).

2   Whether it has harmful side effects in the longer term, for example by teaching children that it is OK to hit people, especially if they love them, or by leading to depression and other psychological problems.

3   The rightness and effect of introducing a blanket 'ban' which interferes with the right of individual parents to act according to their own values.

Study skills: The social science disciplines

One reason why our three debaters disagree is that they come from different social science 'disciplines'. Psychologists, sociologists, economists and political scientists develop their own kinds of arguments. They work from different kinds of questions and seek out different kinds of evidence. So answers from one discipline don't necessarily make a lot of sense in relation to the questions in a different discourse. Psychological enquiry tends to focus on what goes on inside a person, for example exploring how a child's behaviour changes in response to a particular regime of discipline and punishment. Sociology looks more at the relationship between people and society, for example at whether, as families have changed, parents' attitudes to disciplining children have changed. Social policy specialists try to understand how political and economic forces can be channelled to produce new ways of organising society. As a result, it is very easy for 'experts' from the different disciplines to talk *past* rather than *to* each other.

A practitioner like Bernice has to learn to live with these differences and take what seems to be most relevant from each discipline. But sometimes a choice has to be made to give one set of ideas priority over another. For example, you might be convinced by the psychologists' evidence that physical punishment works, but nevertheless decide that it is too risky to allow because of the sociologists' evidence of its association with violence in later life. The different social sciences will keep coming up with evidence, but it is up to the rest of society to decide whether they are asking the right questions.

Where does this leave Bernice in her deliberations about Sue and her daughter? She still didn't feel 100 per cent sure of her position but she had taken a number of ideas from the reading. First, she was persuaded by Straus that there may be long-term effects from physical punishment and this made her feel more sure that she should take some action. From Larzelere and Rosemond one of the important things she picked up was that Sue is inconsistent in her discipline; she isn't using it to make a point or following through a smack with an explanation or a new activity, so it is largely ineffective as well as potentially damaging. Overall, this suggests that some intervention might be desirable. But she is still unsure about the moral issues: should she intervene between a mother and a child, or should she keep her nose out of other people's business?

Key points

- Smacking is associated with risk of psychological problems in adulthood.

- However, a correlation does not prove that one factor caused another.

- Inconsistent discipline may be as damaging as too harsh discipline.

- Evidence can be gathered scientifically but decisions have to be made and prioritised through moral and political debate.

- Deciding whether to intervene will also depend on views about the role of the state in the lives of families and individual parents and children.

3.3 Some missing links

Punishment can become sexualised

While Bernice was rummaging through the last week's newspapers she came upon a somewhat humorous article by Barbara Ehrenreich called 'Getting to the bottom of naughtiness' which linked spanking with sex and which shed light on the discomfort Pat expressed about the punishment she had received at her father's hands.

Activity 10   Spanking and sex

Allow about 20 minutes   Read 'Getting to the bottom of naughtiness' on page 96 now. Make some notes on the connections the author makes between spanking and sex.

Comment   The article hints at the sexualisation of punishment, something which the British have a reputation for abroad ... (le vice anglais).

There is a connection between spanking and erotica.

There are double standards: people who condemn pornography in public are also willing to stand up for physical punishment of children and wrong-doers.

Ehrenreich takes a fairly relaxed view of what adults do to each other but concludes her article by challenging those who insist on their right to spank the 'under-aged and non-consenting'. In doing so she anticipates one of the key issues we will be looking at later in this unit in terms of the definition of sexual abuse.

This is not one of the issues explored in the spanking debate discussed earlier, or in the mainstream agenda on children and punishment. Why is this? I came up with two responses.

1   What research can handle

My first response is that it is very difficult to carry out systematic research into the links between sex and punishment. What would count as 'evidence' that a person derived sexual pleasure from spanking? It isn't the sort of thing many parents would readily admit to in an interview or even an anonymous questionnaire. And the children would not necessarily be reliable witnesses, either at the time or in later years. What is more, the whole notion runs so contrary to popular ideas about families and parenthood that a researcher might run into a lot of resistance and aggression. It would take a subtle and painstaking line of enquiry to make progress in an area like this.

Ehrenreich's arguments are based on such cases as the internet web site. But this might have been set up by one individual and be accessed by very few people. A social science researcher would not know what confidence to place in this kind of one-off 'evidence' and would tend to ignore it. The same applies to the personal experience and anecdotes that Ehrenreich draws in. They have not been gathered systematically enough to find their way into a scientific report. Although anecdotes are often the way that people who are powerless get their stories on to the official agenda, such evidence tends to be filtered out of scientific discourses.

Getting to the bottom of naughtiness

Barbara Ehrenreich

Maybe it all started with those voluptuous images of young Michael Fay facing down a Singaporean spanking squad, because suddenly there's a rush to paddle the bottoms of America's youth. Prodded by the Christian right, with its militant concept of 'parental rights', school districts all over the country are debating bringing back the paddle, and a bill before the New Hampshire legislature would subject teenage graffiti vandals to public bare-bottom spankings – administered, no doubt, by the legislators themselves.

Spanking advocates like California Assemblyman Mickey Conroy laugh off 'ivory towers' studies showing that corporal punishment only deepens the incorrigibility of the young – after all, he was paddled as a boy himself and look how he turned out. Conroy, who keeps a collection of paddles in his office and enjoys carrying one around, seems to have grasped one of the more bizarre themes from the sexual underground: that whatever else it is – 19th-century nastiness or enlightened tough love – spanking can be fun!

What to do when confronted with another trend straight from the dark recesses of the Republican id? One goes to the source: in this case, to venues such as the urban weeklies' 'Anything Goes' personal ads or the Internet's alt. sex.spanking news group, which are chock full of invitations to party with paddles and pants down. Our pro-spanking guardians of law and order should find plenty of kindred spirits in ads such as 'Good looking white male, prof, early 40s, looking for naughty girl in need of firm, bare-bottomed OTK [Over The Knee]'. Or maybe they'd want to contact the 'Naughty boy' who feels his transgressions have earned him a 'bare-butt spanking, hard!'.

The Christian right, which has otherwise done so little to open up the frontiers of human sexual experience, has been campaigning vigorously for the corporal punishment of children for well over a decade. One of their flagship groups, Focus on the Family, advocates it as a means of safeguarding 'family values', and the right's original Family Protect Act, first floated in 1980, would have prohibited any federal attempt to outlaw spanking or strengthen the statutes against child abuse. So at last we know what it is they like so much about 'the family': where else, except in a Calvin Klein ad, will you find a group of nubile young people whose every gesture and sneer seems to cry out for a little OTK?

No doubt the pro-spanking fellows would insist that their interest in paddling is purely asexual, and that the depraved practices of consenting adults have nothing to do with the loving correction of bad little children. But as the spanking personals make all too clear, the adult practice of 'erotic spanking' derives its erotic charge entirely from fantasies of kinky incest. In alt.sex.spanking, for example, stern 'dads' routinely advertise for 'naughty' spankees, or offer to share their family fun, as in 'My teenaged step-daughter has been bad again. I had to put her over my knee to warm her butt. Turned out it warmed us both up! ... Pictures and audio available.'

Perhaps you think this sort of stuff doesn't belong in a family newspaper – but then what is it doing in a 'pro-family' agenda? If a neighbour starts ranting about bare buttocks or the efficacy of various paddling devices, you'd probably keep the kids locked indoors. But if he does the same thing in a legislative chamber, there's a heartfelt applause for his commitment to 'old-fashioned values'.

Far be it from me to condemn anyone's erotic proclivities, but surely nothing would be lost by getting the spanking freaks out of the legislatures and into the 'adult' milieus that specialise in their peculiar tastes. Let the spanking advocates of the political right take a tip from savvy recreational spankers, and seek out the potential spankees on alt.sex.spanking or thereabouts. As for those who continue to insist on their right to spank the under-aged and non-consenting: the challenge will be to come up with some form of punishment, preferably administered by bands of teenage vigilantes, that these miscreants will not enjoy.

(*Guardian*, 17 May 1996, p. 21)

2   Gender differences in attitudes to punishment

My second observation is about the gender and vested interests of the people who control the debate. The debate you analysed was conducted solely by men. It is interesting that the 'experts' on punishment happen to be men when most child rearing in Western societies is done by women. You saw something similar in Unit 1, where it was pointed out that the theory of maternal deprivation was developed by a man, John Bowlby, and that many of the expert voices telling women how to be good mothers were also male.

One in-depth research study which sheds some light on the gender issues at the heart of the punishment debate was conducted by Angus (1988). In a book on Catholic schooling in Australia he refers to physical violence as 'the steel that reinforces the cement of masculine culture' (p. 103) and recounts an incident in which boys from years seven and eight were strapped in front of their classmates in an assembly. In one school he was studying such 'displays of physical violence' were infrequent, but 'performed in public with the rituals of theatre [so that] the impact on pupils is maximised' (p. 103). Attitudes among the other teachers varied but most disapproval came from the few women teachers of the boys in this age group. Their disapproval, he reports, was not so much about the rights and wrongs of the punishment itself but at 'being asked to leave the scene of public humiliation before the strapping could proceed'. The women teachers felt their authority was greatly undermined by such polarisation and by the reliance of male teachers on the use of physical punishment which was not something they could fall back on. The author suggests that the presence of women teachers has implicitly challenged the pre-eminence of physical modes of control and discipline and attitudes have changed significantly about this issue as a result.

Key points

- Corporal punishment features heavily in pornography and smacking or caning can become sexualised. This is rarely addressed openly in the debates about punishment or discipline.

- The reasons for the omission of this aspect of the debate are connected to the difficulty of conducting reliable research on the matter and the relative power of men to set the terms of public debate.

The voice of children

Not only are women less prominent in the debate but so are children, the recipients of 'discipline' – the Save the Children survey on page 83

appeared to be the first to ask children what they thought of smacking. When people tell you 'it did me no harm' they are usually adults looking back. It is difficult to get an objective view from children about punishment they have been on the receiving end of. If we have been punished by parents who we believe love us, how can we reconcile this with rejecting their actions?

Alice Miller, a prominent German psychoanalyst, has written a great deal about childrearing, partly because of her belief that enforced 'obedience' in childrearing techniques in pre-war Germany contributed to the culture which gave rise to the Nazi regime.

She uses the concept of 'idealisation' to explain how it is that children often do not remember or blame their parents for hurting them. They would rather accept that they 'deserved' any punishment, however severe, than lose their ideal of a good and loving parent. She argues that:

> *The child's dependence on his or her parents' love ... makes it impossible in later years to recognise these traumatizations, which often remain hidden behind the early idealization of the parents for the rest of the child's life.*

(Miller, 1987, p. 4)

In her work she tries to count the costs of severe punishment in emotional rather than behavioural terms. She writes:

> *An enormous amount can be done to a child in the first few years: he or she can be moulded, dominated, taught good habits, scolded and punished – without any repercussions for the person raising the child and without the child taking revenge ... If he is prevented from reacting in his own way because the parents cannot tolerate his reactions (crying, sadness, rage) ... then the child will learn to be silent. This silence is a sign of the effectiveness of the pedagogical principles applied but at the same time is a danger signal pointing to future pathological development. If there is absolutely no possibility of reacting to hurt, humiliation, and coercion, then these experiences cannot be integrated into the personality: the feelings they evoke are repressed, and the need to articulate them remains unsatisfied, without any hope of being fulfilled. It is this lack of hope of ever being able to express ... relevant feelings that most often causes severe psychological problems.*

(Miller, 1987, p. 7)

Think before you SMACK!

Are you going to smack because of something your child has done or because you are at the end of your tether?

If it is because of your stress, will taking it out on your child really make you feel better?

If it is because of something your child has done, how will a smack make things better?

Think before you SMACK and then – DON'T!

Her view could be summarised as 'it works but sometimes at a terrible cost'.

According to this view, Sue's daughter may be storing up trouble for the future: we saw that she was not allowed to cry when she was slapped in the supermarket, although this was her first reaction. She is too young not to need her mother's approval, which she seeks by showing her paintings and activities, for example, and she certainly can't challenge her mother's actions. According to Miller, she may well explain the hurt she is experiencing as being her own fault, or a sign that her mother loves her and that 'love equals hurt'. This ties in with Straus's idea of punishment as having a hidden agenda about 'hitting people you love'.

Key points

- Young children are not in a position to question the behaviour of their parents or to express their feelings of rage or humiliation.

- Children may internalise too harsh punishment as being 'deserved'.

3.4 Deciding whether to intervene

Bernice found one more helpful article. It summarises many of the steps we have taken so far in this unit. This time it deals very directly with the issue she was grappling with of whether Sue's parenting had crossed the threshold of seriousness to the extent that intervention was warranted. This paper draws together lessons from a number of recent programmes of research on child protection issues about the problems of definition.

Activity 11   **Steps to a decision**

Allow about 20 minutes

Read the extract from the Dartington Social Research Unit's *Messages from Research* in the Reader, Chapter 27.

Note down the steps Bernice might work through to reach a decision she feels comfortable with.

Comment   This outline clarifies a number of steps which Bernice went through in making her judgment.

(a)   It asks if there are single, isolated acts which could be said to be abusive but concludes that many happen in ordinary, non-abusive households too, so ...

(b)   It sets up the idea of a 'threshold' within which an act is placed:
- on a continuum and
- in a context.

(c)   It asks what harm may come of the action in the long term and sets out the consequences of 'low warmth, high criticism' parenting styles, arguing for input which helps to bolster support for families to reverse this.

So what do you think Bernice might decide? The 'low warmth, high criticism' framework seemed to sum up Sue's parenting style and the harm it could do to her daughter. It might also be a partial explanation of the different ways in which Allan and Pat's brother responded to their respective fathers' discipline. Bernice decided to make a formal report to the social worker who liaises with the playgroup within the next few days. Is that what you would have decided?

We have considered the issue of physical abuse in relation to children and we have also spent time considering 'society's' views about children, discipline and punishment. We make decisions within all these reference points – Bernice for example accepts the arguments for limited discipline and feels comfortable with the way her parents brought her and Allan up, where any punishment was counterbalanced by a lot of encouragement and support. It is the absence of these positive emotional qualities as much as the presence of the physical punishment which led her to decide to intervene in relation to Sue. By reporting the incident to social services, who carry the official mandate for 'child protection', Bernice moved this relationship into the public arena to be scrutinised by professionals.

Key points

- While smacking children is very common, it may still be harmful.

- The debate about punishment tends to switch between considering whether or not it works and whether or not it is 'right': these are separate questions.

- Scientists can test the questions asked but choosing and prioritising the questions may be as significant as finding answers.

- Physical punishment is a risk factor for psychological problems in the long term.

- A low warmth, high criticism style of parenting is considered to be the worst of both worlds for a young child.

3.5 What about the grown ups?

We have considered the rights and wrongs of hitting children at length but Sue's daughter is not the only person who has been hit in the last two weeks. Allan was hit by the man outside the pub. What Pat did not know was that:

- Pat's mother has been hit by her father who got frustrated by her wetting the bed

- Jesse (Pat and Allan's son) has been hit by a school bully

- Sue has been hit by her boyfriend.

How are these incidents 'constructed' and what responsibility do we have as workers or as citizens if we 'know' about or anticipate such violence? Does 'society' have any right to get involved in these other situations at all or is the relationship between parents and children a special case? The Dartington Report acknowledges that:

Society continually reconstructs definitions of maltreatment which sanction intervention ... The State remains selective in its concerns and there is a difference between behaviour known to be harmful to children and behaviour which attracts the attention of child protection practitioners. For example, professionals' interest in school bullying is not as great as parents and children would wish it to be and domestic violence is only just beginning to achieve salience as a cause of concern.

(Dartington Social Research Unit, 1995, p. 15)

The state is selective not only in relation to children but also when it comes to violence directed against adults. In these instances of physical violence, the incident involving Allan was the only one where the police were involved. Why? Is it because:

- it occurred in public
- they are not members of the same family
- they are both men?

If you compare this with Sue's situation, you can see that all three factors were absent, which could explain the lack of any public intervention.

- Sue's partner hit her in the privacy of their own home, not in public.
- Sue and her partner can be seen as part of one nuclear family.
- Sue is a woman, her partner is male.

On the other hand, Pat's mum was also hit in private, by a member of her family, and by a man – but there is a difference. She is an older person in receipt of limited community care services (she has several hours of domiciliary care a week), and would fall within the remit of her local social services adult protection policy as a vulnerable adult because she is someone:

> *... who is or may be in need of community care services by reason of mental or other disability, age or illness; and who is or may be unable to take care of him or herself, or unable to protect him or herself against significant harm or exploitation.*

(Lord Chancellor's Department, 1997)

We noted in Block 1 how care in families becomes an issue worthy of public attention when it is exceptional. Here is another instance where family life is potentially open to public scrutiny and regulation because Pat's mother has care needs over and above the norm. But this does not mean that her situation will necessarily come to light. Pat's mother would consider it disloyal to mention such a thing to an outsider. She doesn't even tell her daughter in case it worries her.

Sue, on the other hand, will not be covered by the adult protection policy. She is afraid she will get hurt and feels hopeless because she has nowhere to go. These examples show that being acknowledged as someone deserving of protection is something of a lottery if you are

Would you want to be called a 'vulnerable adult'?

being abused within the home/family or within residential care. Just as a degree of physical violence is thought to be legitimate between parents and children if it is construed as discipline or punishment, so an element of control is often accepted, and even approved of, in relationships between men and women, or between carer and cared for.

Some of the confusion of moral values on these matters in society at large is reflected in popular culture – music, drama, newspapers, TV, cinema. I have selected four songs to illustrate how violence between men and women merges into accepted images of romantic and marital relationships and how this ideology is internalised by women. The songs span a 30-year period.

Activity 12 Domestic violence in popular culture

Allow about 15 minutes

Listen to Audio Cassette 5, side 1, part 3 and look at the Media Notes. On it are four songs:

(a)   Louis Jordan, 'Gal, you need a whipping', 1954

(b)   The Crystals, 'He hit me (it felt like a kiss)', 1962

(c)   Sandy Posey, 'Born a woman', 1966

(d)   The Police, 'Every breath you take', 1983.

Note down how the themes of each song indicate a cultural acceptance of violent behaviour in male–female relationships.

Comment

The first song, 'Gal, you need a whipping', rehearses the notion, prevalent in both white and black communities, that men are entitled to a 'service' from women and to apply sanctions if they do not come up to scratch. This song illustrates graphically the confusion between love and control, sex and punishment.

The second song, 'He hit me (it felt like a kiss)', reinforces this notion and shows how these attitudes persisted into the so-called permissive 1960s.

The title encapsulates the way violence can be redefined as an act of love and is all the more powerful because it is sung by women, for women.

Goodbye to bliss

Hard to believe, but pregnancy can mean the start of domestic violence.

In romantic films, an expectant mother can expect flowers, chocolates and congratulations from her delighted husband. It's such a seductive stereotype that even those who should know better, such as midwives and gynaecologists, cling to it. Yet research suggests that pregnancy may trigger domestic violence rather than domestic bliss. Studies in the US and Canada show that up to 21 per cent of pregnant women have been abused by their partners, with many of the women first experiencing violence during pregnancy.

(*Guardian*, 11 June 1997)

Sign of the crimes

For the first time, UNICEF has included in its annual Progress of the Nations report a specific section on violence against women.

... The feminist rhetoric being used is staggeringly bold. There is a new category, 'gender crime', bringing together practices such as bride burning, dowry crimes, domestic beatings and genital mutilation which have recently been examined in isolation. The change is particularly significant because no one seems to be worrying any more about accusations of cultural imperialism. Previously, the fear of judging other cultures sometimes halted feminist criticism of attacks on women in other countries.

(*Guardian*, 24 July 1997)

The third song shows how individual women internalise this ideology of control until what exists in the outside world as a set of values forged out of unequal power relations becomes wrapped up as a 'natural' part of 'being a woman'.

The last song, 'Every breath you take', also reinforces the idea of ownership ('you belong to me', 'I'll be watching you' ...), a construct which is borne out by the fact that individual women are most at risk of life-threatening violence when they attempt to leave or have recently left a violent partner (see Holder *et al.*, 1994, p. 5). The song shows what a fine line there is between the two sides of romantic ideology – presented as being about love it can easily tip over into control and threat.

The hierarchical relationship which underlies these songs is one which is referred to by feminists as 'patriarchal' and is strongly supported within major world religions: it provides a structure and order but at the cost of suppressing women's interests within the private and public spheres. Some theorists see sexist oppression as a mirror of, or compensation for, the economic oppression which men were/are subjected to in their working lives. Even though these lyrics might seem rather extreme, these attitudes remain very central to our culture and institutions and can become ingrained in the way individuals fantasise about and conduct their relationships.

Many police forces are now seeking to reverse the practice of treating domestic violence as a *private* matter and are developing closer links with other agencies and services. This will be discussed in more detail in the next unit.

Should we tolerate any violence in personal relationships?

Key points

- Violence between adults is treated differently depending on issues such as the age, gender, race and ethnicity of the victim.
- Some degree of violence by men towards women is often condoned within marital and sexual relationships.
- Vulnerable people often have no way of telling anyone what is happening to them.
- Some individuals, like Sue, are both victim and perpetrator and need support and intervention in both cases.

Section 4
Sexual abuse

In Section 3 we worked through the process of evaluating *physical* abuse as it relates to children and briefly considered some of the anomalies which occur when considering such abuse towards adults. We started by examining the debate around the smacking of children as part of 'normal parenting'. We saw that, because of the ways we think about children and smacking in contemporary Britain, witnessing a single incident would probably not be enough to warrant intervention under child protection procedures even if it were quite severe. Do the same considerations come into play when it is *sexual*, rather than physical, abuse at issue? In the extract from *Messages from Research* which you read in Section 3, a number of differences are suggested:

- Whereas for other forms of abuse a single event would probably not be enough to trigger intervention, in relation to sexual abuse even a relatively minor incident may require immediate and definite action.

- The thresholds which define a sexual act are more clear-cut: there is less of a continuum and more agreement about what constitutes a sexually abusive act.

- Sexual abuse of children is less context specific: it cannot be justified and there are no extenuating circumstances which excuse abuse within family relationships.

Sexual abuse is also more likely to be a serial and repeated form of behaviour by abusers, leading to ongoing risk to other children or vulnerable adults if no action is taken. It is not situational; that is, it is not brought on by a particular set of circumstances. Evidence from abusers suggests that they actively set up the circumstances and relationships within which they abuse by targeting suitably vulnerable children or adults and working their way into positions of trust (see for example Waterhouse *et al.*, 1994).

Where there is some support for physical punishment by parents there is a vehement outcry against any sexual abuse of children, and increasingly against the sexual abuse of vulnerable adults. But we have seen in relation to physical assaults that it makes a difference who the victim is, whether they are seen as blameless and worth protecting and whether they can access anyone to whom they can disclose what is happening. We will see that this is equally true of sexual abuse.

Key points
- There is more consensus about the threshold at which sexual acts committed against children are deemed to be abuse and to trigger intervention.
- Even a single act might lead to decisive action being taken.
- Sexual abusing tends to be repeated by perpetrators and often involves deliberate and planned targeting of children or vulnerable adults.

4.1   The centrality of consent

In this section we will briefly look at what makes a sexual act abusive and unpack this to include a more detailed consideration of capacity and consent. After all, people often want to have sex with each other and sex with someone you want to have sex with is prized within Western societies. So consent is a critical defining issue and adds an extra step into the process of definition which we worked through in relation to physical abuse. Consent may cut across the evaluation of the actual act or damage which has been done. For example, in the celebrated 'Spanner' case a group of gay men were convicted for engaging in consenting sado-masochistic acts. The acts themselves were very damaging and serious and the state argued that they were inherently indecent, but the men's defence was that they had entered into them voluntarily.

In contrast to this, a case in the United States which occurred at about the same time was 'met with horror and incredulity' because it concerned a woman who had been raped and had subsequently become pregnant despite being in a coma. Here there could be no question but that the man convicted had intended to exploit the woman: there were no mitigating factors, he could not argue that she had gone along with it, had given double messages or had in some way contributed by 'asking for it' – arguments which are often made by defence lawyers in criminal rape trials. It was a cut and dried case and what made it so was the very obvious lack of consent on the part of the woman concerned and the extraordinary ethical issues raised by her pregnancy.

Coma rape victim pregnant

Ian Katz in New York

Even in a country accustomed to a daily diet of criminal grotesqueries, the rape of a woman aged 29 who has been in a coma for 10 years has been met with horror and incredulity.

The reaction of the woman's parents has shocked the United States almost as much as the crime itself: they have refused to abort the resulting pregnancy on religious grounds.

The case has sparked a debate among doctors and medical ethicists about what rights can be ascribed to the woman, whose identity has been withheld, the foetus, and the family.

'The woman's body is being used as a vessel, reducing her to more of a thing than a person' bioethicist Ellen Moskowitz told USA Today. 'It could be offensive to her humanity.' If she is permanently unconscious, however, 'the wrong done to her is not profound'.

The attack was discovered in December after nursing staff at the Westfall Health Care Centre in Rochester, New York, noticed a slight swelling of the woman's stomach. Tests quickly showed that she was four to five-and-a-half months pregnant.

The woman's family was told that if the pregnancy was not terminated, she should have given birth in May. Her parents said they would not sanction an abortion because of their religious beliefs, and because they wanted a reminder of their daughter. Though there is no record of a comatose woman becoming pregnant, there have been numerous cases of patients giving birth while in a coma.

The pregnant woman was a devout Catholic, and friends say she strongly opposed abortion. She had just been accepted for the prestigious Cornell College when she was injured in a car crash at the age of 19.

She has remained in a coma ever since, breathing without assistance but fed by a tube.

No one has been arrested in connection with the rape, believed to have taken place in August. A former aide who worked at the centre at the time was charged in November with sexually abusing a disabled patient aged 49.

(*Guardian*, 31 January 1996, p. 1)

These issues are spelt out in the next Offprint article you will be reading, which focuses on consent issues in the context of sexual abuse of adults with learning difficulties. The paper starts by setting out the same kind of continuum which we sketched out in relation to physical abuse, with sexual acts put on a scale from teasing and innuendo (non-contact abuse) through to touch, masturbation and penetrative sex (contact abuse). But as we saw earlier in the unit, such a classification is not in itself a sufficient indicator of the seriousness of any incident. The paper introduces factors which have been highlighted in relation to child sexual abuse around power, authority and dependence, and translates these into the situations in which adults with learning difficulties find themselves. It then goes into more detail about what valid consent means, dealing separately with whether the person has given consent, their capacity to consent, and 'barriers' and inequality in the form of authority, force or pressure which undermine their ability to freely consent.

Activity 13

Allow about 30 minutes

Sexual abuse and adults with learning difficulties

Read Offprint 26.

When you have read it, listen to Betty Fisher, who speaks on side 2 of Audio Cassette 5. She describes how her son was sexually abused by a member of his church.

(a)   Listen to what she has to say and decide for yourself whether you consider this to have been abuse. Use the framework summarised in Table 2 of Offprint 26. Did Garry consent, could he consent, did the man exert undue force or control over him?

(b)   How serious do you consider this abuse to have been? Look back to the criteria of seriousness in Section 2.3 and use these as a reference point. On a scale of 1–10 (where 10 is the most serious) where would you place this incident?

(c)   How could this incident have been prevented?

(d)   In what ways did the legal process create barriers to Garry's receiving justice?

Comment

(a)   Yes, this does seem to have been abuse. It was perpetrated within an ongoing relationship between people of unequal power. The perpetrator intended to take advantage of Garry, who:

- did not consent to the sexual contact
- probably lacked the capacity to consent, and
- was both tricked into it and then forced to endure it.

Any one of these would have been enough to define this act as non-consenting and abusive. Although the man was not a member of staff, he had 'authority' as a member of the church, which he used to get access to Garry and to avoid questions about his intentions or behaviour.

(b)   I would place this incident at the more serious end of the scale. The incident has had a lasting impact on Garry's mental health and has caused great distress to his family. The man seemed to have deliberately targeted Garry as a vulnerable person and, given what we know about the serial nature of sexual offending, is likely to gravitate towards abusing other vulnerable adults unless he is stopped. What did you think?

(c)   Betty queried why the service had not checked up on the man, where he lived, how suitable and accessible this would be for Garry, or what the arrangements would be for Garry's stay. She says they were 'naive'. They assumed everything would be OK because the man was a member of the church. Although it is not normal to have friends vetted, in this case it might have prevented considerable distress.

(d)   The court proceedings were not helpful to Garry. In court Garry was asked inappropriate 'double negative' questions, he was asked to take the oath, and he had to come face to face with his abuser without a screen or video loop being made available. Betty says there was no attempt to 'establish a relationship' with him as a person with learning difficulties who was acting as a witness in court. This lack of attention to the special needs of people with learning difficulties is a barrier to their receiving justice.

Justice for all?

Consent is a complex issue and one where unstated assumptions often confuse judgments. For instance, in rape and sexual assault cases it is often implied that a woman who has been out for dinner with a man has consented to sex, or that her consent on one occasion implies her consent at all times, and these attitudes permeate the legal system (Lees, 1996). A woman's right to withhold her consent to sex within marriage has only recently been conceded. Women's testimony is sometimes undermined as irrational or malicious. These problems in guaranteeing personal autonomy in sexual encounters affect *all* women. As Doyal says, 'women have often lacked the social or economic autonomy to underpin sexual choices' (1995, p. 60). Even in marriage their consent may be co-opted as a part of the economic and personal service bargain. For some, the issues are even more complex and difficult. The issue, as we saw in the offprint, is not only whether the person gave consent on a particular occasion but whether they were able to make that judgment, in other words whether they had the 'capacity' to make that decision. We considered capacity as an issue in relation to Tony and the discussion about whether he should be tagged. It comes up again as a complex issue in relation to sex – this is something which someone else can't decide on your behalf in a case conference, so what happens if you can't decide for yourself?

Consider these three examples:

1   Pat's mother increasingly demonstrates symptoms of dementia and is losing her capacity to make decisions for herself but her husband still wants and expects to have sex with her. At what point does this become an infringement of her rights? How is anyone likely to find out if Pat's mother dislikes the sex or wants it to stop: she may well not say anything or communicate her distress about so personal a matter. If Pat were aware of this side of her parents' relationship, should she intervene, and if so how?

2   A woman cited in Brown and Keating (in press) had been admitted to a psychiatric hospital under a section and while in hospital she entered, seemingly willingly, into a sexual relationship with a fellow patient. Afterwards she argued that the hospital staff should have prevented her from doing so because she had lacked capacity. She claimed that this was not a relationship she would have entered into if she had been well.

3   The girlfriend of Pat's cousin Derek is a young woman with severe learning difficulties and although she likes Derek and enjoys the status of 'having a boyfriend' she does not really understand what sex involves or any of the risks which go with it. According to the law (Sexual Offences Act 1956) she is deemed unable to give her consent because of the level of her learning disability. Derek might be able to argue that he did not appreciate her inability to give consent and this would be a defence in the unlikely event that their relationship were ever to lead to a court case: it is much more likely that it would be left to the staff of the service or professionals to make a judgment about whether the relationship should be allowed to continue, a point that was made in Unit 18.

In these three examples the central issue is capacity to consent, but the issues surrounding it and the subsequent problems in assessment and intervention are very different. While Pat's mother is losing her capacity to consent, the woman with mental health problems has fluctuating capacity to make her own decisions and it is possible that Derek's girlfriend is never going to be able to exercise capacity in relation to sexual relationships.

Meanwhile, as we saw for Garry, a further issue is not only whether someone can and does give their consent, but the context within which they do so. Many people at some time in their lives have sexual relationships in which they may be left feeling exploited or deceived. At what point does this invalidate their consent? Clearly, if you have consented to something at knife point you have not consented freely, but what if you believed your partner loved you, or might marry you, and you later found out (s)he didn't? Does that level of deception cut across or invalidate your 'informed' consent? Moreover, there may be situations in which one person doesn't have to use force, but can draw on the persuasive power of the pinstripe or the credit card and effectively buy consent. At an individual level this might look like, and be defended as, individual choice, but when it adds up it can be seen that inequality substantially disadvantages many people in their sexual lives. Once again, the issue of power becomes a central one in deciding on such a question and it is something you will be exploring more in the next unit. Perhaps the material basis of what looks like a freely entered into sexual transaction is most clear in relation to prostitution, but poverty is the bottom line which effectively shapes and limits many people's sexual options and relationships. Kelly *et al.* (1995) argue, 'the sex industry relies upon, and trades in, all forms of inequality' (p. 12). It also confuses issues of responsibility and blame. I started out by asserting that there is almost universal condemnation of sexual abuse against children, but if that were so how could it be that until 1997 when girls under 16 were involved in prostitution it was they, and not their punters, who were cautioned, 'for what in effect, and in law, is an offence against them' (Kelly *et al.*, 1995, p. 31)?

Translated on to a global level, we see inequality between countries fuelling a trade in 'sex tourism'. Issues of geography, race, gender and age are transcended by the argument that:

> *The majority of children in the world who are victims of sexual exploitation come from poor, often but not exclusively Black, countries. What connects these children with children abused from rich western countries is that they are trying to find ways to ensure their own physical survival. Children and young people in desperate circumstances, like many women, learn fairly quickly that if they have nothing else to sell they can sell their bodies ...*
>
> *(Kelly* et al., *1995, p. 12)*

If you think about what makes a 'good' victim it is anyone who is marginalised, unsupported, isolated and not likely to be believed. An abuser would hardly need to use force to abuse such a person.

Key points

In assessing consent there are several considerations:

- whether consent has been given at all
- whether an individual has the capacity to consent at this time
- whether inequality, violence or exploitation negates a child's or adult's consent and 'choice' in sexual matters
- in extreme forms this inequality may boil down to the child's or adult's need for physical survival.

Conclusion

The core questions for Unit 19 were:

How is 'abuse' defined?

- There is no such thing as an objective definition of abuse. The line between abuse and ordinary behaviour is constantly being redrawn. Actions are interpreted in a different light as new issues are brought under the spotlight of research and debate, and new information shapes perceptions. This does not mean that abuse is not real. It means that our acknowledgement of abuse depends on who has the power to challenge the way they are treated, or is seen by others as deserving of protection.

- In this and the previous unit we have seen that there are different responses to personal or sexual violence depending on who is involved and how the relationship is interpreted.

What are the different legal and professional contexts for child and adult protection?

- There is more consensus when abuse occurs in relation to children than there is in relation to adults.

- The legal and professional frameworks within which action can be taken are clearer for children than for vulnerable adults.

- However, as our worked example of corporal punishment of children by their parents showed, there is a great deal of ambiguity when it comes to drawing the line between discipline and abuse.

What criteria can be used for judging the seriousness of different kinds of abuse and abusing?

- The criteria for deciding on seriousness include: the victim's consent; their capacity to consent; the misuse of power by someone in authority; the impact on the person abused, and others; the level of deliberate intention exercised by the abuser; whether the act is against the law; and the likelihood of the abuser repeating the abuse.

Why does abuse happen and what pressures can lead to abusive behaviour?

- Abuse most often happens in circumstances of inequality, including inequalities of age, sex, economic and social power.

- Cultural beliefs also make abuse more of a possibility. For example, the confusion between love, control and possession reflected in popular culture can serve to make violence in intimate relationships between men and women socially acceptable. In relation to children, beliefs about discipline legitimise behaviour which, if it were between adults, would be considered unlawful and abusive.

What part do gender, race, age and poverty play in the dynamics of abusive relationships?

- As we saw above, the key issue is inequality, which is bolstered by ideologies which assert that unequal power is inevitable and 'natural' by claiming that one race or sex is superior and justified in controlling others.

Thinking about these issues is important because as well as being a student of this course you are probably also a carer, a relative, someone on the receiving end of care, or possibly a victim or survivor of abuse. In any of those roles, you have to be clear about where the threshold lies between legitimate control, physical or sexual contact and abuses of power which can lead to significant harm. Taking action against abuse can be a difficult thing to do, but it helps to have the confidence which comes from knowing that you have reached a thoughtful decision.

In the next unit, where we look at what can be done about abusive practice or relationships, the discussion is taken one step further.

Study skills: Managing during the summer

Late July and August – what the newspapers call 'the silly season' – can be an awkward time for OU students. Many find it harder to concentrate on study when the evenings stay light and the weather outside is more inviting. And then school holidays and going away on holiday can cut right across normal patterns of life, throwing study plans into confusion. Also, the OU study centres close, leaving a gap in the tutorials; your tutor too may be unavailable for a spell. Yet your study programme continues.

K100 allows a two-week break to be taken at your convenience (probably during your study of Block 6). Block 6 is the usual four units in length, but the gap between TMA 05 and TMA 06 is six weeks. Of course, you don't *have* to take the break. You can keep right on and get to the end of the course with a couple more weeks for your exam preparations. Or you can use the two extra weeks to slow down and spread your work out, rather than have a complete break.

But even with the extra two weeks, if your summer arrangements are really disruptive you may still fall behind. If so, don't despair. Just work out the best solution you can. If necessary, you may have to cut some corners – not cover everything you might otherwise have done. Whatever happens, don't let yourself lose momentum, or lose heart, just because things get tricky for a few weeks. Having reached this far (past the two-thirds mark), you owe it to yourself to push on to the end of the course.

References

Angus, L. (1988) Continuity and Change in Catholic Schooling, Falmer Press, Lewes.

Brown, H. and Keating, F. (in press) '"We're doing it already ..." adult protection in mental health services', *Journal of Psychiatric Nursing*.

Brown, H. and Stein, J. (1998) 'Implementing adult protection policies in Kent and East Sussex', *Journal of Social Policy*.

Dartington Social Research Unit (1995) *Child Protection: Messages From Research*, HMSO, London.

Department of Health (2000) *'No Secrets: Guidance on developing and implementing multi-agency policies and procedures to protect vulnerable adults from abuse'*, TSO, London.

Department of Health, Home Office, Department for Education and Employment (1999), *Working Together to Safeguard Children*, London, The Stationery Office.

Doyal, L. (1995) *What Makes Women Sick: Gender and the Political Economy of Health*, Macmillan, Basingstoke.

Eastman, M. (1993) 'Fighting it right', *Community Care*, Vol. 6, No. 5, p. 20.

Farmer, E. and Owen, M. (1995) *Child Protection Practice: Private Risks and Public Remedies – Decision Making, Intervention and Outcome in Child Protection Work*, HMSO, London.

Holder, R., Kelly, L. and Singh, T. (1994) *Suffering in Silence: Children and Young People who Witness Domestic Violence*, Domestic Violence Unit, Hammersmith and Fulham.

Kelly, L., Regan, L. and Burton, S. (1991) *An Exploratory Study of the Prevalence of Sexual Abuse in a Sample of 16–21 Year Olds*, Child and Woman Abuse Studies Unit, University of North London.

Kelly, L., Wingfield, R., Burton, S. and Regan, L. (1995) *Splintered Lives: Sexual Exploitation of Children in the Context of Children's Rights and Child Protection*, Barnardo's, Ilford.

Lees, S. (1996) 'Unreasonable doubt: the outcomes of rape trials' in Hester, M., Kelly, L. and Radford, J. (eds) *Women, Violence and Male Power*, Open University Press, Buckingham, pp. 99–117.

Lord Chancellor's Department (1997) *Who decides?: Making decisions on behalf of mentally incapacitated adults*, CM303, The Stationery Office, London.

Mason, M. and Gambill, E. (eds) (1994) *Debating Children's Lives*, Sage, Part 3, Debate 12.

Miller, A. (1987) *For Your Own Good: The Roots of Violence in Child Rearing*, Virago Press, London.

Stevenson, O. (1996) *Elder Protection in the Community: What Can We Learn from Child Protection?*, Age Concern Institute of Gerontology, London.

Sundram, C. (1984) 'Obstacles to reducing patient abuse in public institutions', *Hospital and Community Psychiatry*, Vol. 35, No. 3, pp. 238–43.

Waterhouse, L., Dobash, R.P. and Carnie, J. (1994) *Child Sexual Abusers,* The Scottish Office Central Research Unit, Edinburgh.

Williams, C. (1993) 'Vulnerable victims? A current awareness of the victimisation of people with learning disabilities', *Disability, Handicap and Society,* Vol. 8, No. 2, pp. 161–72.

Acknowledgements

Grateful acknowledgement is made to the following sources for permission to reproduce material in this unit:

Text

P. 77: Hunter, L. (1996) 'Are you in an abusive relationship?' *19 Magazine*, 8–13 December 1996, IPC Magazines Ltd with permission from Robert Harding Syndication; p. 83: Thomson, A. (1996) 'Blair admits smacking his children – and feeling remorse', *Times*, 6 June 1996, © Times Newspapers Ltd, 1996; p. 97: Ehrenreich, B. (1996) 'Getting to the bottom of naughtiness', *Guardian*, 17 May 1996, © Guardian Newspapers 1996; p. 104 (centre): Knight, J. 1997, 'Goodbye to bliss', *Guardian*, 11 June 1997, © Guardian Newspapers Ltd 1997; p. 104 (bottom): Coward, R. (1997) 'Sign of the crimes', *Guardian*, 24 July 1997, © Guardian Newspapers Ltd 1997; p. 109: Katz, I. (1996) 'Coma rape victim pregnant', *Guardian*, 31 January 1996, © Guardian Newspapers Ltd 1996.

Illustrations

Pp. 61 and 98: NSPCC. Photographs posed by models; pp. 72, 80: NSPCC/Corinne Day; p. 99: Leaflet – Think Before You Smack, courtesy of End Physical Punishment of Children; pp. 103 and 111: Pam Isherwood/Format; p. 104 Jacky Fleming; p. 105: Bryan McAllister; p. 106: Courtesy of Edinburgh District Council Women's Unit, Zero Tolerance Division/Copyright The Estate of Franki Raffles.

Unit 20
Power and Vulnerability in Care Relationships

Prepared for the course team by Tom Heller

New for the 2003 edition of K100

While you are working on Unit 20, you will need:
- Course Reader
- Offprints Book
- Audio Cassette 5, side 2
- Wallchart
- Care Systems and Structures

Contents

Introduction

As we discussed in Unit 4, and as you have seen at several other points of the course, particularly in Units 18 and 19, care relationships are not evenly balanced. Carers tend to hold various kinds of power and those being cared for tend to be vulnerable to misuse of that power. But care situations may often be quite complicated, with several carers involved, making it unclear who is caring for whom and who is vulnerable to whom. In this unit we explore some of the ambiguities and vulnerabilities that can arise in a situation where a mother may be in need of support after giving birth to a child, for whom she is herself expected to be a highly committed carer. Various agencies and a range of professionals may become involved in such a situation, each with their own priorities, their own ways of understanding what is going on and their own ideas as to who is in need of what care and who is vulnerable to whom. This is a situation where it may be unclear as to whether care is or is not going wrong. And the competing concerns of different professionals may cloud the picture, adding to the vulnerability of the recipients of their care, unless there is appropriate consultation and interprofessional understanding.

The unit will follow the story of a fictional family who get into difficulties following the birth of their first baby.

This unit discusses issues about feelings and possible distress following the birth of a child. Some of the material might be quite sensitive for you, especially if you have recently had a child yourself or been in a similar situation to the people in the case study. We hope that you will be able to use your own personal experiences during your study of this unit, but also that you will seek assistance if you are particularly affected by any of the sensitive issues that we discuss.

Core questions

- What powers do carers exercise in a context such as a mother experiencing mental distress following the birth of a baby, and what vulnerabilities might these give rise to?

- Does 'postnatal depression' exist as a distinct disease, or is it a convenient label that describes one variant of normality?

- All citizens have rights, but what happens when one person's rights (for example those of a small child) conflict with those of another person's (for example their mother?).

- Can professional services be considered to have the ability to make situations worse for their clients as well as better?

Section 1
Setting the scene

This unit explores the core questions through the use of a fictional story involving 'Jenny' following the birth of her child 'Abby'.

> ### Jenny, Geoff and Abby
>
> Jenny is 30-years-old. She lives in a well-maintained semi-detached house on the outskirts of a small town in the south of Scotland. This is a commuter area where two car families seem to be the norm. Fairly new cars are in evidence in driveways and the area has a feeling of suburban 'normality', with everything apparently in its proper place.
>
> There is a 'SOLD' notice still propped up behind the hedge of Jenny's house because the estate agents have not come to collect it in the time since Jenny and her husband, Geoff, aged 42, moved in three months ago.
>
> But the neighbours have noticed that all is not well. Jenny has been seen in the garden hanging up the washing and apparently sobbing at the same time, and Abby seems to be crying for a long time before she gets comforted ... On a couple of occasions the neighbours think that they have heard Jenny shouting at her new baby and then breaking down in tears herself.
>
> Maureen, a local health visitor, had undertaken a routine home visit when Abby, their child, was two months old. The available notes from previous health professional encounters told her only that this is Jenny's first child and that the family has changed address three times in the last year.

Activity 1   Conjecture

Allow about 15 minutes

Read carefully through the brief description that introduces Jenny, and consider her situation. Are there any features that you feel might make her susceptible to mental distress following the birth of her child?

You do not need to have specialist knowledge to undertake this activity. Just try to imagine (empathise about) what it must have been like for Jenny to have given birth at this point in her life. What features can you imagine from the brief outline given that could contribute to the way that she might be feeling at this time? Feel free to use the full extent of your imagination in conjecturing about this scenario.

Comment   Externally it appears that this new child has been born into a situation with considerable social advantages. This is unlikely to develop into a story involving great poverty, or the desperation of living in a deprived neighbourhood. What could be more delightful than the birth of a first child? Of course change and disruption are inevitable when a new baby is introduced into the complex equation that creates and sustains a relationship. But what does actually go on 'behind the curtains' in the networks, systems, relationships and, indeed, in the internal psychological world that we all create for ourselves? Does this façade of 'normality' hide tensions and stresses?

What is the hard 'evidence' in this scene? We know that Jenny and Geoff have recently moved to this new house. Might the trauma of moving house and the inevitable disruption have become particularly difficult for any reason? Has this family become disconnected from previously supportive networks of relatives and friends? Could changing addresses three times in the last year be an extra factor? Why had they moved at this time when the birth of their new baby was so near? Might the **combination** of factors such as a new baby **and** a new neighbourhood bring special problems for a family with new responsibilities?

We also know very little about Jenny, Geoff or Abby themselves. What sort of people are they and why have they come to live in this specific place? Is more detective work appropriate in this situation? Could the presence of the SOLD notice in the front garden, several months after the sale, be a pointer? Is it a simple blunder by the estate agent, which is of no significance at all? Or is the new family so preoccupied that they can't find the time or energy to ring the agent to take the sign away or otherwise dispose of it themselves?

At this stage in the story we know the ages of the three members of the immediate family. Does this provide us with any 'evidence' that can be used to start to build up a picture of the stresses and strains within this particular family? Probably not, but it may be an indication of some of our own pre-conceptions and act as an indication of some of the 'baggage' that all professional workers bring to their work. In previous units you have explored a range of values and attitudes and considered how easy it can be to jump to conclusions based on our own constructed views of what is 'right' or 'normal'. Objectively in our case study there is no evidence to suggest that there are problems that might arise from age differentials. However, some people might feel that the ages of 30 and 42 carry a special significance; is this 'about right' as an age to start a family? Or in some people's eyes might this conceal other difficulties? Do you consider that this 'age gap' might be a 'problem'? Was Jenny wondering for a long time whether to 'sacrifice' her own professional career in order to start a family? Has there been pressure from her partner or from other family members to 'produce' a baby?

There are, as yet, big unknowns about the thoughts and feelings of the family we are focusing on ... What sort of expectations did they have about the birth of a baby and the expansion of their family? What about their own upbringings and the ways they were parented themselves; might this influence their current mental state and the interactions within their relationship?

Behind the façade of normality and suburban respectability there may well be family discord or problematic inter-relationships

All mothers with young children in our society are 'observed' by health and sometimes social care workers in authority. This is an example of the power that professional workers have over other people within society. After the birth of a new baby, midwives, health visitors and other primary care team professionals make it their business to observe and collect data on the family. Even when they are welcomed into the family their role is not social. When concerns arise, such as about the mother's mental health, a wide range of individuals and agencies could become involved. This unit will explore ways in which these agencies might be helpful, and also what happens if they create confusion or further disruption to the way that the new family is trying to cope.

The focus of the unit so far has been on your own understanding of the situation that is developing for our family. But what happens when professional workers become involved? Is guessing about what might be going on for this family the 'correct' approach for professional workers? There is always the danger of prejudice. Perhaps Maureen, the health visitor, has strongly held views based on negative experiences regarding the birth of her own children ... or perhaps she doesn't have children of her own. Both of these possibilities will influence the way she observes, judges and interacts with the family. And the power that health and social care workers possess gives extra significance to their opinions and actions.

Activity 2   **Values and opinions**

Allow about 15 minutes

Look again at the initial case study and your answer to Activity 1.

In what ways do you think that your response to the activity could be seen as being based on your own opinions and experiences?

Comment

Activity 1 asked you to use your imagination about the position that this family find themselves in. In this situation (and perhaps in all professional and human situations) it is difficult not to bring ourselves and our own feelings into the way that we think about, describe, and ultimately judge, other people. You will have your own particular view of parenting based on your own experiences. For myself parenting has been a central part of my life. Having four children has affected the way I behave and the 'prism' through which I view other people; both those with children and those without. In particular the birth of our first children (identical twins) changed me and my relationship with my partner, with our friends, with relatives and with wider networks and agencies. A new label and entirely new social networks were opened to me (such as toddler groups), while other familiar ones became more difficult to access (such as the political group I belonged to which held its meetings at times which clashed with the babies' bath time). Since that time being a parent has affected my lifestyle, my life choices and my entire outlook on life as well as the risks that I may or may not take. Most particularly it affects the way that I see, and potentially make value judgments about, other people during the course of my professional life as a doctor.

Before going up the drive to meet Jenny, Geoff and Abby all professional workers will have a full range of opinions and prejudices about what life 'must' be like for a family in a suburban area with a new small child. And of course members of different professions may well have different ways of observing, analysing and commenting based on their specific professional backgrounds and teaching.

Key points

- Complex stresses and strains for individuals and families might be concealed behind an apparently 'normal' exterior.

- A new baby in the family changes many of the previous dynamics, but not necessarily in predictable ways.

- Those whose job it is to observe these dynamics bring their own thoughts, feelings, experiences and prejudices into their assessments of the situation.

- The power held by professional workers gives added significance to their opinions and actions.

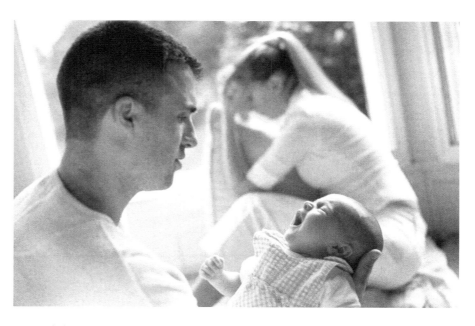

A new baby can lead to unpredictable changes in family relationships

1.1   Information gathering

For any professional workers collecting and collating information can be rather like detective work. Certainly Maureen's first interview with Jenny uncovers quite a lot of additional 'clues' or data:

Jenny, Geoff and Abby: continued

On direct enquiry Maureen, the health visitor, finds out that Jenny and Geoff moved to this location because Geoff's job as a computer manager and IT specialist for a large national firm required speedy relocation. They have been married for three years and have known each other for about five years in total.

Jenny was married previously at age 17, but divorced when 24-years-old after a combative, childless marriage. She, herself, was the single child of a couple who separated when Jenny was seven-years-old.

Abby was born eight weeks ago. She was not planned and had, indeed, arrived at a difficult time for Jenny and Geoff. Jenny had been about to complete a lengthy professional course of study to become a quantity surveyor. Nor had the pregnancy been easy. Jenny had a lot of sickness, ankle swelling and low back pain for the duration of the pregnancy. She developed high blood pressure and the necessary follow-up appointments were disrupted by a move to temporary accommodation while awaiting the final move to their current address.

Activity 3   **Sifting data**

Allow about 20 minutes   Which parts of this unfolding story do you think might be relevant to professional workers if there are concerns about Jenny's levels of stress and even her mental health status?

Are there any signs that you could gather from the story at this stage that might make you wonder about her vulnerability to postnatal stress?

Again we do not expect you to be experts in mental health diagnosis, or even know much about postnatal depression or other things that might happen to women after childbirth. Just try to think yourself into the situation as it relates to Jenny herself.

So, write down all the features of the story that you think might impact on Jenny's stress levels following the birth of Abby.

Comment   The simple answer is that **all** the features outlined could be relevant to the way that Jenny might be feeling. It can be difficult to be sure exactly which factors in a person's life might 'cause' particular stress-related problems at a later stage. At one level Jenny's story does not appear to be very much out of the ordinary, since mental distress can be quite unpredictable and there may be no obvious problems in a person's background.

Many of the things that have happened to Jenny over the years are quite common and could be part of almost anybody's life story. However, it may be important to try to consider those features, or combinations of features, which increase the risk of significant mental distress after childbirth.

From the story so far several features have emerged that might be worth further exploration. Our preliminary list might be something like this:

- Social position: Jenny, Geoff and Abby are not living in poverty, but is there any reason to expect that income is linked to the incidence of postnatal mental distress?

- Social isolation: it seems from the story that Jenny may be socially isolated in her current home. Might this create stress at this time in Jenny's life?

- Age of parents at time of birth of first child: is the age of the parents relevant?

1.2   Using research to increase your understanding

As well as direct evidence that we can gather ourselves it might be helpful to consider the results of research done by others. Epidemiology is the study of patterns of illness within a community. In exploring postnatal depression, epidemiology can help us to discover whether certain factors in people's individual stories increase the likelihood of that person going on to develop significant mental distress.

However it is always important to use research findings carefully. Research findings may contradict each other and should always be viewed with caution. For example, although research might indicate that mental distress is more likely to occur in certain circumstances, or in particular groups of women, this doesn't mean that the condition only happens in those 'high-risk' groups ... or that everyone in 'high-risk' groups will develop the condition. *Any* new mother can develop mental distress following the birth of her child.

Social class, social isolation and poverty

Many studies have indicated, as you would expect, that women living in poor social conditions and with diminished support networks have an increased risk of developing mental distress after the birth of their babies (Seguin, 1999).

> *Poor housing conditions, financial difficulties, long-term health problems and negative interpersonal relationships may bring about such feelings of chronic stress for a new mother.*
>
> *(Seguin, 1999, p. 5)*

Ritter (2000) studied a sample of inner-city women in the USA and found that just about all women with low incomes were mentally stressed:

> *Few, if any, women could be categorised as truly experiencing low stress at average annual incomes below $10,000.*
>
> *(Ritter, 2000, p. 582)*

Social support, particularly from the father of the baby (O'Hara, 1996) and from other mothers (Mauthner, 1995) seems to be crucial to the prevention of mental distress after having a baby.

Cultural understanding

In western classifications women who are significantly distressed following the birth of a child are often described as suffering from 'postnatal depression' (PND). This is often used as a convenient label for clinical and research purposes. Cross-cultural studies seem to show something very similar happens in many different cultures all around the world although it may be given a different 'label' (Kumar, 1994; Affonso, Cox, 1996; Cox, 1999; 2000; Huang, 2001).

Mauthner (1998) introduces a feminist perspective into the search for cultural understanding of the phenomenon of PND. She considers that women in many different cultures often find themselves in subservient positions and that within relationships they may feel themselves unable to voice their true feelings:

> ... all (the mothers with low mood in the study) seemed to have experienced conflicts between their experiences and expectations of motherhood. Faced with these conflicts, the mothers had difficulties accepting their actual and concrete mothering experiences. They suppressed their own feelings, struggled to fulfil their ideals, and concealed their needs and feelings from other people.

> (Mauthner, 1998, p. 347)

The broader picture

As well as considering individual research evidence a technique called meta-analysis attempts to gather together the results of all the research on the causes of a particular disease. For example, a meta-analysis of 59 research studies of PND throughout the world (a total of 12,810 women) found that nearly one in seven of all women experience postnatal depression (O'Hara, 1996). This form of analysis has found that the most common time for women to develop this type of mental distress is during the first three months following the birth, with the peak time being in the first four – six weeks (Cox, 1993).

Beck (2001) has recently undertaken a meta-analysis of 84 research studies of PND and found thirteen significant predictors of postnatal depression listed below. They are shown in decreasing order of their effect.

Depression before the birth of the baby

Self-esteem

Childcare stress

Anxiety before the birth of the baby

Life stress

Social support

Marital relationship

History of previous depression

Infant temperament

Maternity blues

Marital status

Socio-economic status

Unplanned or unwanted pregnancy

Is it all to do with hormones?

Many of the bodily changes that occur in women throughout their pregnancy are regulated by chemicals called hormones. There are enormous hormone changes during pregnancy. The hormones called oestrogen, prolactin and progesterone all rise to high levels and there are changes also in cortisol and thyroid hormones (Harris, 1996). All these hormones, except prolactin in women who breast feed, fall rapidly following the birth of the child (Abou-Saleh, 1998). Although there is no direct evidence that these changes in hormones directly affect women's mood, the hypothesis remains that the hormones can affect the way that the nerves and their networks work within the brain, which in turn might affect mood (Pajer, 1995; Wieck, 1996).

There is little evidence, however, that hormone based treatments are effective in treating or preventing postnatal depression (Lawrie, 2001). Thus the consensus remains that psychosocial factors are more important triggers for PND than the hormone changes that occur during each pregnancy and delivery.

A stereotypical view of women as weak and 'suffering' from depression has existed for centuries

1.3 Is postnatal depression a disease at all?

There is no doubt that quite large numbers of women do experience a period of low mood at some time following the birth of their baby. Usually this is quite short lived and may last just a few hours or days. This mood dip is well recognised and often called 'baby blues'. In addition a small number of women develop potentially very serious mental distress, which has come to be labelled by the medical profession as 'puerperal psychosis'. In this severe condition, which is fortunately very rare, women may become very confused, have fluctuating moods and 'disordered thinking', which may include irrational preoccupations, hallucinations or delusions.

 For further information about 'puerperal psychosis' you can visit this website: www.mama.org.uk/puerperalprint.htm [accessed 25.6.02]

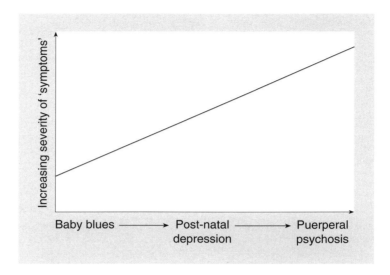

Figure 1   A spectrum of mental distress?

Most professional health workers have come to accept postnatal depression as a specific mental health problem that falls somewhere between 'baby blues' and 'puerperal psychosis' (see Figure 1). Certainly to label Jenny's distress as 'baby blues' would be rather belittling, but on the other hand she could not be considered to have lost the ability to engage with reality. But what evidence is there for postnatal depression being a specific 'disease'? Although there is no doubt that quite large numbers of women do have the symptoms that could be classified as 'depression' following the birth of their baby, some research studies have found that women are just as likely to become 'depressed' at other stages in their lives:

> *... there is very little evidence from the best controlled studies that the post-partum period (the time after the birth of the baby) is a time of increased risk for non-psychotic depression.*
>
> *(O'Hara, 1996, p. 45)*

Other studies (Ritter, 2000; Evans, 2001) have found that pregnancy itself was as stressful, or more stressful, than the time after delivery of the child:

> *... the study challenges a long-held doctrine that the time of high risk for depression is postpartum (after the birth). Rather for these women (in the study), confronting the fact of their pregnancy was the high-risk period.*
>
> *(Ritter, 2000, p. 583)*

Mandy (1998) looked at three groups of women and compared women who had just given birth with women who had recently had surgery and others who had experienced neither. This research found that the likelihood of developing 'depression' was similar across all three groups. However the women who had given birth experienced significantly more positive mood on average than women in the other groups.

Najman (2000) considers that many of the 'cases' of depression that are categorised as postnatal depression are in his opinion *'exacerbations or continuations of a pre-existing set of symptoms of depression'.* Controversially he concludes, *'it appears that the postnatal period is possibly a period of optimum mental health for the mother'(p. 25).* This is backed up by other research which found that elation was a more common 'mood disturbance' in women and their partners following childbirth than depression itself (Lane, 1997). In other words some women are also happy after the birth of a new child!

So why has there been such an acceptance of the concept of postnatal depression (or PND) as a definite disease? This might relate to the fact that a proportion of women, perhaps similarly to Jenny, certainly do get very low moods following the birth of their baby, but the *implications* of this may be more severe for them and their family than at other times of their lives. This is at least in part due to the *vulnerability* of the family and all the individuals within it at this time. Professional services seem to be alert to this possibility and focus considerable attention on families after the birth of a baby. As we will see for Jenny, the effects on her and her child, Abby, are highly significant at this vulnerable time.

Do men get postnatal depression?

In the story so far Geoff has remained rather in the background. But there have been significant advances in the understanding of the factors that seem to cause depression in both women and men (Harris, 2001). Using this framework it appears that recent stressors (such as the birth of a baby), can trigger feelings of powerlessness, loss and humiliation in men or women who may have had negative early life experiences themselves. Matthey (2000) certainly found that men as well as women developed PND, but that men had a lower incidence. This research provided evidence that men *reported* distress less frequently than women, indicating that some at least of the difference in quantity might be accounted for in gender differences in support-seeking. Men may be less likely than women to acknowledge their own emotional distress, and less likely to seek appropriate help. Ballard (1996) found that depression does exist in men after the birth of their children, but that it is not clear whether the number is higher than amongst other young married men who have not recently had children:

'Depression amongst fathers is associated with having depressed partners, having an unsupportive relationship and being unemployed.'

(Ballard, 1996, p. 65)

Study skills: Using evidence to test hypotheses

A key skill of studenthood is learning how to search for and weigh up evidence from research studies. Part of this skill is to understand the role of evidence in testing hypotheses.

Testing hypotheses

You saw how the search for information began with some guesses, or 'hypotheses', about the possibility that Jenny's social circumstance might have contributed to her low mood. A hypothesis is a brief statement of what you think might be true, which you can then test against available evidence. The value of a hypothesis is that it guides you as to what evidence to look for. In the passage above you saw that the hypothesis that social circumstances can influence low mood in the post-natal period seemed to be supported by available research evidence. On the other hand, in Box 1, you saw that the hypothesis that post-natal mood swings are *directly* caused by hormone changes did not seem to be supported by evidence. Though 'the hypothesis remains' that hormone changes affect a mother's mood in *indirect* ways.

Meta-analysis

However, the search did not stop there. There have been many studies investigating other hypotheses about factors that might contribute to post-natal low mood. So, researchers such as O'Hara and Beck have researched the research studies, to try to draw out the common findings from many studies. Their meta-analyses drew attention to a variety of other factors linked to post-natal distress. These findings in turn suggest new questions and hypotheses.

New hypotheses

For example, Beck found that the most likely predictor of post-natal depression was pre-natal depression. This suggests that it may not be the consequences of birth itself that influence low mood, but more general features of the mother's situation. The same conclusion could be drawn from the other 'predictors' in the list. This leads us to a different kind of hypothesis: that the way mood is influenced in the post-natal period is *not* significantly different from other periods of life; in other words, that PND is not a special kind of depression, but ordinary depression at a special time.

This is typical of scientific enquiry. Rather than just plodding along looking for answers to the same question (i.e. testing the same hypothesis), researchers turn questions inside out to see whether they can argue the opposite case. The idea is to test a variety of hypotheses to destruction and see which ones are left standing. In our case the new hypothesis, challenging the idea of PND as a special disease, seemed to be supported by a number of studies. Thus the search for evidence to test a variety of hypotheses led us to a much broader approach to our original question. Instead of taking PND for granted, as a 'disease' that afflicts mothers, we see that we should consider other hypotheses and look at Jenny's low mood much more broadly.

Evidence based practice

It is important to understand the relationship between evidence and hypotheses, because there is a growing emphasis on the idea that care practice should always be based on sound evidence. That means that instead of taking the ideas underpinning established practice for granted, alternative hypotheses should be generated and then tested. Don't worry if this language and way of thinking seems rather confusing right now. The discourse of scientific enquiry gradually comes to seem 'natural' as you gain practice in reading and writing it.

Key points

- Professionals bring their own 'baggage' to their assessment of situations. It is important to recognise the subjective nature of much professional observation. The professional's own opinions and values can impinge on the way that information is gathered and used.

- Don't believe everything you read in 'scientific' journals. Research findings about possible causes of distress can help your understanding, but should always be treated with caution.

- Postnatal depression attracts a lot of attention because families are so vulnerable at this stage. This is reflected in the ways that professional and statutory services focus on families at this time.

- The use of the label 'postnatal depression' is called into doubt by some theorists, but can be useful shorthand to use for descriptive or research purposes.

Section 2
Professional involvement

Professional health workers, particularly health visitors, have a duty enshrined in law to look after women and their new babies (Nurses and Midwives Council, 2000). In most areas of the UK it is the duty of the midwife to provide certain services and support the new family for the first 28 days after the delivery of any child. After this time responsibility moves to the health visitor, who has usually made a legally required (statutory) visit on the tenth day after delivery (Holden, 1996). If there are any problems, particularly if the care and safety of the child seem to be involved, then an inter-agency approach, including social workers, is recommended (Department of Health, 1999a).

So far in the development of the story concerning Jenny, Geoff and Abby there is very little firm evidence that any significant problems are occurring in the household. The neighbours have observed some tears, but not reported these to anyone in authority. We have just been using our imaginations to consider possible things that might be going wrong. We do not have the benefit of any detailed notes from previous professional workers to provide further clues. Maureen, the health visitor, visited the family as a routine following notification from a hospital in Brighton where Abby was born prior to the move to Scotland. These are the notes from Maureen's first visit.

HV notes

31-year-old mother, first baby. Non-smoker. Recently moved to area. Delivery normal in a Brighton hospital. Husband employed. Bottle-feeding. Child's birth weight 3.4 Kg. Current weight 4.01 Kg. Bowels OK. No parental concerns. Discussed immunisations. See in clinic 2w.

2.1 What else can professional workers use?

It seems as though Maureen has failed to check whether her 'client' has a significant level of mental distress. She is not alone:

> *There is some evidence that health workers use postnatal visits identifying and exploring parents' concerns about bodily functions, leaving only a few minutes for psychosocial inquiries.*

> *(Minde, 2001, p. 803)*

Health visitors and other professionals should always ask relevant questions about feelings. Even if the situation seems quite satisfactory, asking the questions directly allows the mother either to confirm this impression ... or disclose emotional difficulties. The ordinary suburban setting with apparently standard domestic arrangements failed to alert Maureen to the possibility that Jenny was struggling to cope with her own feelings. And of course Jenny had put on her best show for the visit. In the time between the arrangement of the visit and the visit itself Jenny had made concerted attempts to keep her persistent tears under control and tidy up the front room. Women may well find themselves reluctant to volunteer that they are feeling stressed or low following the birth of their baby. In one study in Scotland only 26 per cent of those later diagnosed as being depressed had sought help themselves (McIntosh, 1993). Most of the women in this study had thought that medical help was inappropriate and many had feared that seeking professional help would lead to them being labelled 'mentally ill', given pills, or even that their baby might be taken away. This is an indication of the power relationship between professional workers and their clients.

Professionals for these reasons may 'miss' up to 50 per cent of significant postnatal depression (Briscoe, 1986; Seeley, 1996; Hearn, 1998). Are there any ways in which professional workers can be helped to make sure that fewer women 'slip through the net'? In some areas schemes have been developed to ensure that new mothers are visited by more experienced, volunteer local mothers. These projects are intended to make new mothers feel more confident in their developing skills. The hope is that because of the more equal power relationships the mothers may be more likely to confide feelings of distress to another mother (Eastwood, 1995; Jones, 1995). The administration of a questionnaire has been suggested as another way of making sure that all health workers visiting after the delivery of a child concentrate for some time at least on the mental health of the mother (Cooper, 1998).

The Edinburgh Postnatal Depression Scale (EPDS) is a questionnaire which has been developed in Scotland for exactly this purpose (Cox, 1987). It is currently in common usage throughout the United Kingdom. You can see the full questionnaire, which the mother fills in herself, in the box which follows. It consists of ten short statements that are designed to indicate how the mother has been feeling over the previous week. It usually takes about five to ten minutes to complete and the health visitor can help the mother to complete the questionnaire if there are problems with literacy or comprehension. If the mother scores over 12 points then this is an indication that there might be the need for further investigation to explore the extent of any possible mental distress (Leverton, 2000).

The EPDS has been accepted by many agencies as an effective way of detecting low mood that might be labelled as depression in women following childbirth (Murray, 1990). If this questionnaire is given to women on several occasions it can also be used to detect whether the condition is improving, or indeed getting worse. The scale can also be used as a research tool as a way of measuring the different incidence of this problem between various communities of women.

However the use of a questionnaire might feel rather impersonal to some women and it certainly can not replace the clinical skills of professional workers who come into contact with women. The questionnaire may also present problems when used by women from some minority ethnic groups or whose first language is not English. As you can well imagine listening and using intuition can sometimes be more sensitive than administering a questionnaire. Leverton (2000) found that the health visitor's simple description of women as 'fed-up' or 'depressed' was more accurate than the EPDS questionnaire used by itself. Certainly health visitors and other clinical workers need detailed training in administering the questionnaire and in interpreting the results (Seeley, 2001).

Edinburgh Postnatal Depression Scale (EPDS)

Instructions for users

1   The mother is asked to underline the response which comes closest to how she has been feeling in the previous 7 days.

2   All ten items must be completed.

3   Care should be taken to avoid the possibility of the mother discussing her answers with others.

4   The mother should complete the scale herself, unless she has limited English or has difficulty with reading.

5   The EPDS may be used at 6-8 weeks to screen postnatal women. The child health clinic, postnatal check-up or a home visit may provide suitable opportunities for its completion.

Name:

_____

Address:

_____

Baby's Age:

_____

As you have recently had a baby, we would like to know how you are feeling. Please UNDERLINE the answer which comes closest to how you have felt IN THE PAST 7 DAYS, not just how you feel today.

1   I have been able to laugh and see the funny side of things

As much as I always could

Not quite so much now

Definitely not so much now

Not at all

2   I have looked forward with enjoyment to things

As much as I ever did

Rather less than I used to

Definitely less than I used to

Hardly at all

*3   I have blamed myself unnecessarily when things went wrong

Yes, most of the time

Yes, some of the time

Not very often

No, never

4   I have been anxious or worried for no good reason

No, not at all

Hardly ever

Yes, sometimes

Yes, very often

*5   I have felt scared or panicky for not very good reason

Yes, quite a lot

Yes, sometimes

No, not much

No, not at all

*6   Things have been getting on top of me

Yes, most of the time I haven't been able to cope at all

Yes, sometimes I haven't been coping as well as usual

No, most of the time I have coped quite well

No, I have been coping as well as ever

*7   I have been so unhappy that I have had difficulty sleeping

Yes, most of the time

Yes, sometimes

Not very often

No, not at all

*8   I have felt sad or miserable

Yes, most of the time

Yes, quite often

Not very often

No, not at all

*9   I have been so unhappy that I have been crying

Yes, most of the time

Yes, quite often

Only occasionally

No, never

*10   The thought of harming myself has occurred to me

Yes, quite often

Sometimes

Hardly ever

Never

Response categories are scored 0, 1, 2, and 3 according to increased severity of the symptoms. Items marked with an asterisk are reverse scored (i.e. 3, 2, 1, and 0). The total score is calculated by adding together the scores for each of the ten items.

(Cox, 1987)

Key points

- Several groups of professional workers are responsible for the care and welfare of women in the potentially highly vulnerable time following the birth of their babies.

- Professional workers have the 'power' to determine what factors are looked for during a professional interview. Care can go wrong if the wrong choices are made.

- Professional health workers and others may miss signs of mental distress in the people they come into contact with.

- The use of questionnaires or rating scales might help in the detection of mental distress, but can not replace the skills and training of experienced professional workers.

Study skills: Checking out the numbers

Are you getting into the habit of checking out numbers as you encounter them? Did you notice that the McIntosh study reported 26% of depressed mothers seeking help, whereas Hearn and others had suggested that up to 50% of cases are missed?

- Did you wonder what happened to the other 24%?

- Or did the numbers just wash over you?

- Or did you immediately spot that there is no inconsistency here, because the 24% would be cases identified by professionals?

If about 25% of depressed mothers seek help themselves, and about 25% were identified by professionals, that would give 50% being identified and 50% being missed. (You would not expect the numbers to tally perfectly anyway, because the first study was in Scotland, whereas we are not told in the case of the others.)

You are not expected to try to remember numbers like these as you read them, but try to make the effort to make sense of them, so that you take in the general gist.

2.2 Postnatal depression and the media

How do people form their ideas and opinions about situations such as becoming a mother? How have Jenny, Geoff and indeed Maureen come to believe the things they do about parenting? Some of our thoughts and feelings are certainly influenced by the media. In particular the media has a longstanding and complex relationship with the subject of mental health and mental distress. Often tabloid journalists portray people who have complicated personal histories in the most lurid terms: 'Madman runs amuck in knife frenzy!' 'Crazy mum in city centre siege!'. There often seems to be a link made in the media between mental distress and danger. Postnatal depression itself can be portrayed in very different ways by various sections of the media in their search for sensationalism. Sometimes this focuses on the most dramatic or tragic consequences of the situation, or on the incompetence or unavailability of helping agencies.

On the other hand, Jenny might have been exposed to quite sensitive items on the topic of mental distress that she comes upon in the media. These may highlight heart-warming stories in which people appear to have 'beaten the tragic disease', or otherwise have an uplifting story to tell. These stories may be accompanied by contact addresses of self-help organisations or advice on how to get help.

Activity 4 **Media reports on postnatal depression**

Allow about 25 minutes   Read the following article that appeared in a newspaper during January 2002.

What effect do you think that reading this article might have had on Jenny when she started to feel low following the birth of her baby?

TRAGIC TOLL OF MOTHERS WHO CAN'T GO ON

AROUND 30 women a year commit suicide before their baby's first birthday as a result of post-natal depression or other psychiatric problems, says a new survey.

Doctors believe some deaths could have been avoided if health workers had been more alert to risk factors and women had access to special psychiatric mother and baby units. Up to 80 per cent will suffer the 'baby blues'. Ten per cent will get post-natal depression.

PND is most common with a first pregnancy, but can recur with subsequent pregnancies.

TWO thirds of women who had previously had PND had some form of recurrence after subsequent pregnancies.

PND is thought to be linked with the changes in hormone levels that can occur after giving birth. Stress, exhaustion and life changes also play a role.

SYMPTOMS can include crying for no apparent reason, feeling anxious, lethargic, suffering obsessional thoughts, rejection of the child, problems with concentration, loss of libido, sleeping problems or pains that have no medical cause.

PND may not become evident until many weeks after the birth.

WOMEN are more vulnerable to PND if they have a family history of depression, have suffered major life events, such as bereavement, in the year before birth or were traumatised by the birth. Support throughout a pregnancy reduces the chance of PND.

THE condition can be helped by rest and the opportunity to talk about feelings.

OTHER treatments include counselling and psychotherapy, and relaxation techniques.

For further information, call the Edinburgh-based postnatal depression project on 0131 538 7288 or the Meet A Mum Association on 0208 7680123 (7pm to10pm).

(*The Mirror*, 17 January 2002)

Comment   It is hard to be sure what Jenny might feel if she were to read this particular article. She may well recoil from the subject of suicide. 'This surely doesn't mean me? I won't be in that small number who harm themselves.' She may be quite upset that a subject like this, which may feel very personal to her, has come under the public gaze. She may be vulnerable to the imagery constructed around 'non-ideal' motherhood, which influences her own thinking and the thinking of others she encounters (including Geoff).

On the one hand she might be pleased to discover that she is not the only woman to have developed unusual and disturbing feelings following the birth of her baby. She might be quite relieved to know that this is a condition that seems to be recognised by the 'experts' and that various forms of help might be available if the situation gets out of hand. She may take note of the different organisations that are available to help and contact them to discuss her specific situation.

On the other hand she may not be able to connect with other people's stories at all; they seem so different to her actual situation and they have been told in a way that emphasises the problems and difficulties. Of course she would never harm herself or her child.

Other people, including professional workers like Maureen, and indeed other family members, are also influenced by the general messages portrayed in the media.

Media reporting of mental distress is often sensationalised and can make matters worse for people who are users of mental health services

Articles such as this tend to set the mood for the way that the general public, including people such as Jenny, view mental distress. Philo (1994), in a survey of the public's response to Scottish and national press coverage of mental health issues, found that the media can play a significant role in fuelling beliefs which *'contribute to the stigmatisation of mental illness'*. This research seemed to indicate that media coverage helps to link mental distress with violent and extreme behaviours, exactly as the article you have just studied did. Baby blues (a common problem) is linked with suicide (a very rare event indeed). Even when the media coverage was largely sympathetic and apparently informative the resulting impression of people with mental distress was of *'a group of helpless 'victims' in need of 'expert' advice ...'* And the same conclusion could be derived from the short article you have just read.

Even those articles which specifically set out to provide information on the subject of postnatal depression or 'baby blues' can give partisan or conflicting messages. The news article you have just read certainly seems to do this. Martinez (2000) identified 27 recent articles on PND which had appeared in American journals and found that they favoured a medical model of the condition. (You will remember from your study of Unit 2 about the power of this model.) The articles also contained contradictory information about PND and the authors generally assumed that their readers were heterosexual, married and middle class.

2.3 Lower and lower ...

Back in our story where the situation seems to be deteriorating.

Jenny, Geoff and Abby: further deterioration ...

Over the next couple of months Geoff notices that Jenny's mood seems slowly to be getting lower and lower. She appears to be lost without the structure and routine of her previous job. Most days she can not be bothered to get changed and she spends the day in her dressing gown doing more or less the minimum care for Abby, who cries a lot of the time. He has heard Jenny shouting at Abby and has observed her being quite rough with her on occasions. Geoff is out at work most of the day and brings take-away suppers home on his return. He is pretty much exhausted by his new job and he finds Jenny quite hard to communicate with. Abby is delighted to see him, he feeds and baths her and puts her in her cot for the night. She cries a lot in the evenings and often wakes several times in the night.

Geoff's sister, Gwen, arrives for a brief visit and is quite shocked about the situation that she finds in the new house. She has recently seen an article (perhaps similar to the one you have just studied), about the 'horrors of PND' in the paper ... She is determined to alert the authorities ...

Jenny does seem to be feeling worse and worse. She is starting to exhibit 'symptoms' that indicate to her family that her internal, psychological world is becoming increasingly distressed. Many of these signs and symptoms are apparent to her friends and family and other social contacts.

 The box below contains a description of 'postnatal depression' taken from the Health Education Board for Scotland website: www.hebs.com [accessed 25.06.02].

Extract from 'Talking about depression'

Each woman is affected in her own particular way. These are some of the feelings and experiences which women often report. Feeling:

- depressed and tearful. Everything can seem a struggle. You feel bad about yourself and about everything around you

- anxious and worried about your own health, the baby's or the rest of the family's. You may feel genuinely frightened of being alone at home, or of going out even to the local shops

- irritable and frustrated. You may snap at your children and get in a rage with your partner or your friends

- exhausted both physically and emotionally

- unable to cope with the many demands on you

- guilty at not behaving like 'a proper mother', or about the angry feelings you may have.

You may also notice changes in the way your body functions and the way you behave:

• concentrating on even the simplest task can be difficult

• your usual sleep patterns may be upset. You may feel you want to sleep all the time. Or it may be hard to fall asleep or sleep long enough

• your appetite can be affected so that you lose all interest in food, or eat much more than usual for comfort

• your body may seem to slow down. Making decisions of any sort, even about what to wear, can seem impossible

• or you may feel full of nervous energy and keep constantly busy, but not really achieve much

• you may lose any interest in sex.

(Health Education Board for Scotland, 2002)

How do you think that Jenny might react to seeing this list? Do you think she may be able to recognise herself, or do you think she might be shocked and disturbed by the way that people such as herself are talked about in the media?

If Jenny ever gets to see a psychiatrist then he or she will be checking to see if Jenny's 'signs and symptoms' fit into the description of a known mental 'disease'. Read the following description, taken from the most authoritative catalogue of classification of 'mental disorders' entitled *Diagnostic and Statistical Manual of Mental Disorders*, fourth edition (American Psychiatric Association, 1994).

What is depression? The official description

DSM IV

MAJOR DEPRESSIVE EPISODE

A. Five (or more) of the following symptoms have been present during the same 2-week period and represent a change from previous functioning; at least one of the symptoms is either (1) depressed mood or (2) loss of interest or pleasure.

Note: Do not include symptoms that are clearly due to a general medical condition, or mood-incongruent delusions or hallucinations.

(1) depressed mood most of the day, nearly every day, as indicated by either subjective report (e.g., feels sad or empty) or observation made by others (e.g., appears tearful). **Note:** In children and adolescents, can be irritable mood.

(2) markedly diminished interest or pleasure in all, or almost all, activities most of the day, nearly every day (as indicated by either subjective account or observation made by others).

(3) significant weight loss when not dieting or weight gain (e.g., a change of more than 5% of body weight in a month), or decrease or increase in appetite nearly every day. **Note:** In children, consider failure to make expected weight gains.

(4) insomnia or hypersomnia nearly every day.

(5)   psychomotor agitation or retardation nearly every day (observable by others, not merely subjective feelings of restlessness or being slowed down).

(6)   fatigue or loss of energy nearly every day.

(7)   feelings of worthlessness or excessive or inappropriate guilt (which may be delusional) nearly every day (not merely self-reproach or guilt about being sick).

(8)   diminished ability to think or concentrate, or indecisiveness, nearly every day (either by subjective account or as observed by others).

(9)   recurrent thoughts of death (not just fear of dying), recurrent suicidal ideation without a specific plan, or a suicide attempt or a specific plan for committing suicide.

B.   The symptoms do not meet criteria for a Mixed Episode.

C.   The symptoms cause clinically significant distress or impairment in social, occupational, or other important areas of functioning.

D.   The symptoms are not due to the direct physiological effects of a substance (e.g., a drug of abuse, a medication) or a general medical condition (e.g., hypothyroidism).

E.   The symptoms are not better accounted for by Bereavement, i.e., after the loss of a loved one, the symptoms persist for longer than 2 months or are characterized by marked functional impairment, morbid preoccupation with worthlessness, suicidal ideation, psychotic symptoms, or psychomotor retardation.

(*American Psychiatric Asociation, 1994*)

Study skills: Coping with alternative descriptions

You have now come across three quite different looking descriptions of depression:

• Box 3: the Edinburgh Postnatal Depression Scale

• Box 4: 'Talking about depression'

• Box 5: What is depression? The official description

Why do there have to be so many? Could professionals not get together and agree to one of them?

Actually, these descriptions are addressed to different audiences and serve different purposes, so there is need for all three. None is more 'correct' than the others. The first is designed to produce a reliable test, which is easily understood and as straightforward as possible to answer. The second is more descriptive and aimed at helping mothers to explore and understand their own feelings. While the last covers depressions of all kinds and aims to help professionals classify the severity of specific cases.

It may seem confusing to have a variety of overlapping but different descriptions of roughly the same thing. One of the challenges of studying is to become comfortable with there not being one 'true' account of anything, but rather a variety of attempts to describe the world to particular audiences for particular purposes.

If you want to find out more about the way that psychological problems are classified by professionals using the Diagnostic and Statistical Manual of Mental Disorders then visit the website: www.psych.org/clin_res/dsm/dsmintro81301.cfm [accessed: 25.06.02].

Key points

- The media can be an important source of information and advice about mental health issues, but can also sensationalise, stigmatise and create an atmosphere which creates difficulties for vulnerable people with mental distress.

- Lay descriptions, such as those that appear in self-help literature or in the media, might be helpful for non-professional people to understand their situation and recognise these signs and symptoms in themselves or people they know.

- Official descriptors of mental 'disease' are used by health professionals to describe and classify signs and symptoms, but lay accounts should also be valued.

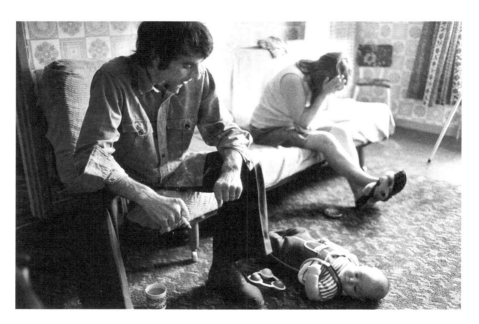

When one person has a period of mental distress all the other members of the family are affected

2.4 Getting help

In a situation like the one that is unfolding for Jenny and her family you could make a long list of agencies that could be approached for help. But Jenny and Geoff might be so entrenched in their own problems that they are unable to seek help for themselves. The situation has slowly built up and they may not be aware of the extent of their 'problems' or how serious their situation might be.

McIntosh (1993) researched the experience of 60 first-time mothers, of whom nearly two thirds reported that they had felt depressed for at least two weeks in the nine months following the birth of their baby:

> *Despite the disruption and misery which (feeling depressed) created, the majority of sufferers did not seek assistance for their depression from any source. Professional agents were regarded either as threatening or as inappropriate to the solution of the problem.*

> *(McIntosh, 1993, p. 183)*

Some people may be relieved to know that their situation has a recognised 'label' or diagnosis, but others find that such labels threaten their own identity and self-esteem. Small (1994) found that although most women in their research study had perceived themselves to be depressed, a third of them did not want to label the experience as postnatal depression:

> *Women who reported feeling depressed believed the contributing factors to be lack of support, isolation, fatigue and physical ill health. Only two in five of the case group had sought any form of professional assistance. Half the women in the case group had sought help from non-professional sources, mainly friends.*

> *(Small, 1994, p. 89)*

It can also be difficult for friends, neighbours or relatives to know when and how to alert the relevant agencies. You will remember that Jenny's neighbours had observed that both Jenny and Abby were crying. But what is 'normal', and when is calling for help from official agencies seen as unwarranted prying, or stigmatising labelling?

Jenny, Geoff and Abby: Gwen comes to visit

Geoff's sister Gwen is not in very regular contact with Geoff and Jenny. She lives in Devon and has come to visit the new family on her way to a holiday in the Scottish Highlands. She works as a legal secretary for a firm of solicitors.

On her visit to Jenny and Geoff she is quite shocked at what she discovers. Jenny seems in a bad way, even to her untrained eye, and she is anxious that Abby is not getting the care and attention that she needs.

Gwen takes matters into her own hands and without telling anyone else telephones several local agencies and paints a vivid picture of the scene that she has witnessed in Jenny and Geoff's house. She is very anxious about the changes that she has noticed in Jenny since the last time they met about two years previously. She has also become alarmed by florid publicity about the tragic death of a mother which has been in all the newspapers and on TV recently. In her phone calls to local organisations she stresses the darkest aspects of Jenny's outlook on life and how she seems unable and unwilling to look after herself, the house and particularly Abby. In some ways Gwen could be considered to be using her power at a time when Jenny is at her most vulnerable. At other times she would not have dreamed to take such action without a full discussion with the people directly involved.

Gwen manages to get through to the community psychiatric nursing team based at the local Community Mental Health Trust day centre. She stresses the emergency nature of the situation and Jack, a qualified community psychiatric nurse (CPN), is dispatched to find out more.

Gwen has also contacted the local social work team. After an allocation meeting they send the new social worker, Stephanie, round.

Maureen, the local health visitor, is also contacted and is concerned that she may have missed something on her first visit to the family and is keen to make amends.

There are so many places to turn to for help with mental distress that the choice might create confusion

---

Activity 5 | **Involving several agencies**

Allow about 15 minutes | Gwen has managed to get social workers, psychiatric workers as well as the initial health visitor concerned about and involved with the situation. What do you think that the impact on the family might be from the involvement of several different agencies?

What do you think are the possible advantages and disadvantages when several agencies become involved in a situation where significant mental distress seems to have been uncovered?

Make a list of what you consider might be the advantages and a list of the disadvantages.

Comment There may well be **advantages** associated with the involvement of several agencies:

- A single agency might not have all the necessary resources or expertise to help, and a 'partnership approach' is now recommended in complex situations, or where the welfare of children might seriously be threatened (Department of Health, 1999a).

- The involvement of more than one agency might also help to provide various checks and balances over the actions, or indeed the inactivity, of another agency.

However, multi-agency involvement may create **disadvantages**:

- There is the possibility of duplication of effort, or of poorly defined roles.

- Usually communication is more difficult between agencies than within agencies and conflict between the ways that different organisations work is always a possibility.

- People who make use of the services may not understand the different roles and responsibilities that various agencies have and may find accessing help more difficult.

- Jenny may be confused by all the different people contacting her from different agencies and will have to repeat her story with each worker.

- It may be more difficult to be assertive, or to insist on one's rights when more than one agency is involved.

- It will be especially difficult for Jenny, or for the rest of her family, to establish a relationship with any of the workers if there is confusion or overlap of roles.

Official policy statements recommend a multi-agency approach, especially where harm to children or young people might be possible:

> *Promoting children's well-being and safeguarding them from significant harm depends crucially upon effective information sharing, collaboration and understanding between agencies and professionals. Constructive relationships between individual workers need to be supported by a strong lead from elected or appointed authority members, and the commitment of chief officers.*

> *(Department of Health, 1999a, para 1.10, pp. 2–3)*

But in practice there can often be confusion, overlap and a clash of 'cultures' between different agencies. A consistent and coherent approach is very hard to sustain and can present enormous difficulties for people attempting to use those services. In addition to the practical problems that may be associated with the involvement of different agencies there may also be difficulties associated with the different 'models' or theoretical approaches that a variety of agencies and their workers might adopt. In a situation such as Jenny's, where there is a possible diagnosis of postnatal depression, many interpretations and approaches may be applied by different agencies, or indeed by different workers within the same agency. Professionals may work to different models because they were exposed to them during their own training or within their particular professional culture. And of course different agencies have varying amounts of power and authority with which they can insist that 'their' model gains preference over others.

Possible theoretical models used by the various workers from different agencies include: the medical model and psychodynamic, psychosocial and systemic approaches.

The **medical model,** which you also examined in Unit 2, would insist on an assessment of Jenny's mental state, with a view to determining whether she has the features of depression as set out in various recognised guidelines. General practitioners, psychiatrists and many community psychiatric nurses might use the medical model as the underpinning basis for their work. For example DSM-IV (American Psychiatric Association, 1994), which you studied earlier in the unit, might be used. A mental health worker might ask specifically about the 'symptoms' which indicate that a firm diagnosis of 'depression' can be made. Often the medical model implies that there is some form of chemical disturbance in the brain chemistry of the person who has the symptoms. In turn the diagnosis (label) of 'depression' will lead, almost inevitably, to trigger specific types of medical intervention, including the use of antidepressant medication.

A **psychodynamic approach** to Jenny's situation would attempt to understand her feelings in terms of the experiences she has had in her own past. Significant features, such as the parenting that she was exposed to, become important pointers to the way she has developed as a human individual and the emotional apparatus she has at her disposal to respond to life events. This approach attempts to understand the world from the point of view of Jenny's own psychological world as it has developed. The implications for helping Jenny are that therapy would be undertaken to help her to understand for herself that her reactions and feelings have been shaped by these elements from her past and help her to redefine her situation in terms she finds less distressing.

A **psychosocial analysis** of Jenny's predicament might look at many of the significant social and practical features of her life that may have affected her current mental health status. Brown (1996) analysed the sorts of psychosocial features in women's lives that make the onset of depression more likely. A social worker might base their work with Jenny on a model like this. In particular, a feminist critique might involve examining the way that women in general, and Jenny in particular, have been treated within society. For example Jenny was 'expected' to move away from her own sources of support because of her husband's needs, which took preference. Her own educational and employment needs may have been considered less important than those of the men around her. Many people find a sense of identity through their job or occupation. When Jenny left her job it is possible that this undermined her sense of self-worth and made her vulnerable to feelings of low mood. Ways of helping using this viewpoint would include the development of a joint understanding with Jenny of the factors that have given her low self-esteem throughout her life and establishing ways of defining herself more positively.

A **systemic approach** would make an attempt to see Jenny in the context of all of her social and personal relationships. Using this approach it is apparent that it is not just Jenny who has created the current situation, but it has evolved because of the complex interactions between herself and the other 'players' within the dynamic. The way that Jenny feels is a result, at least in part, of the way that she has interacted with Geoff. A therapeutic approach using systems therapy would include helping both Jenny and Geoff to see themselves as part of the dynamic which has led to the current situation. The approach would seek not to blame or locate the cause in either or both parties, but to come to some mutual understanding about the ways that their interactions have developed during their relationships.

Study skills: Competing models

You have just encountered four 'models' of the way depressions arise and how they can be treated. Why should there be different models? Why not simply agree on the best and leave the others aside?

A central aim of academic research and debate is to construct 'models' of how various aspects of the world work. (You will remember the biomedical model of health and disease, back in Unit 2.) Models enable us to plan actions. By giving us ways of understanding how things work, they enable us to predict what will happen if we act in particular ways. However, we can *never* know that a model is 'true'. Reality is generally far too complicated to be represented by any single model. Yet we have to use models, even though we know they are only approximations of 'reality'. They are all we have. Without them we would be helpless. However, we need to keep testing them and improving them. And we must always be ready to see their limitations and recognise that they may mislead us.

In complex situations (such as Jenny's) it is often an advantage to have several models available, so that you can try them out in turn and consider which seems to fit the circumstances best. Then if your initial actions seem not to be working, you can switch to an alternative strategy. In academic study you need to become mentally flexible: capable of understanding and applying different models and comparing the 'truths' they produce.

Jenny, Geoff and Abby: confusion and competition

Since the initial telephone calls from Geoff's sister, Gwen, the three agencies that she contacted have all become involved.

The social worker, Stephanie, has made regular visits and spends at least an hour each week with Jenny. She uses a 'psychodynamic' approach in her work. The focus during these sessions is on Jenny's background and the problems she had as a small child. Jenny doesn't engage much during these sessions and is feeling too weepy to bother about thinking about things in the past. She can't understand the relevance of going back to feelings from her own childhood. Stephanie is concerned that Jenny has not 'disclosed' possibly serious events from her childhood.

Maureen, the health visitor, is so concerned that she 'missed' the initial diagnosis that she is spending at least two hour-long sessions at the house each week. During these appointments she is trying to get Jenny more interested in playing with Abby. Jenny isn't really able to respond to these suggestions and still interacts with Abby in a distracted manner.

Jack, the community psychiatric nurse, is concerned that Jenny may have a serious 'mental health problem'. He visits and starts to introduce the idea of medication to Jenny and suggests that she might benefit from attendance at the local mental health day centre in the centre of town.

Jenny and Geoff become increasingly confused by the different advice they are getting from each of the people representing the various agencies. They feel that in spite of all the unasked for attention they are getting, the situation is not improving.

Key points

- There may be many agencies available that can potentially give help and support to individuals and their families to enable them to cope with difficult situations.

- If more than one agency is involved in a situation there are opportunities for this to be advantageous, but also for complications, overlaps and disputes to arise.

- Different professional workers may use very different models to analyse the situation and in their attempt to provide appropriate help.

Section 3
Potentially serious problems with professional involvement

Jenny, Geoff and Abby: what if abuse is occurring?

A multi-professional conference is organised by the social services department. The social services, the health visitor and the mental health team are all represented at the meeting and Jack, the local community psychiatric nurse (CPN), is appointed as the 'key worker' for Jenny. Maureen is asked to concentrate only on Abby's needs. Note that this is, once again, a meeting of powerful people deciding things about the absent Jenny. As a result of the meeting Jack starts to visit Jenny on a more regular basis. After some time of awkwardness between them they start to have good 'sessions', during which Jenny is able to tell Jack about many of the features that she feels have made her depressed following Abby's birth. She is able to reveal important things about her relationship with Geoff. Jack is a good listener and when the tears come he feels able to put his arms round Jenny's shoulders. He also tells her of the problems that he has recently been having in his own family life.

More recently he has started to visit Jenny in the evening when he knows that Abby will be asleep and that Geoff will be away on business trips ...

Activity 6

Allow about 25 minutes

Aspects of professionalism

(a)   What is going on in the relationship between Jenny and Geoff and their new professional worker, Jack, the community psychiatric nurse? Write down your thoughts about the possible dynamics in this fictional situation.

(b)   Read *Enfield Social Services 'Guidance on professional boundaries between staff and service users'*. This has been printed as Offprint 24. How does this guidance help your understanding of the boundaries and power relationships in this situation?

Comment

(a)   The scenario certainly changes with the introduction of Jack. We have deliberately described an ambiguous situation that could be interpreted in several ways. It may be that Jack is a highly skilled, intuitive worker: he knows that Jenny needs an uninterrupted period of time during his visits to be able to disclose safely about the important features of her life. The fear of being disturbed during his visits would make Jenny less likely to unburden herself to him. People may use third parties (a child etc.) as a diversion, consciously or subconsciously, in order to avoid getting to grips with their own deepest issues. Jack's use of touch, putting his arm round Jenny's shoulders as she sobs, may be a good way of helping her feel supported while she deals with the most difficult things she has ever had to face. It may be an entirely benign and acceptable symbol of the empathy that he feels towards his client.

On the other hand, a more problematic interpretation is possible. Jenny is in a highly vulnerable state. She finds herself not entirely in control of her emotions or actions, and overwhelmed by fears and feelings. She has not had an easy emotional life. She is starting to disclose things to Jack, who seems to have everything that the previous men in her life were lacking. He is attentive and lets her talk, he seems full of empathy, and claims to understand how she is feeling. The arm round her shoulder is warm and comforting. But where are the boundaries to this increasingly intense relationship?

(b)   The Enfield Social Services guidelines help to clarify the situation. Jack certainly is in a position of power in his relationship with his client. He has arranged the consultations to occur at a time and place when he and Jenny will not be disturbed. He does seem to be breaking professional boundaries with his use of touch and by visiting Jenny when she is alone. He is also positioning himself as a major figure in Jenny's already stressful emotional world. Will she be able to cope with the consequences of either further involvement, or a withdrawal of his presence?

Counsellors and other health workers should always be aware that they have considerable power within any therapeutic relationship

3.1 Is this an abuse of power?

Is this situation with Jack (the CPN) and Jenny becoming an issue of sexual abuse in which Jack uses his power as a professional health worker to take advantage of Jenny? The extent to which sexual abuse of clients takes place within psychiatric settings will always be hard to determine. However studies have shown that it may be quite a common occurrence (Pope, 1986; Rutter, 1989; Borys, 1989; Jehu, 1994).

Sex between therapists and clients has emerged as a significant phenomenon, one that the profession has not adequately acknowledged or addressed. Extensive research has led to recognition of the extensive harm that therapist-client sex can produce. Nevertheless, research suggests that perpetrators account for about 4.4% of therapists (7% of male therapists; 1.5% of female therapists) when data from national studies are pooled.

(Pope, 2001)

It certainly seems as though Jack has a problem in maintaining an appropriate boundary between his work as a professional worker and himself as an individual with his own needs. Some debate might be developed on the nature of boundaries in counselling or mental health work in general. For example Hermansson (1997) considers that effective counselling might demand, in a qualified way, boundary crossing. He argues that counsellor aloofness, with rigid boundaries, might in itself become potentially abusive. However, it does appear in the situation in which Jack and Jenny find themselves that the potential for sexual abuse has developed. Although situations like this might be explicable they are never excusable (Home Office, 2000). Jack might be under pressure in his work situation with an enormous, draining workload and feel the need for warmth and some level of intimacy from his clients. A psychodynamic profile of therapists who have been found to sexually exploit their clients discovered, not surprisingly, that they have severe problems with their own sexual identities and experience a considerable amount of sexual anxiety and guilt in their personal relationships (Hetherington, 2000). It also appears that many professional therapists who do stray across the 'boundary' and develop inappropriate sexual or social relationships with their clients may have been recently separated, divorced or are experiencing personal difficulties of their own (Blunden, 2001).

> *If practitioners are to avoid abusive and exploitative relationships with their clients, they should ensure that they properly assess the potential risks of any personal difficulties for their counselling practice. They should also be aware when particular clients, or their behaviour, causes them professional difficulties. This is not a sign of weakness. In these circumstances, the good practitioner will always seek appropriate support and supervision.*

(Blunden, 2001)

Rather as in the relationship between Jenny and Jack the abusive situation might develop slowly and clients who are being abused may not understand the full significance or nature of the abuse. The Department of Health has produced a booklet (Department of Health, 2001a) that helps people to understand the therapies that they may be having. The booklet sets out warning signs (below) that help in the recognition of potential abuse by therapists.

 This booklet is also available on the Department of Health website at: www.doh.gov.uk/mentalhealth [accessed: 25.06.02].

Warning signs

A therapist or counsellor should not:

- be defensive, upset or angry when you ask questions or end therapy
- visit you at home uninvited or arrange to meet you socially
- make close physical contact without your consent
- ask you inappropriate questions about your sex life
- be unpredictable or threatening in their behaviour
- talk frequently and in detail about their personal life
- regularly go over the allocated time for therapy sessions.

(Department of Health, 2001a)

3.2 Complaining about services

As the story develops it becomes increasingly clear that Jack is abusing Jenny. This a misuse of his power as a professional worker. He has stayed longer and longer in the evenings alone with Jenny and his comforting 'arm around the shoulder' has developed into more explicit touching. In this situation professional boundaries have certainly been breached and there are definite grounds for complaint.

Jenny may be ambivalent about the attention that she is receiving from Jack, and feel that in some ways she herself is implicated in the situation that has developed. She might think that her ability to complain is reduced because of her own feelings of guilt and powerlessness. Indeed she may not want to complain because she feels flattered by the attention she has received – but this doesn't make the relationship any less abusive.

Lay people such as Jenny, Geoff or any member of their family, friends or networks have a number of opportunities to make their concerns known about possible inappropriate or abusive professional relationships, but the process of making a complaint can be quite daunting and although there are a number of checks and balances that govern the work of professional health workers, finding the right way of entry into the system can be confusing (Department of Health, 2001b). Once again the power usually rests in the hands of the professionals.

NHS complaints process

First discuss your concerns with the person concerned or other staff members in the department – they should try to sort the problem out.

If you are not satisfied, ask to speak to the manager of the service.

If the matter is not resolved, or if you prefer to complain in writing, write to the manager of the service or the Chief Executive. They should acknowledge your letter promptly and investigate your concerns.

If you are still not satisfied, discuss the matter with your local health authority.

If you have exhausted the complaints procedures open to you and are still not satisfied you can complain to the Health Services Ombudsman.

(Department of Health, 2001b)

Because Jack is a worker within the NHS it is possible to use the NHS complaints procedure. Making complaints through the NHS complaints system can be quite confusing and gruelling for lay people, and this may be especially true if the person complaining is feeling unwell or upset on behalf of others. Abuse in Therapy is an organisation in the UK which exists to provide support and advocacy for people who have been abused by 'trusted professionals'. Between 1991 and 1998 they were approached by 137 clients only 69 of whom felt willing or able to pursue a formal complaint against their abuser (Currie, 2002).

 To find out more about organisations which assist people who may have been abused in therapy visit the following website: The Prevention of Professional Abuse Network (POPAN) www.popan.org.uk [accessed: 25.06.02].

A new system called the Independent Complaints Advocacy Service (ICAS) is being established to provide independent support for people wishing to make a complaint. ICAS services are intended to give people who want to complain the support they need to do so. This service will replace the previous Community Health Council advocacy role (Department of Health, 2001c). In addition Patient Advice and Liaison Services (PALS) are being established in England although different services will be developed in the other countries of the UK. PALS are designed as a means of providing on-the-spot help for patients within NHS trusts. They will be employed by and responsible to trusts (NHS Confederation, 2002). PALS will aim to resolve problems and concerns quickly before they become serious and inform people of the complaints procedure and put them in touch with the specialist, independent advocacy services when they wish to complain formally.

 To find out more about these new systems visit their website: www.doh.gov.uk/patientadviceandliaisonservices/index.htm [accessed: 25.06.02].

3.3 Complaints to the relevant professional body

Because Jack is also a qualified nurse, it is possible to make a complaint to his regulatory body, the Nursing and Midwifery Council (NMC). The NMC is the regulatory body for nursing, midwifery and health visiting:

> *The core function of the Nursing and Midwifery Council is to establish and improve standards of nursing, midwifery and health visiting care in order to serve and protect the public.*
>
> *Our key tasks are to:*
>
> - *maintain a register listing all nurses, midwives and health visitors*
> - *set standards and guidelines for nursing, midwifery and health visiting education, practice and conduct*
> - *provide advice for registrants on professional standards*
> - *quality assure midwifery and nursing education*
> - *set standards and provide guidance for local supervising authorities for midwives*
> - *consider allegations of misconduct or unfitness to practise due to ill health.*

 To find out more about the work of the Nursing and Midwifery Council visit their website: www.nmc-uk.org/cms/content/home/ [accessed: 25.06.02].

Professional workers can also complain

Jack is behaving inappropriately and his behaviour should be of serious concern to his fellow professional workers within his own organisation and in other agencies. It is possible that one of his co-workers has noted that Jack's behaviour is inappropriate. It may fit into a pattern that has been observed previously, or be the result of a chance remark or incidental observation ... his car may have been noticed outside Jenny's house late in the evening. In this situation it is quite legitimate for one of his colleagues to make representations or complaints. Sometimes this is called 'whistle-blowing' and it may have far reaching implications, both for the person who is being complained about, and also for the professional making the complaint. It has been said that whistle-blowers are rather like bees, they have only one sting to use, and using it may lead to career suicide (Yamey, 2000). This is especially true when the whistle-blower makes a complaint against their own organisation and some of the practices that occur at an institutional level. Many organisations seem to be deeply threatened by any possible 'epidemic' of ethical and moral responsibility which might bring about the destruction of that organisation's 'ethical autonomy' (Alford, 1999). Indeed a survey of American whistle-blowers found that 86 out of 87 whistle-blowers had experienced retaliation from their organisation (Soeken, 1987).

> *Whistleblowers face economic and emotional deprivation, victimisation, and personal abuse and receive little help from statutory authorities.*

> *(Lennane, quoted in Yamey, 2000)*

Within the United Kingdom the government has recently recognised some of the problems that employees might face if they disclose information that might be considered 'whistle-blowing'. The Public Interest and Disclosure Act 1998 has been designed to give: '*Significant statutory protection to employees who disclose information reasonably and responsibly and are victimised as a result*' (NHSE, 1999).

> *The fear of being labelled a trouble maker, the fear of appearing disloyal and the fear of victimisation by managers and colleagues are powerful disincentives against speaking up about genuine concerns staff have about criminal activity, failure to comply with a legal duty, miscarriages of justice, danger to health and safety or the environment, and the cover up of any of these in the workplace.*

> *In recent years the public has been shocked by disasters and scandals that have claimed lives and damaged others. The enquiries set up to uncover the facts behind these catastrophes have revealed all too often that they had been a consequence of a pattern of poor practice over a long period of time and that, although not officially recognised, were often known about by employees who had been too scared to speak up, or who had raised the matter only to find their concerns ignored.*

> *(NHSE, 1999, p. 2)*

Activity 7   **A whistle-blower's story**

Allow about 30 minutes   Adrian, whose story you are going to hear, is real and this incident actually happened. Adrian Hughes is now head of a social services' inspection and registration unit, but he started his career as a childcare worker in a residential school for children, where he learnt about abuse at first hand.

    Listen now to the interview with Adrian Hughes which you will find on side 2 of Audio Cassette 5. In the first part of the interview you will hear Adrian describe how difficult it was for him to report this abuse and get it put on the record, but he then goes on to say how, in his current practice as an inspector, he attempts to overcome some of those pressures.

When you have listened to the whole interview go back to the beginning and jot down all the reasons Adrian gives as to why he found it difficult to be a whistle-blower.

Comment   The list might include the following:

- Adrian was new and, as he said, 'a bit green'.

- He didn't have much status in the home.

- He felt 'part of the abuse' because he had asked the senior worker for help and he had been drawn into it by holding his colleague's watch.

- He was put off by a senior worker who challenged his judgment and inexperience.

- He didn't want to jeopardise his livelihood or his future career.

- He didn't know whom he could go to outside the establishment.

Adrian was not able to confront the abuse partly because he had been drawn into it himself. When Adrian did eventually say something to a manager who was senior both to him and to the worker who had abused the child, what he said was discounted. His lack of status in the home and the lack of agreed guidelines worked against his complaint being taken seriously by management. Adrian did question the actions of his senior but was told that the way this incident had been handled might have been 'appropriate'. Adrian described this as a 'conspiracy' of senior staff. Although a clear hierarchy existed, the management did not offer guidance or support – a feature identified by Wardaugh and Wilding in the Course Reader, Chapter 24, which you read at the end of Unit 18.

Adrian felt inhibited from pursuing his complaint because he was afraid he would lose his livelihood and, as he said, he had rent to pay and food to buy. Being a whistle-blower involves taking risks which cut into the very basics of life. It can involve being intimidated, threatened or harassed.

Pilgrim (1995) highlights two kinds of whistle-blowing:

> *The first is where a professional draws attention to the conduct of colleagues which **violates** norms ... the second is where a professional **challenges** the norm itself and thereby raises the question of whether it should be changed.*

Which type do you think Adrian was faced with? He started by thinking that the behaviour he had witnessed would be as unacceptable to his managers as it was to him, but his manager's response made it clear that his colleague's abusive behaviour conformed to the prevailing view of how to deal with such incidents. Adrian had come up against the proverbial brick wall: to take his complaint further would have involved challenging the whole regime and its values – a very difficult thing for a new worker to do.

Key points

- Professional workers can often be in a position in which they can misuse their power in ways that are harmful to the people they are entrusted to care for.

- Written guidance on professional boundaries may be helpful in determining whether abuse of power is taking place.

- Individuals do have opportunities to complain when they consider that abuse of power is taking place, but often the way to make such complaints is unclear and can be fraught with difficulties.

- It can be very difficult for health or social care workers to challenge the bad practice of colleagues or senior workers.

- To make effective complaints or to report abuse, workers need to know what steps they should take both inside and outside their immediate agency.

Section 4
Different needs and conflicting rights

> ### What is happening to Jenny, Geoff and Abby?
>
> Jenny's mental health continues to deteriorate. Jack, the CPN, has been suspended pending investigations and no other worker is currently allocated as key worker. Abby is now 14-months-old, but she remains quite a 'difficult' baby. She finds it hard to sleep, and often seems to cry persistently. Jenny spends more and more time in bed while Abby does her best, playing on the bedroom floor amongst the domestic debris ... and the electric sockets ... Geoff is increasingly fed up with the disruption of his working life and has already had a warning from his managing director about timekeeping and unscheduled days off work.
>
> The health visitor, Maureen, visits again, notes the scene, chats to Jenny, plays with Abby for a while and writes the following report:
>
> *HV notes:*
>
> Jenny seems to be significantly depressed. She is not interacting well with Abby. Abby is often left to her own devices and Jenny does not always respond adequately to the clues which her child shows. Abby may be left in potentially dangerous situations. There are now increasingly serious concerns whether Jenny can look after Abby satisfactorily.

Activity 8　**Individual needs?**

Allow about 15 minutes　Read carefully the above section of the case study which outlines the development of this increasingly serious situation.

The three family members have their own needs. We do not expect you to be a specialist in this area, but from your own imagination and general knowledge make three sets of observations:

(a)　Comment on the situation as it relates to the needs of the mother, Jenny.

(b)　Comment on the situation as it relates to the needs of the father, Geoff.

(c)　Comment on the situation as it relates to the needs of the 14-month-old child, Abby.

Comment　All three family members in this scene have major needs. Their situation has deteriorated and they do not seem to be able to rely on each other to have their needs met within the family unit.

(a)　**Jenny** seems to have become rather unresponsive to Abby's cues for attention. Her 'flatness' isn't much fun for Abby who has tended to withdraw from contact with Jenny, and indeed from other adults. Her insecurity shows in her persistent crying, she is less involved in play.

Other 'negative behaviours' may well start to creep into the situation ... In turn this makes it less likely that Jenny will want to look after her ... And the downward spiral continues.

Jenny has many significant needs. She has 'lost' her career and contact with family, local friends and workmates no longer provides her with support. She is not looking after herself or her own child. Jenny has also become isolated within her relationship with Geoff.

(b)   **Geoff** also has needs. The hopes he had of a new job, new house and new family seem to be crumbling around him. His expectations have taken a dramatic turn for the worse, and men also need a time of adjustment following the birth of a child. He is certainly not getting any support from Jenny. For some couples the new baby may strengthen the relationship, while for others the addition to the family feels like an intrusion which gets in the way of their relationship and competes for the attention of the mother. Men can be left out of consideration in postnatal depression where so much attention becomes focused on the mother and child.

(c)   **Abby**, at age 14 months, could be considered to be the most vulnerable member of the family. While adult 'players' within the family dynamic do have a measure of control over their own actions, reactions and destiny, the same can not be said for entirely dependent children. At 14 months Abby is entirely reliant on others for her physical and emotional needs. In situations like this professional workers have a duty to assess whether these needs are being met by her family ... or whether additional support or intervention might be needed.

Abby's needs are manifestly not being met and she could well be considered to be 'in need' under the terms of the Children Act.

4.1   Where do rights come in?

The previous section considered some of the *needs* that each individual in this small family unit might be considered to have. Looking at each member of the family triangle in turn can help to illuminate these needs, but what about each person's *rights*? Does each have rights? And do the rights of some take precedence over others?

Jenny is suffering from apparently increasingly serious mental distress. Her life is in torment and she is not functioning well. At this stage of her problems Jenny is probably not in need of the protection of the Mental Health Act (1983). This is a major piece of legislation, currently being revised and updated, which is a formal attempt to define the requirements of people who are in need of mental health services but who may not understand the consequences of their actions. The Act also attempts to consider the needs of society in general, which may require protection from people whose mental distress has taken them 'beyond reason', and whose actions might be harmful to themselves or to others. More recently the government has officially recognised the need for regulating the services for people with mental distress and put in place in England a National Service Framework for Mental Health (Department of Health, 1999b). This contains a number of 'standards'.

Conflicting rights

Activity 9

Allow about 10 minutes

National Service Framework Standards for Mental Health

Read carefully the first three standards from the National Service Framework for Mental Health, set out in the box below.

Make notes on these standards in relation to the problems that Jenny is facing.

National Service Framework for Mental Health

Standard one

Health and social services should:

- promote mental health for all, working with individuals and communities

- combat discrimination against individuals and groups with mental health problems, and promote their social inclusion.

Standard two

Any service user who contacts their primary health care team with a common mental health problem should:

- have their mental health needs identified and assessed

- be offered effective treatments, including referral to specialist services for further assessment, treatment and care if they require it.

Standard three

Any individual with a common mental health problem should:

- be able to make contact round the clock with the local services necessary to meet their needs and receive adequate care

- be able to use NHS Direct, as it develops, for first-level advice and referral on to specialist helplines or to local services.

(Department of Health, 1999b)

Comment

Although the standards that are set out in the NSF are desirable, they are not always applicable to specific local situations. We simply do not know about the levels of service provision in all localities. Local services may be unable to deliver services that meet these standards, or indeed may not have the capacity to provide Jenny with the specific help that she requires. Tyrer (1999) discussed the NSF standards soon after they were published and concluded that they were probably utopian and certainly hard to measure or implement.

4.2 Conflicting rights?

Other pieces of legislation might also come into consideration in the situation with Jenny, Geoff and Abby which conflict with Jenny's rights as an individual user of mental health services. For example the Children Act 1989 has applied to families in England and Wales since 1991, and it came into force in Northern Ireland in 1996. The law in Scotland is slightly different but is covered by the Children (Scotland) Act 1995 (Scottish Office, 1995). However the basic principles remain the same in all UK countries (see Care Systems and Structures). In general the Act considers that the welfare of children is paramount. The belief remains that children are best looked after within their family, with both parents playing a full part. Legal proceedings should be avoided and parents are encouraged to seek agreement whenever this is possible and arrangements for access and childcare should be decided as quickly as possible. The law will step in when parents are in fundamental disagreement, or when there are doubts about the capability of one or both parents to make satisfactory arrangements.

> *Unless the court orders differently, both parents are expected to retain their parental responsibilities and rights and to be active players in deciding how their children grow and develop. This emphasises that both parents continue to have responsibilities for their children, even if they separate or divorce.*
>
> *(A brief guide to the Children (Scotland) Act 1995: Section 2, Family Law, www.scotland.gov.uk/library/documents4/sc-ch-04.htm – [accessed: 25.06.2002])*

Abby is in a highly vulnerable situation. She is entirely dependent on the care of others and very sensitive to the quantity and quality of communication from adults, especially her parents. You will remember from your study of Unit 1 the importance of early childhood experience. In the scenario which is unfolding in Abby's family these vital elements of development seem to be either inconsistent or absent, and her longer-term prospects may well be significantly affected. The detailed way in which parents relate to their children is of enormous importance to the way that the child develops. The early months following birth should be one of the most active and social periods of development, during which the 'sense of core self' is formed (Stern, 1985). When this is disrupted and the child is exposed to their parent's reduced or disturbed attention and in the absence of alternative sources of consistent care there may be implications beyond the period of that disturbance, and cognitive, emotional and social development can be affected (Emanuel, 1999; Edhborg, 2001). Even at a much later time Abby may still be vulnerable. Murray (1999) followed up children whose mothers had been depressed shortly after giving birth. Even at age five years, when the children were in school, it was found that they exhibited a high level of disturbed behaviour with their mothers, and the content and social patterning of play at school was also 'abnormal'.

In addition to the possible longer term damage that might be caused by a failure of parenting care at this age, it is possible that Abby is also at more immediate risk. Postnatal depression can be associated with an increased risk of physical abuse (Cadzow, 1999). Professional workers do have to make some sort of risk assessment regarding the levels of risk that Abby is currently facing. The Children (Scotland) Act 1995, and it's equivalent in other UK countries attempts to define the nature of 'need'.

Service and support for children

'The Children Act defines 'need' broadly. A child is in need of care and attention if:

- he or she is unlikely to achieve or maintain, or to have the opportunity of achieving or maintaining, a reasonable standard of health or development unless services are provided for him by a local authority

- his or her health or development is likely to be impaired, or further impaired, unless such services are so provided

- he or she is disabled, or affected adversely by the disability of a member of the family.'

A brief guide to the Children (Scotland) Act 1995: Section 2, Family Law, www.scotland.gov.uk/library/documents4/sc-ch-04.htm [accessed: 25.06.02].

If you work with children and families and have concerns that a child is being abused you can look at DoH guidelines for safeguarding children at www.doh.gov.uk/ safeguardingchildren/index.htm. Alternatively, contact your Social Services Department for advice.

Key points

- All the individual family members in a complex situation have their own needs and different levels of vulnerability.

- Only some of these needs will be covered by 'rights' enshrined in law, although under current UK law the needs of children are paramount.

- Legal solutions should only be used to settle complex family problems when other methods have proved unsuccessful.

- The quality of relationships in the early years of child development is important and should be reflected in the interventions provided.

4.3 Principles of good practice

Throughout this course you have been asked to consider five principles of good practice listed in Unit 5 (Block 1):

The K100 principles of good practice

- enable people to develop their own potential

- enable people to have a voice and be heard

- respect people's beliefs and preferences

- promote and support people's rights to appropriate services

- respect people's privacy and rights to confidentiality.

Activity 10   Applying the five principles

Allow about 20 minutes   How do you think that these five principles could have been put into practice by the professional workers who came into contact with Abby and Jenny?

Comment   The five principles of good practice are important guidelines for all professional workers who might come into contact with this family.

- **Enable people to develop their own potential**

  Each of the people in our scenario is having problems regarding the development of their own potential. Jenny's life seems virtually 'on hold' and the notion of 'developing her own potential' must feel a long way off for her. She has lost her focus in life, her job no longer provides her with structure, and her family life has deteriorated. Once the issue of abuse was cleared up the professional workers have tried, through their therapeutic efforts, to help Jenny to recover her sense of self-esteem. All the different models of care are aimed at making life better for Jenny. As soon her mood is improved and her feelings about herself become more positive she will be able to develop her own potential. Abby also seems to be at significant risk of not being able to start to develop her own potential which is significantly linked to the way that her parents behave towards her. As their situation improves Abby herself will be more likely to achieve her potential and develop the skills and qualities she needs.

- **Enable people to have a voice and be heard**

  It is difficult to imagine what it really might mean to 'give an infant a voice'; inevitably people will be speaking on her behalf. Were the situation to deteriorate further and court proceedings become necessary, then a 'guardian ad litem' might be appointed by the court on Abby's behalf. The guardian ad litem acts as an advocate for children and helps the court to make decisions that take into account the best outcome for those children. In some ways Gwen has acted as an informal advocate for this family, although she was not asked to take on this role. She intervened in a situation in which she felt that all members of the family, especially Abby, were vulnerable.

Jenny might initially find it difficult to summon up the energy to access the support groups that will help her to allow her voice to be heard. But such groups do exist (see later), and it is the duty of professional workers to make sure that women and other family members are aware of these self-help services.

- **Respect people's beliefs and preferences**

We just don't know from the story whether Jenny's particular beliefs and preferences have been elicited, or respected. Good professional practice, however, will always be aware that each individual has beliefs and preferences, as well as rights and responsibilities, and that these should always be taken into consideration. Perhaps Jenny should be consulted about which professional worker she felt would be most appropriate for her own needs, and indeed which types of therapy she felt would help her most. There is certainly a question about childrens' development of beliefs and preferences, and debate about whether a child of Abby's age could be said to have these.

- **Promote and support people's rights to appropriate services**

In this story recognition of the potential problems came late and when several services were involved the potential for confusion arose. The notion of 'appropriate services' assumes both competent and non-harming services. Jack, the CPN, has breached his own professional guidelines and sought to use his power as a health worker to exploit the vulnerability of one of his clients.

- **Respect people's privacy and rights to confidentiality**

In complex situations like the one that has engulfed Jenny and her family we have seen that many different agencies have become involved. As the story develops even more people and services might become involved. There is a fine balance that has to be drawn between people's right for privacy and confidentiality and the necessary sharing of important information between the people who really do need to know details about this family's problems. Questions remain regarding the exchange of information between agencies and professionals and how far this should go and whether Jenny should be forced to accept help if she does not want it.

Activity 10 considered Jenny and Abby's situation. Often the focus of concern is centred around women and their children, but what about Geoff? Geoff is vulnerable in his own way. Some fathers consider that their needs and rights are not taken into account sufficiently and have formed support group and self-help organisations to represent their views. Perhaps the best known current support organisation is called Families Need Fathers. This organisation acts as a link for isolated fathers and will help fathers get support locally. They also lobby nationally to attempt to make the voice of fathers heard when legislation is being developed.

Possible sources of help

We include these in case you wish to study these topics in more detail. You do not need to follow up these contacts for your study of the course.

Association for Postnatal Illness
145, Dawes Road, London SW6 7EB
Helpline 020 7386 0868
www.apni.org/ [accessed: 25.06.02].

Meet A Mum Association (MAMA)
Waterside Centre
25, Avenue Road
London SE25 4DX
Helpline 020 8768 0123
www.mama.org.uk [accessed: 25.06.02].

National Childbirth Trust
Helpline 020 8896 1625
www.nctpregnancyandbabycare.com [accessed: 25.06.02].

There is a national telephone helpline: Women and Mental Health
0845 3000911

Families Need Fathers
134, Curtain Road
London EC4 3AR
0207 613 5060
www.fnf.org.uk/ [accessed: 25.06.02].

4.4 What helps women with PND get better?

With professional help most women similar to those in Jenny's situation who become depressed following the birth of a child do manage to get better again (Drug and Therapeutics Bulletin, 2000), although there is usually considered to be an increased risk of further periods of low mood following the birth of any subsequent babies (Richards, 1990). Often evidence-based practice is cited as an important principle to guide professional workers responsible for providing treatment. This involves focusing on treatment that has been shown to be effective through research studies. For many traditionally trained psychiatrists drug therapy has become the mainstay for the treatment of depression, often with little recognition of the possible benefits of other types of intervention. However the evidence for the effectiveness of antidepressant medication in treating postnatal depression is surprisingly scanty. A recent review (Hoffbrand, 2001) discovered only one recognised research trial which has been conducted to evaluate the effectiveness of antidepressant drugs and compare their effectiveness with other forms of treatment for women with postnatal depression. This single trial (Appleby, 1997) demonstrated that one drug (fluoxetine/ Prozac) was as effective as a course of cognitive-behavioural counselling in the short term. Similarly there is little evidence for hormone based treatment (Lawrie, 2001). Drug therapies may create problems for breast-feeding and cause sedation and possibly other side effects. Women may also be reluctant to take medication (Appleby, 1999).

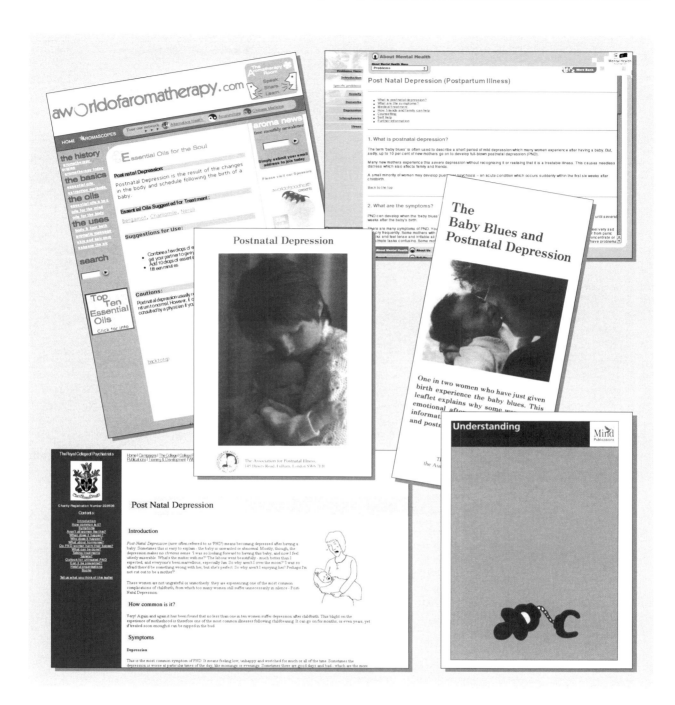

Help with postnatal depression

Other research using randomised controlled trials have shown that non-directive counselling and cognitive behavioural counselling are effective treatments, and that they can be 'delivered' by non-specialists in mental health, such as health visitors (Holden, 1996; Appleby, 1999). Other types of effective treatment, which all follow a broader social and holistic approach to treatment, are set out in the box below. Most recently the research of McArthur (2002) has shown that the way care services are delivered has a profound effect. Allocating resources to those families most in need really does work!

What works in the treatment of postnatal depression?

Partner support

Difficulties in the marital relationship have been shown to be good predictors for the development of PND, and partners who are generally unsupportive in childrearing are a source of considerable stress for the mother. Research has shown that women experience a more rapid recovery from the symptoms of PND when the partner is supportive (Ray, 1998; Misri, 2000).

Psychological and psychosocial intervention

Various psychological interventions have been shown to be effective in the treatment of PND. This includes group cognitive-behavioural programmes (Milgrom, 1999), interpersonal psychotherapy (O'Hara, 2000) and interpersonal psychotherapy in group settings (Klier, 2001).

Various simple counselling interventions delivered by health visitors have also been shown to be effective (Elliott, 1989; Holden, 1996).

Infant massage and other alternative therapies

A recent study has suggested that mothers learning the practice of infant massage is an effective treatment for facilitating mother-infant interaction for mothers with postnatal depression (Onozawa, 2001). Other 'alternative and complementary' therapies have been shown to be effective in treating depression, although there are not many trials specifically focusing on PND. For example, St. John's Wort (hypericum) is a well tolerated herbal medicine which has been shown to be as effective as antidepressants in the treatment of mild to moderate depression (Woelk, 2000).

Support group intervention

Chen (2000) provides evidence that participation in support groups for postnatally distressed women provides quantifiable psychosocial benefits. Interestingly the approach to support groups has now extended to electronic support via the internet (Jean, 2001).

Support from an understanding partner is one of the most effective ways that help women recover from PND

Key points

- The principles of good practice apply to mental health work as well as to all other aspects of care work.

- Research has demonstrated that a number of non-drug based treatments are effective in helping women to get better.

Conclusion

As the story has unfolded Jenny, Geoff and Abby have become increasingly involved in problematic situations, not always of their own making. One of the main principles of any service is that it should at least do no harm. We hope for this family that local services eventually pull themselves together to provide satisfactory help for Jenny, Abby and Geoff. In addition, after such a difficult time for the services themselves, a review of the 'critical incidents' should be undertaken to determine how better care could have been provided for this family. Ideally this review and reflection should involve all the agencies that have been involved and include examination of the behaviour of individual professionals and of the agencies as a whole.

Finally you might like to consider if your study of this unit has helped you to answer the unit's core questions:

What powers do carers exercise in a context such as a mother experiencing mental distress following the birth of a baby, and what vulnerabilities might these give rise to?

Jenny and Abby were both vulnerable to the way that representatives of different care services interpreted their roles. Initially both were vulnerable to a lack of recognition of their needs, while at a later stage over-involvement became a serious problem. In particular Jenny's vulnerability as a new mother seems to have resulted from a combination of factors including the nature of modern family life; being shut off from many networks; isolation from family and previous friends because of the recent move; and the possible effects of losing her role and status at her place of work.

In their intensely vulnerable state both Jenny and Abby had become susceptible to the exertion of power by others. This occurred within the family (for example when Gwen intervened without consulting them), and when professional workers used and abused their considerable power (for example when Jack pursued his own ends within the relationship).

Does 'postnatal depression' exist as a distinct disease, or is it a convenient label that describes one variant of normality?

The unit has explored in quite a lot of detail the feelings of mental distress that some women experience following the birth of a baby. Some women definitely do experience this, but there is doubt whether this represents a distinct 'disease'. Some commentators suggest that this form of mental distress is the same as that which can occur at any time, but it is the vulnerability of the family after the birth of a baby that gives it particular significance for services. Throughout the unit we have used the expression 'postnatal depression' to help us think about these feelings and to understand some of the research into the causes and the treatment that is available for women at what can be a difficult and emotional time.

All citizens have rights, but what happens when one person's rights (for example those of a small child) conflict with those of another person's (for example their mother)?

Throughout the case study there have been issues that highlight the conflict between Abby's rights as a small child, with those of her mother, Jenny. Often attempting to achieve a balance between these potentially conflicting rights is the most complex part of any service's task. Jenny, as a user of mental health services, has access to the mechanisms that have been developed to protect the rights of this vulnerable section of society. Similarly Abby, as a small child, is protected by those people who are designated by society to serve and protect the rights of children.

Can professional services be considered to have the ability to make situations worse for their clients as well as better?

This case study has been designed to show that services do, indeed, have to be constantly aware of the effect that they are having on their clients. Clients remain highly vulnerable to the timing and quality of interventions and of course failure to intervene can also have serious consequences. The various professions that have impinged on the family in our case study have each come with their own world-view, values and practices. The ensuing problems developed throughout our story as a direct result of these competing models and the lack of co-ordination and co-operation between the services. When care goes wrong and professional services make serious mistakes, either of action or inaction, the consequences for vulnerable people such as Jenny, Abby and Geoff can be profound.

References

Abou-Saleh, M., Ghubash, R., Karim, L., Krymski, M. and Bhai, I. (1998) Hormonal aspects of postpartum depression, *Psychoneuroendocrinology*, Vol. 23, No. 5, pp. 465–75.

Affonso, D., Anindya, K., Horowitz, J. and Mayberry, L. (2000) An international study exploring levels of postpartum depressive symptomatology, *Journal of Psychosomatic Research*, Vol. 49, No. 3, pp. 207–16.

Alford, C. (1999) 'Whistleblowers: how much we can learn from them depends on how much we can give up', *American Behavioural Scientist*, Vol. 43, No. 2, pp. 264–77.

American Psychiatric Association (1994) *Diagnostic and Statistical Manual of Mental Disorders – fourth edition (DSM-IV)*, American Psychiatric Association, Washington.

Appleby, L., Warner, R., Whitton, A. and Faragher, B. (1997) 'A controlled study of fluoxetine and cognitive behavioural counselling in the treatment of postnatal depression', *British Medical Journal*, Vol. 314, pp. 932–6.

Appleby, L., Koren, G. and Sharp, D. (1999) 'Depression in pregnant and postnatal women: an evidence-based approach to treatment in primary care', *British Journal of General Practice*, Vol. XX, pp. 780–2.

Ballard, C. and Davies, R. (1996) 'Postnatal depression in fathers', *International Review of Psychiatry*, Vol. 8, pp. 65–71.

Beck, C. (2001) 'Predictors of postpartum depression: an update', *Nursing Research*, Vol. 509, No. 5, pp. 275–85.

Blunden, F. and Nash, J. (2001) 'Prevention of client abuse in counselling relationships', www.popan.org.uk/articles/004.htm [accessed 25.06.02].

Borys, D. and Pope, K. (1989) 'Dual relationships between therapists and clients: a national study of psychologists, psychiatrists and social workers', *Professional Psychology: Research and Practice*, Vol. 20, No. 5, pp. 283–93.

Briscoe, M. (1986) 'Identification of emotional problems in postpartum women by health visitors', *British Medical Journal*, Vol. 292, pp. 1245–7.

Brown, G. (1996) 'Life events, loss and depressive disorders', in Heller, T., Reynolds, J., Gomm, R., Muston, R. and Patisson, S. (eds) *Mental Health Matters*, Macmillan, London.

Cadzow, S., Armstrong, K. and Fraser, J. (1999) 'Stressed parents with infants: reassessing physical abuse risk factors', *Child Abuse and Neglect*, Vol. 23, No. 9. pp. 845–53.

Chen, C., Tseng, Y-F., Chou, F-H. and Wang, S-Y. (2000) 'Effects of support group intervention in postnatally distressed women', *Journal of Psychosomatic Research*, Vol. 49, pp. 395–9.

Cooper, P. and Murray, L. (1998) 'Postnatal depression', *British Medical Journal*, Vol. 316, pp. 1884–6.

Cox, J., Holden, J., Elliott, S., McKenzie, P., McKenzie, J. and Cox, J. (1987) 'Development of the 10-item Edinburgh Postnatal Depression Scale', *British Journal of Psychiatry*, Vol. 150, pp. 782–6.

Cox, J., Murray, D. and Chapman G. (1993) 'A controlled study of the onset, duration and prevalence of postnatal depression', *British Journal of Psychiatry*, Vol. 163, pp. 27–31.

Cox, J. (1996) 'Perinatal mental disorder – a cultural approach', *International Review of Psychiatry*, Vol. 8, pp. 9–16.

Cox, J. (1999) 'Perinatal mood disorders in a changing culture: a transcultural European and African perspective', *International Review of Psychiatry*, Vol. 11 (2–3), pp. 103–10.

Currie, V. (2002) 'Statistics from the Abuse in Therapy Support Network in the UK', www.advocateweb.org/hope/aitstats.asp [accessed 25.06.02].

Department of Health (DoH) (1999a) *Working together to safeguard children: a guide to inter-agency working to safeguard and promote the welfare of children*, Department of Health, Home Office and Department of Education and Employment, Stationery Office, London. www.the-stationery-office.co.uk/doh/worktog/worktog.htm [accessed 25.06.02].

Department of Health (DoH), Patient Advice and Liason Services (PALS), www.doh.gov.uk/patientadviceandliaisonservices/index.htm [accessed 10.9.02].

Department of Health (DoH) (1999b) *National Service Framework for Mental Health: Modern standards and service models*, TSO, London.

Department of Health (DoH) (2001a) *Choosing Talking Therapies?* www.doh.gov.uk/mentalhealth [accessed 25.06.02].

Department of Health (DoH) (2001b) *Reforming the NHS Complaints Procedure: A listening document,* www.doh.gov.uk/nhscomplaintsreform/listening.htm [accessed 25.06.02].

Department of Health (DoH) (2001c) *Involving Patients and the Public in Healthcare: A discussion document*, www.doh.gov.uk/involvingpatients [accessed 25.06.02].

Department of Health and Welsh Office (1983) Mental Health Act, London. www.doh.gov.uk/mhact1983.htm [accessed 25.7.02].

Drug and Therapeutics Bulletin (2000) 'The management of postnatal depression', *DTB*, Vol. 38, pp. 33–6.

Eastwood, P. (1995) 'Promoting peer group support with postnatally depressed women', *Health Visitor*, Vol. 68. No. 4, pp. 148–50.

Edhborg, M., Lundh, W., Seimyr, L. and Widstrom, A-M. (2001) 'The long-term impact of postnatal depressed mood on mother-child interaction', *Journal of Reproductive and Infant Psychology*, Vol. 19, No. 1, pp. 61–71.

Elliott, S. (1989) 'Psychological strategies in the prevention and treatment of postnatal depression', *Balliere's Clinical Obstetrics and Gynaecology*, Vol. 3, pp. 879–903.

Emanuel, L. (1999) 'The effects of post-natal depression on the child', *Psycho-analytic psychotherapy in South Africa*, Vol. 7, No. 1, pp. 50–67.

Evans, J., Heron, J., Francomb, H., Oke, S. and Golding, J. (2001) 'Cohort study of depressed mood during pregnancy and after childbirth', *British Medical Journal*, Vol. 323, pp. 257–60.

Harris, B. (1996) 'Hormonal aspects of postnatal depression', *International Review of Psychiatry*, Vol. 8, pp. 27–36.

Harris, T. (2001) 'Recent developments in understanding the psychosocial aspects of depression', *British Medical Bulletin*, Vol. 57, pp. 17–32.

Health Education Board for Scotland (2002) *Talking about Postnatal Depression*, www.hebs.com [accessed 25.06.02].

Hearn, G., Iliff, A. and Jones, I. (1998) Postnatal depression in the community, *British Journal of General Practice*, Vol. 48, pp. 1064–6.

Hetherington, A. (2000) A psychodynamic profile of therapists who sexually exploit their clients, *British Journal of Psychotherapy*, Vol. 16, No. 3, pp. 274–86.

Hermansson, G. (1997) 'Boundaries and boundary management in counselling: the never ending story', *British Journal of Guidance and Counselling*, Vol. 25, No. 2, pp. 133–46.

Hoffbrand, S., Howard, L. and Crawley, H. (2001) 'Antidepressant treatment for postnatal depression' (Cochrane Review), in *The Cochrane Library*, 4, Update Software, Oxford.

Holden, J. (1996) 'The role of health visitors in postnatal depression', *International Review of Psychiatry*, Vol. 8, No. 1, pp. 79–86.

Home Office (2000) *Setting the boundaries*, TSO, London.

Huang, Y-C., Mathers, N. (2001) 'Postnatal depression – biological or cultural?: a comparative study of postnatal women in the UK and Taiwan', *Journal of Advanced Nursing*, Vol. 33, No. 3, pp. 279–87.

Jean, F., Lewis, G., MacLeod, C. and Taylor, S. (2001) 'A postpartum depression electronic support group', www.ume.maine.edu/~ithcra/Sproj6/ [accessed 25.06.02].

Jehu, D. (1994) *Patients as Victims: Sexual abuse in psychotherapy and counselling*, Wiley and Sons, New York.

Jones, A., Watts, T. and Romain, S. (1995) *Health Visitor*, Vol. 68, No. 4, p. 153.

Klier, C., Muzic, M., Rosenblum, K. and Lenz, G. (2001) 'Interpersonal psychotherapy adapted for the group setting in the treatment of postpartum depression', *Journal of Psychotherapy Practice Research*, Vol. 10, pp. 124–31.

Kumar, R. (1994) 'Postnatal mental illness: a transcultural perspective', *Social Psychiatry and Psychiatric Epidemiology*, Vol. 29, No. 6, pp. 250–64.

Lane, A., Keville, R., Morris, M., Kinsella, A., Turner, M. and Barry, S. (1997) 'Postnatal depression and elation among mothers and their partners: prevalence and predictors', *British Journal of Psychiatry*, Vol. 171, pp. 550–5.

Lawrie, T., Herxheimer, A. and Dalton, K. (2001) 'Oestrogens and progestogens for preventing and treating postnatal depression' (Cochrane Review), in *The Cochrane Library*, Vol. 4, Update Software, Oxford.

Leverton, T. and Elliott, S. (2000) 'Is the EPDS a magic wand?' *Journal of Reproductive and Infant Psychology*, Vol. 18, No. 4, pp. 279–96.

Mandy, A., Gard, P., Ross, K. and Valentine, B. (1998) 'Psychological sequelae in women following either parturition or non-gynaecological surgery', *Journal of Reproductive and Infant Psychology*, Vol. 16, pp. 133–41.

Martinez, R., Johnston-Robledo, I., Ulsh, H. and Chrisler, J. (2000) 'Singing 'the baby blues': a content analysis of popular press articles about postpartum affective disturbances', *Women and Health*, Vol. 3 (2/3), pp. 37–56.

Matthey, S., Barnett, B., Ungerer, J. and Waters, B. (2000) 'Paternal and maternal depressed mood during the transition to parenthood', *Journal of Affective Disorders*, Vol. 60, pp. 75–85.

Mauthner, N. (1995) 'Postnatal depression: the significance of social contacts between mothers', *Women's Studies International Forum*, Vol. 18, No. 3, pp. 311–23.

Mauthner, N. (1998) '"It's a woman's cry for help": a relational perspective on postnatal depression', *Feminism and Psychology*, Vol. 8, No. 3, pp. 325–55.

McArthur, C., Winter, H., Bick, D., Knowles, H., Lilford, R., Henderson, C., Lancashire, R., Braunholtz, D. and Gee, H. (2002) 'Effects of redesigned community postnatal care on women's health 4 months after birth: a cluster randomised controlled trial', *Lancet*, Vol. 359, pp. 378–85.

McIntosh, J. (1993) 'Postpartum depression: women's help-seeking behaviour and perception of cause', *Journal of Advanced Nursing*, Vol. 18, pp. 178–84.

Milgrom, J., Martin, P. and Negri, L. (1999) *Treating postnatal depression: a psychological approach for health care practitioners*, John Wiley, Chichester.

Minde, K., Tidmarsh, L. and Hughes, S. (2001) 'Nurses' and physicians' assessment of mother-infant mental health at the first postnatal visits', *Journal of the American Academy of Child and Adolescent Psychiatry*, Vol. 40, No. 7, pp. 803–10.

Misri, S., Kostaras, X., Fox, D. and Kostaras, D. (2000) 'The impact of partner support in the treatment of postpartum depression', *Canadian Journal of Psychiatry*, Vol. 45, pp. 554–8.

Murray, L. and Carothers, A. (1990) 'The validation of the Edinburgh postnatal depression scale on a community sample', *British Journal of Psychiatry*, Vol. 157, pp. 288–90.

Murray, L., Sinclair, D., Cooper, P., Ducournau, P., Turner, P., and Stein, A. (1999) 'The socioemotional development of 5-year-old children of postnatally depressed mothers', *Journal of Child Psychology and Psychiatry*, Vol. 40, No. 8, pp. 1259–71.

Najman, J., Anderson, M., Bor, W., O'Callaghan, M. and Williams, G. (2000) 'Postnatal depression – myth and reality: maternal depression before and after the birth of a child', *Social Psychiatry and Psychiatric Epidemiology*, Vol. 35, pp. 19–27.

NHS Confederation (2002) *Involving Patients and the Public in Healthcare*, Briefing No. 53, NHS Confederation, London.

NHSE (1999) *The Public Interest Disclosure Act 1998: Whistleblowing in the NHS*, Health Service Circular, HSC 1999/198 tap.ccta.gov.uk/dohcoin4.nsf/page/HSC-1999-198?OpenDocument [accessed 25.06.02].

Nursing and Midwifery Council (2000) *Modernising Regulation - The New Nursing and Midwifery Council; A consultation document*, NHS Executive, London, www.doh.gov.uk/nmcconsult/ [accessed 25.06.02].

O'Hara, M. and Swain, A. (1996) 'Rates and risk of post-partum depression – a meta-analysis', *International Review of Psychiatry*, Vol. 8, pp. 37–54.

O'Hara, M., Stuart, S., Gorman, L. and Wenzel, A. (2000) 'Efficacy of interpersonal psychotherapy for postpartum depression', *Archives of General Psychiatry*, Vol. 57, pp. 1039–45.

Onozawa, K., Glover, V., Adams, D., Modi, N. and Kumar, C. (2001) 'Infant massage improves mother-infant interaction for mothers with postnatal depression', *Journal of Affective Disorders*, Vol. 63, pp. 201–7.

Pajer, K. (1995) 'New strategies in the treatment of depression in women', *Journal of Clinical Psychiatry*, Vol. 56, pp. 30–7.

Philo, G., Secker, J., Platt, S., Henderson, L., McLaughlin, G. and Burnside, J. (1994) 'The impact of the mass media on public images of mental illness: media content and audience belief', *Health Education Journal*, Vol. 53, pp. 271–81.

Pilgrim, D. (1995) 'Explaining abuse and inadequate care', in Hunt, G. (ed.) *Whistleblowing in the Health Service: Accountability, Law and professional practice*, Edward Arnold, London.

Pope, K. and Bouhoutsos, J. (1986) *Sexual intimacy between therapists and patients*, Westport, Praeger.

Pope, K. (2001) 'Sex between therapists and clients', in Worell, J. (ed.) *Encyclopaedia of Women and Gender: Sex similarities and differences and the impact of society on Gender*, Academic Press, New York, www.kspope.com/sexencyc.html [accessed 25.6.02].

Ray, K. and Hodnett, E. (1998) *Caregiver Support for Postpartum Depression*, Cochrane Library, Oxford Update Software, Oxford.

Richards, J. (1990) 'Postnatal depression: a review of recent literature', *British Journal of General Practice*, Vol. 40. pp. 472–6.

Ritter, C., Hobfoil, S., Lavin, J., Cameron, R. and Hulsizer, M. (2000) 'Stress, psychological resources, and depressive symptomatology during pregnancy in low-income, inner-city women', *Health Psychology*, Vol. 19, No. 6, pp. 576–585.

Rutter, P. (1989) *Sex in the Forbidden Zone: When men in power – therapists, doctors, clergy, teachers and others – betray women's trust*, Fawcett Crest, New York.

Scottish Office (1995) The Children Act (Scotland) 1995, The Scottish Office, Edinburgh. www.scotland.gov.uk/library/documents4/sc-ch-00.htm [accessed 25.06.02].

Seeley, S., Murray, L. and Cooper, P. (1996) 'The outcomes for mothers and babies of health visitor intervention', *Health Visitor*, Vol. 69, pp. 135–8.

Seeley, S. (2001) 'Strengths and limitations of the Edinburgh Postnatal Depression Scale', in *Postnatal Depression and Maternal Mental Health: A public health priority*, CPHVA, London.

Seguin, L., Potvin, L., St. Denis, M. (1999) 'Depressive symptoms in the late postpartum among low socio-economic status women', *Birth*, Vol. 26, No. 3, pp. 157–63.

Small, R., Brown, S., Lumley, J. and Astbury, J. (1994) 'Missing voices: what women say and do about depression after childbirth', *Journal of Reproductive and Infant Psychology*, Vol. 12, pp. 89–103.

Soeken, K. and Soeken, D. (1987) *A Survey of Whistleblowers: Their stressors and coping strategies*, Laurel, Maryland: Association of Mental Health Specialities.

Stern, D. (1985) *The Interpersonal World of the Infant: A view from psychoanalysis and developmental psychology*, Basic Books, New York.

Tyrer, P. (1999) 'The national service framework: a scaffold for mental health: implementation is key to determining whether it's a support or a gallows', *British Medical Journal*, Vol. 319, pp. 1017–8.

Wieck, A. (1996) 'Ovarian hormones, mood and neurotransmitters', *International Review of Psychiatry*, Vol. 8, pp. 17–25.

Woelk, H. (2000) 'Comparison of St. John's wort and imipramine for treating depression: randomised controlled trial', *British Medical Journal*, Vol. 321, pp. 536–9.

Yamey, G. (2000) 'Protecting whistle blowers', *British Medical Journal*, Vol. 320, pp. 70–1.

Acknowledgements

Grateful acknowledgement is made to the following sources for permission to reproduce material within this unit.

Text

p.138 Cox, J. L. *et al.* 'Edinburgh Postnatal Depression Scale (EPDS)', British Journal of Psychiatry, June 1987, Vol. 150. Royal College of Psychiatrists, Gaskell Publications Department; *p.141*: 'Tragic toll of mothers who can't go on', January 17, 2002. The Mirror Newspaper. Mirror Sydication International; *p.145*: Reprinted with permission from the Diagnostic and Statistical Manual of Mental Disorders, Fourth Edition, Text Revision. Copyright 2000 American Psychiatric Association.

Illustrations

p.126: Courtesy of Emily Pennifold; *p.127*: Chris Rout/Bubbles Photo Library; *p.131*: Mary Evans Picture Library; *p.142, 148, 163*: Maggie Guillon; *p.146*: Steve Benbow/Impact Photos; *p.154*: David Buffington/ PhotoDisc/Getty Images; *p.169, top left*: A World of Aromatherpy website; *p.169, top right*: Mental Health Foundation - Post Natal Depression (Postpartum Illness) website; *p.169, middle left*: Post Natal Depression Leaflet. Mind, Association for Postnatal Illness; *p.169, middle right*:The Baby Blues and Postnatal Depression Leaflet - Front cover only. Mind, Association for Postnatal Illness; *p.169, bottom left*: Post Natal Depression. Royal College of Psychiatrists, Gaskell Publications Department; *p.169, bottom right*: Clouette, P. Understanding Postnatal Depression Leaflet - Front cover only. Mind, Association for Postnatal Illness; p.171: Powerstock.

Every effort has been made to contact copyright holders. If any have been inadvertently overlooked the publishers will be pleased to make the necessary arrangements at the first opportunity.

Unit 21
Managing Boundaries and Risk

Prepared for the course team by Hilary Brown

Updated by Jo Warner

With thanks to Jan Walmsley for editorial comments and to Anthea Sperlinger for input on 'difficult behaviour'

While you are working on Unit 21, you will need:

- Course Reader
- *The Good Study Guide*
- Getting a Vocational Qualification
- Audio Cassette 5, side 1, part 1; and Audio Cassette 6, side 1
- Media Notes
- Skills video

Contents

Introduction

This is the last of the K100 'skills units'. In this unit we will be continuing to develop your practice skills by helping you to:

- put difficult areas of caring work into words in a way which allows them to be more openly acknowledged and addressed

- reflect on your role and the extent (and limits) of your responsibilities

- acknowledge how generic skills, such as assessment and planning, can help in situations where people have been, or are at risk of being, abused.

In the context of the issues dealt with in this block, we shall be reviewing two key areas:

- how to manage boundaries

- how to manage risk in situations where children or vulnerable adults might have been abused.

Throughout the course you have been considering some of the principles which should underpin good practice in social care. Previous skills units have helped you to get to grips with practice through observation and rehearsing specific study skills such as working with numbers or writing reports. In this unit we will be bringing together a number of the skills and insights you have been developing to see how you can apply your knowledge in the difficult and sometimes ambiguous situations which we have been exploring in Block 5.

Unit 21 focuses on:

- managing boundaries

- managing risk in situations where abuse is suspected

- reading graphs

- gearing up to revision

- developing writing skills.

You have seen that although everyone hopes that abuse doesn't 'happen here' in their service, neighbourhood or family, it is wise to be alert to the fact that it *can* happen anywhere. Prevention often hinges on having structures in place which guarantee openness and advocacy for more vulnerable people while also safeguarding their privacy and right to confidentiality: a difficult balance to achieve. It is often as important to think about *how* a decision should be made as *what* it should be and to have a clear view of what one is hoping to achieve for the person(s) concerned.

Block 5 has focused on dilemmas about what is private in public settings and what is of public concern in private settings. We have shown throughout the course that care relationships do not just happen 'naturally', they are shaped by economic and social factors which combine to create a situation in which women tend to take on informal care roles and gravitate into low paid care jobs. You have learnt how gender, race and poverty interact with the more formal aspects of hierarchy and that less powerful staff in residential settings often feel almost as powerless as service users. You have also seen how, in community settings, people like Bernice are often in a double bind: if they take action they risk being perceived as interfering, whereas if they stand by while someone comes to harm they may be held responsible. (Ruth, who you will meet on the skills video, also finds herself in this difficult situation.)

In exploring some of these dilemmas, Block 5 has covered a wide range of different types of 'underpinning' knowledge:

- knowledge about behaviour, how it is learnt, what purpose it serves and how to assess it (as we learnt in relation to Rosalie)

- knowledge about institutions and dynamics in residential care

- knowledge gained from debates on values, and the place of scientific evidence in such arguments

- knowledge about ideologies (systems of belief like the ones revealed in the songs you listened to on the tape), which mask unequal power and social or material inequalities behind assumptions about what is normal or natural

- knowledge gained from first hand accounts, by listening to survivors who have come through difficult situations or people who have tried to bring concerns about wrongdoing into the open

- knowledge about different kinds of research and how it links into public and professional awareness

- knowledge about service planning, service development and organisations.

Balancing acts

Because abuse is so complex this unit does not focus on any one area of values in isolation but looks at how they must all be held in balance. Abuse is not a *separate* area of work, neatly cordoned off from other aspects of day-to-day practice. Nor is it work which demands a completely different approach. It is a set of situations in which these approaches are put to the test. Abusive situations and relationships often challenge what we assume to be good practice and make it necessary to balance one principle against another: for example, the need to respect confidentiality has to be set against the need to share information in order to protect someone from harm.

The five principles of good practice which we have emphasised throughout the course are to:

- enable people to develop their own potential

- enable people to have a voice and be heard

- respect people's beliefs and preferences

- promote and support people's rights to appropriate services

- respect people's privacy and rights to confidentiality.

Each has a particular relevance to situations in which abuse is suspected. They will help to define situations where people are not being respected. They will also act as a guide in seeking appropriate support and redress for people who have been harmed.

You will, however, find that conflicts arise, such as between principles of:

- confidentiality and openness

- independence and protection

- control and freedom, and

- autonomy and intervention.

And don't think that if you don't get involved then the vulnerable child or adult will be automatically empowered. It isn't a case of minimum intervention equals maximum autonomy. It might be the opposite in cases where someone's autonomy is being undermined by a more powerful other. It might be that your intervention is the only thing which can guarantee the person's safety and autonomy.

Respect for individuals and the choices they have made is central – but so is acknowledgement of intimidation or coercion, which may make it look from the outside as if someone is colluding with an abuser or 'choosing to be abused' when actually they have few options. We saw that where individuals lack capacity to consent, their apparent agreement to sexual acts or financial transactions should not be accepted without scrutiny, and also that where people are economically or socially marginalised, their options may be limited.

You will also inevitably be faced with conflicts of interest, between victim and perpetrator, parent and child, staff and clients, and sometimes between fellow service users whose needs may not always be compatible.

You'll see some of these conflicts on the video, which introduces a character that you might recognise if you are keen on TV 'soaps'. Ruth from 'EastEnders' works in an after-school club. Her concerns about the possibility of abuse involving one of the boys who attends the club lead her into a series of dilemmas. These have a lot in common with those faced by Marie, Bernice and Adrian.

Unit 21 video content

Video Scene 10 'Managing risk: EastEnders' consists of 10 extracts from the BBC soap 'EastEnders'. It covers:

- being alert to signs of possible abuse and recording any concerns
- deciding what is abuse and what is proper discipline
- assessing difficult behaviour and its causes
- knowing who to get support from and when
- passing on concerns through officially recognised channels.

The sequences are as follows:

10(a)	Ruth notices bruises on Adam's arm
10(b)	Ruth talks to Mark about what is normal
10(c)	Adam misbehaves again (view twice, the second time as an exercise in observation)
10(d)	Ruth confronts Adam again
10(e)	Ruth talks to Adam's mother
10(f)	Ruth wonders what to do
10(g)	Ruth talks to Tom, her senior worker
10(h)	Ruth decides to talk to a social worker
10(i)	Ruth questions Adam: does she go too far?
10(j)	The story ends.

Working within the VQ framework

If you are interested in taking a Vocational Qualification (VQ) in Care at level 3 or 4 you will find that much of the work you do in this unit will be useful. First you will find that many of the generic skills you have learnt, such as assessing and planning for individuals or making accurate case notes, are going to be useful in relation to people who are facing abuse in their lives. But conversely you will also find that the specific focus of this block on potentially abusive situations can help you to sharpen your practice skills in more routine situations.

Competences such as:

- assessing and managing aggressive or abusive behaviours
- supporting clients in difficult relationships
- minimising the level of abuse in care environments
- contributing to the protection of individuals
- service planning to meet identified needs

are all covered in this unit. If you are employed in a care setting you will be in a good position to present clear examples for your portfolio.

There are currently three N/SVQ Units which are closely linked to this block. Firstly, at N/SVQ level 2 and 3 there is Unit Z1: 'Contribute to the protection of individuals from abuse'; secondly, in *Promoting Independence at level 3'* there is Unit Z18: Support individuals where abuse has been disclosed. Thirdly, from *Care Level 4* there is SC17: 'Evaluate risk of abuse, failure to protect and harm to self and others (TOPSS, 1999).

Demonstrating competence in this area of work relies on you sharing responsibility appropriately and not working in isolation or making decisions behind closed doors. Each competence will rely on:

- accurate recording
- prompt reporting of concerns
- careful and accurate collation of evidence, and
- formal, as opposed to informal, consultation and decision making.

 For further information on mapping to VQs see Getting a Vocational Qualification which accompanies the course.

Key points

- The focus of this unit is on managing boundaries and making difficult decisions.
- Practice skills centre on record keeping and consultation in the context of risk.
- All the practice values are important even when these lead to conflicts or dilemmas.

Section 1
Managing boundaries

1.1 Being 'professional'

 In Unit 18 you heard from Vicky Golding about Enfield's work in developing guidelines on professional boundaries. You might want to listen to this part of Audio Cassette 5 again (side 1, part 1) to remind yourself about the areas which were covered in these guidelines and some of the controversies arising from this approach. One problem identified was how much personal information a worker should disclose to a client. Vicky Golding talked about the impact of something as common as having a picture of your family on your desk and the inequalities which might be involved in, for example, allowing someone to reveal their marital status but not the fact that they are gay or lesbian. Because boundaries are crossed in care work there is a need for them to be spelt out and sometimes to be restated in the daily interactions between service workers and users, carers and cared for. Activity 1 gives you the opportunity to consider some of these dilemmas in setting boundaries.

Activity 1   **Acceptable boundaries**

Allow about 10 minutes   Read the following extract and then answer the questions below.

Gerald, a man with moderate learning disabilities, had recently moved from a hospital setting to a group home. After a few months, staff asked for help in managing Gerald's 'aggressive outbursts'. On one occasion he had broken the windscreen wipers on a visitor's car, on another he had smashed the same car's headlights. He had also pulled his key worker's hair and threatened to punch her when she remonstrated with him for giving her a bone crushing hug.

On investigation it transpired that Gerald, coming from a male hospital ward with male staff, was convinced that his female key worker's enthusiastic involvement in his progress and well-being was a sign of sexual interest. This misapprehension had been fostered unthinkingly by other members of staff, who at first jokingly agreed with Gerald when he referred to his key worker as his 'girlfriend', then actively promoted this by teasing remarks such as 'poor Gerald, your girlfriend's not here today'.

Gerald's key worker was inexperienced. She had not challenged Gerald's early references to her as 'my girlfriend'. As she said, 'I didn't think there was any harm in it, and he looked so pleased to see me I didn't want to spoil the relationship I was building with him'. Similarly, although she later commented that Gerald's physical approaches increasingly made her feel uncomfortable, she had not objected at first because she knew how emotionally impoverished his life in the hospital had been. The damaged car belonged to the key worker's boyfriend, understandably seen by Gerald as a rival for her affection.

Gerald, with few models to draw upon, was for a time confirmed in his beliefs by the explicit validation and repetition of his verbal claims, and by the acceptance of physical touch. Staff chose to amuse themselves with what they saw as 'only harmless teasing'; Gerald's key worker allowed her boundaries of personal space to be invaded on the mistaken assumption that she was somehow compensating for past deprivation, and that this and the joking remarks were justifiable because they increased the rapport she needed to establish herself as a good key worker.

While members of staff and the key worker were all clear in their own minds where the boundaries lay – that Gerald was not, and would never be, her boyfriend – Gerald had no means of knowing this. The seemingly abrupt volte-face by his key worker and the disapproval of other staff when their limits of tolerance were reached confused and upset Gerald. It required careful reappraisal on everyone's part to arrive at acceptable boundaries of language and touch. Gerald paid an unacceptably high price in terms of his mental health, his self-esteem and self-confidence.

(Craft and Brown, 1994, pp. 4–5)

This extract mentions 'acceptable boundaries of language and touch':

(a)   How could Gerald have been introduced to these boundaries more successfully?

(b)   Are 'acceptable boundaries' different in another setting you are familiar with? If so, what are the differences?

Comment   (a)   We know that Gerald had moved from an all male environment, so we might have anticipated that he would have a lot of learning to do about how to relate to women (particularly young women). The service might have started off being more formal with him to help him establish boundaries – then relaxed when everyone felt comfortable that he could manage them (rather than start off too informal and then have to back off). What did you think?

           (b)   You came across another setting back in Unit 3, involving Lynne and a relationship with a male home carer (one we made up). There the boundaries were different because Lynne lived in a family home, held down a job and had a boyfriend. It is always important to consider what the norms around touching and use of language are – for example when you are working in someone's own home, or in a situation where you have to give intimate care – and for different groups of people – for example, older people, or people from different ethnic backgrounds. In Unit 20 you saw an example of professional boundaries being broken by Jack in the way he behaved towards Jenny.

Well thought out guidance helps workers to draw an appropriate line for themselves. It also assists managers by giving a reference point to use in supervising staff. (Remember the Enfield guidelines, which Vicky Golding says provide a useful tool for management, as well as for staff and users.) As in Gerald's case, it is not only language which can confuse boundaries. For example, services for people with learning difficulties have sometimes encouraged staff to bring their partners or children into work, with the idea that these contacts will help the service users learn to integrate themselves into community networks. This means that staff are being asked to use their personal contacts and lives as a way of creating 'normal relationships', while at the same time maintaining proper professional boundaries.

Activity 2   **Helping staff to get the balance right**

Allow about 10 minutes   We have seen at several points in the block that written guidance can be a helpful way of containing the contradictions built into staff roles. Write about half a page of 'rules', either for Gerald's service, or for a service setting you know, to address:

- teasing
- hugging
- staff bringing their partners into the conversation
- staff involving their partners in the service's activities or holidays.

Comment   Did your rules treat the kind of teasing which went on with Gerald as a sign of warmth or of insensitivity? Did you make allowance for staff to hug service users? Would you have let Gerald know that his key worker had a boyfriend? Would your rules allow/encourage her to involve her boyfriend if she was taking service users out for a social evening? Or would you see it as parading her good fortune in front of Gerald, who does not, at this stage, have the skills to find a partner? Did your rules take any account of whether services users had previously been in hospital environments? Did you come down on the side of 'inclusion' or 'professional distance' in terms of staff revealing details of their private lives, or taking clients into their own homes? How did you balance the need for people in residential settings to give and receive physical and verbal expressions of affection, against the dangers of giving misleading signals? If a home is run by a husband and wife team, is the line between marital and professional relationships even harder for residents and staff to negotiate? Does this require special rules?

Section 2
Managing risk

You saw in Unit 19 that as well as managing and crossing boundaries, care workers also have to manage risk and anxiety about the work they do. They are often faced with ambiguous situations, as Bernice was in relation to Sue and her daughter. They may not have enough information or evidence to act on their concerns about individuals or families with whom they are in contact. Child and adult protection procedures help workers to contain this anxiety by clarifying what they should do and mandating them to share their concerns with their own agency and other agencies such as the police or social services. The lead agency for the protection of children and vulnerable adults is social services, so concerns which persist should be formally investigated or taken forward by them. The video-based activities which follow will help you develop confidence in managing the risk inherent in such situations.

2.1 Using the video

The video clips you are about to view are based on the BBC programme 'EastEnders'. They outline a developing situation in which Ruth, who works in an after-school club in Walford, becomes concerned about a boy called Adam. You will see that she faces a number of dilemmas and sorts them out in a rather *ad hoc* way. She has obviously not received training to safeguard the children she works with and neither has her manager, nor her friend the social worker, whom she calls in. It is evident that none of them have studied K100! So, don't take their actions as 'good practice' but as a basis for addressing the issues yourself. We are going to deal with Ruth's concerns in two parts, focusing first on recording and assessment and second on the need for appropriate consultation.

As you work through each of the 10 sequences you will meet activities. In writing your responses you will be making the kind of record which could be used as evidence if a case like this were to be dealt with formally under child or adult protection procedures. By the time you have completed all the activities you will have an impressive dossier of evidence of your competence in observation and assessment of risk, and of your ability to make use of guidelines in potentially serious situations such as this.

As you work through the activities you will also find two forms or 'job aids' which you could adapt for use in your own service. One is for recording and assessing difficult behaviour and the other is to help you map the avenues open to you if you are concerned about potential abuse.

Instructions for viewing

Now it's time to set to work. It will be better if you do *not* watch all of the Scene 10 extracts in one go, but sequence by sequence, as you would if you were really involved, undertaking each activity as you go.

2.2 Recording and assessment

As you saw in the case study about Bernice, it can be very difficult to be sure what is going on in private relationships, such as those between parents and children. If someone is being harmed an outsider will only get occasional glimpses of the problems and will have to make a judgment based on fragments of information. A picture has to be put together from signs such as bruises, difficult behaviour, disclosures or isolated incidents. Once a worker has an idea that a child or vulnerable adult may be at risk they also have to make a judgment about whether it is serious enough to warrant action. Ruth has to balance both of these uncertainties: she does not know *if* Adam is being abused and *how serious* it might be if this proves to be the case. She is unclear about what she means by abuse and revisits the issues about discipline which you considered in Unit 19.

View each scene and address each of the associated activities.

Activity 3   **Noting signs which might give cause for concern**

Allow about 5 minutes

View scene 10(a) of the video. In this scene Ruth notices bruises on Adam's arm and asks him how they occurred.

This is the first indication Ruth has that all is not well with Adam. Imagine you are Ruth, write a note for Adam's file about the bruises – a few lines will do but make sure you have noted where the bruises are, how you saw them, what questions you asked and what he said about them. Try to report the exchange you had with Adam using your own, and his own, words.

As a matter of information, bruises of different ages/colouring might signal a series of injuries rather than one fall or bump. Also if injuries are evident in soft tissue parts of the body such as the neck, underarms, stomach, genitals or inner thighs these are unlikely to have occurred as a result of a fall or accident.

Comment   My note for the file would include the following information:

- What was happening, i.e. I was calling him over for a story.

- What the bruises looked like and where exactly they were on his arm.

- That I had asked him about the 'marks on his arm' and he said 'Don't know'.

- That I asked if he could remember hurting his arm and he said 'No'.

- That I also asked him if the bruises still hurt and he said 'No'.

Activity 4   **Reference points**

Allow about 5 minutes   View scene 10(b). Ruth is talking to Mark, her partner, in the pub about whether this is normal. Over the next few days she initiates a discussion with her friend Gita and further discussion with Mark about discipline and what is normal.

In scene 10(a) you saw that Adam's bruises triggered Ruth's concern. In the absence of any other concerns, how worried would you be by these bruises? Do you agree with Mark that being 'black and blue' is normal for a boisterous seven year old?

(a)   On a scale of 1–10, where 10 is extremely worried and 1 is not at all worried, where would you stand?

1   10

|..|

(b)   Where do you think Ruth has positioned herself?

1   10

|..|

Comment   I think at this stage I would be less concerned than Ruth apparently is: I thought I might be a 6 and that Ruth had put herself as an 8. What did you think? I did think, however, that I would make a mental note to look out for bruises on Adam again.

This is a reprise of the debate on discipline in Unit 19. Remind yourself where you stand in relation to these issues. Are you with Gita who seems to be firmly against smacking or with Mark who doesn't think there is anything wrong with a 'clip around the ear'? Is hitting a child more serious than shouting? Ruth says her father 'had us so terrified we'd freeze at the sound of his voice'. Do you think there is a gender gap here?

If (and it is still unclear) Adam's bruises had been caused by being smacked or hit at home, do you think this would be 'abuse'? Would you think it was serious enough to do anything about it at this stage?

Activity 5   **Describing Adam's behaviour**

Allow about 5 minutes   View scene 10(c). It shows an incident between Ruth and Adam when he was painting. You will see Adam misbehaving again. Jot down a brief description of what happens as if you were Ruth putting a note on the file just before she goes home that evening.

Comment

You will remember that we looked at difficult behaviour in some detail in relation to Rosalie in Unit 18. Look back at Section 2 to remind yourself of some of the issues. Now look back at what you have written – what kinds of words have you used? Have you written that Adam was 'attention seeking' or just 'winding Ruth up' or did you use terms like 'challenging behaviour'?

Activity 6   **Assessing Adam's behaviour using an *abc* chart**

Allow about 15 minutes

Before you do this task you might want to revisit part 2, side 1 of Audio Cassette 5 where Anthea Sperlinger and Chad Botley discuss the general principles of assessment they applied to Rosalie's situation. Although they were considering difficult behaviour in the context of severe learning difficulties, what they say applies to everyone and might be useful here. They suggest using an *abc* chart as a framework for observation and you can practise using this in relation to Adam now. Look at the *abc* chart on the next page. See what you are being asked to record in detail to help work out the context and function of Adam's difficult behaviour.

Now rewind the video and watch scene 10(c) again. Observe exactly what happens. You will probably find you have to pause the video several times in order to concentrate on the exact sequence of events and use the blank *abc* chart (Job Aid 1 on p. 195) to record your comments (you might want to copy it so you can use it again). You may notice more than one thing happening under each heading. Include *all* your ideas as they could provide valuable clues to Adam's difficulties.

When you have completed the observation briefly review what you have written. What do you think the trigger was? And the consequences?

Comment   My abc chart is on page 196. I could not see a clear-cut 'cause' for Adam's behaviour from this one incident. I thought he might have disliked hearing his friend's work praised, or that he needed to get down from the table. Of course, if this were for real you would need to collect a lot of data to base your judgment on but what was your initial analysis?

Although there isn't a clear 'answer' in many situations like this I hope you found that this structured observation enabled you to begin a process of constructive assessment. This kind of approach can help to take the heat out of a situation, to remove some of the immediate emotional (and sometimes punitive) response and to gather information which will help everyone to analyse what is really going on.

Activity 7   **Playing by the rules**

Allow about 10 minutes

View scene 10(d). In this scene Ruth confronts Adam about playing with his ball in the games room.

Remembering your views from the previous clip, how well do you think Ruth dealt with this incident? In my opinion, she seemed nervous and unsure of herself, and did not deal well with the confrontation. What if the after-school club had rules to guide staff in this situation? What should they say?

Jot down your ideas of 'rules' which would be appropriate to guide staff in dealing with confrontations.

abc chart

Name: _____

Your service: _____

Date	Time	Setting Where was he/she and with whom? (Note which room, who with, and general atmosphere in the room/house/centre etc.)	Trigger What was going on beforehand? (Recall and note what happened just before the behaviour)	Behaviour What did he/she actually do? (Record details of the child's or adult's behaviour – what did they actually do?)	Outcome How did it stop/end? What happened afterwards? (Look to see what the consequences of the behaviour were)	How long did it last? (Note here how long the behaviour lasted)	Signature (Sign your name or initials)
		E.g. • lunch-time • dining room • sitting alone • everyone talking • music on softly (and what music) • with Tom and Ann	• what happened to the person? • what change(s) took place in the environment just before the behaviour? E.g. was the child or adult • given instructions • being left alone • being held or touched • involved in an activity • stopped from doing something • finishing their activity • having a toy, or other possession, taken away • aware that people had moved away • attention was given or withdrawn • people approached		• what happened to the child or adult? • what changed in their environment immediately following the incident? E.g. • activity arranged • food/drink given or offered • attention given • possession given • attention withdrawn • demands ceased • people approach • people go away • difficulty avoided		

Comments: (Note any other observations here)

(Adapted from Felce and McBrien, 1991)

Job Aid 1 *abc* chart

Name: _____

Your service: _____

Date	Time	Setting Where was he/she and with whom?	Trigger What was going on beforehand?	Behaviour What did he/she actually do?	Outcome How did it stop/end? What happened afterwards?	How long did it last?	Signature

Comments: (Note any other observations here)

(Adapted from Felce and McBrien, 1991)

Completed *abc* chart

Name: Adam

Your service: Walford After-school Club

Date	Time	Setting Where was he/she and with whom?	Trigger What was going on beforehand?	Behaviour What did he/she actually do?	Outcome How did it stop/end? What happened afterwards?	How long did it last?	Signature
23 Nov	4.35	Adam was sitting at the table with Patrick. It was quiet. It was before tea.	Patrick was painting quietly. Adam was 'printing' with his hands using water and wet paint. Ruth: (1) Challenged Adam about what he was doing and told him off a bit because he was printing not painting and then (2) said she liked Patrick's painting.	Splashed water over Patrick's painting, got down from the table and walked away.	Adam walked away from the table. Demands on him by Ruth to sit/paint quietly stopped. He was no longer in competition with Patrick.	2–3 mins	HB

Comments: (Note any other observations here)

(Adapted from Felce and McBrien, 1991)

Comment   Workers are likely to be judged on their ability to anticipate and diffuse situations as well as to observe, accurately describe and assess.

I think the rules should say something like this:

- Try to avoid directly confronting a child and instead try to distract him or her into a more appropriate activity.

Comment   - *Don't hit or shout.*

- If you have to intervene to stop him or her damaging property or hurting another child do so as calmly as possible, using the least amount of physical pressure; for example, take him or her quietly outside if you can or hold him or her until he or she has calmed down.

- Write a note about any accidents or incidents in which a child has to be removed from their usual play or activity.

Activity 8   **Setting the rules**

Allow about 10 minutes   View scene 10(e). Ruth is talking to Mrs Woods about how she disciplines Adam (she is also fishing for extra information but we will not dwell on that just yet).

Mrs Woods clearly has her own way of being firm with Adam at home and her own views about how to handle him. This raises the question of whether there is a need for an agreement with parents about how children are to be disciplined when they are at the after-school club. Should there be a written statement and, more importantly, *how* do you think such an agreement should be arrived at?

Think about how you would want these matters to be decided if you were:

(a)   a worker at the after-school club

(b)   a parent sending their child to the after-school club.

Comment   If a statement of rules were circulated by the club then parents could see what the ethos was before they send their children there. Agreeing to the rules could be a condition of enrolling their child; alternatively parents could be consulted through a parents' group or committee. Perhaps you felt that approaches should be agreed on an individual basis?

2.3 Consultation

Ruth is clearly concerned about Adam and is having trouble controlling his behaviour. She still doesn't have enough information to know how best to deal with the situation. What should she do? As we saw in Units 19 and 20 the key to child or adult protection is appropriate and timely consultation, and much of the work which has been done to develop policy has focused on setting out channels for communication within social services and with other agencies. Sharing concerns and information is mandatory in the case of children and advisable in the case of vulnerable adults. We have seen that Ruth is working through a process of logging her concerns about Adam and trying to reach a judgment about whether to pass these on to anyone else or to another agency. She comes to a point where there is:

- enough evidence to warrant concern that Adam has problems (bruises, difficult behaviour and demonstrating fear that he will be hit), and

- an awareness that if this were so it would be wrong not to intervene.

The next issue for Ruth is what she should do, having decided to act – to whom should she address her concerns. In the next series of video clips you will see how Ruth comes to a decision to take her concerns about Adam further and who she consults.

Activity 9   **Sharing concerns**

Allow about 5 minutes

View scene 10(f) in which Ruth is talking to Mark in the pub. He says 'Surely it can't be down to you to sort it out?' and he's right. Who should Ruth talk to first about her concerns?

Comment

I think she should share her worries with her manager in the first instance – what did you think? This is in fact what she does – she initiates a discussion with Tom, the senior worker at the after-school club.

Who would *you* share concerns with in your workplace or particular situation? Such a decision has a different feel to it if you are working within a formal structure such as Ruth's. If you were a concerned neighbour or relative you might find it more difficult to act if it involved contacting an agency like social services 'cold', without any prior contact with them.

Activity 10   **Sticking to your guns**

Allow about 10 minutes

View scene 10(g) in which Ruth talks to Tom, her senior worker.

Tom is not very helpful. When he says 'I don't see any evidence' and 'my sympathy is with his parents' he leaves Ruth, as a more junior member of staff, in an unenviable position.

What do you think he should have said and offered to do? Imagine he has a supervision session with Ruth. What advice could you offer him about how he should conduct the supervision session? List five 'pointers'.

1
2
3
4
5

Comment   It might have helped if he had made time to talk to Ruth in his office away from the children for a few minutes. I thought he should have:

1   listened to Ruth's concerns to find out the extent of her worries and the evidence she has observed; as it is, he dismisses them before he has heard what she has to say

2   asked her to keep a record of any injuries, hints or disclosures, or any further episodes of difficult behaviour

3   given her some concrete guidance on how to deal with Adam's behaviour if he is difficult with her again

4   told her what *not* to do, like not questioning Adam directly or gossiping to anyone

5   told her what kinds of things to look for which *would* give immediate rise to concern

6   agreed a date and time to jointly review the situation – this would ensure that Ruth is not left to shoulder the anxiety alone and give her a structure to work within, making it clear that he is taking responsibility as the senior worker.

Passing on concerns may not be enough. You may find that a senior worker or manager may not immediately share your view. Their response might be as a result of greater experience but could also be because they do not appreciate the gravity of the situation – they might put your concern down to your inexperience or doubt the values you have drawn on in making your judgment.

Activity 11   **Making it official**

Allow about 5 minutes

View scene 10(h) in which Ruth decides to contact her friend who is a social worker.

Rebuffed by her manager, Ruth is increasingly anxious about not sharing her concerns with someone more experienced. As Adrian in Unit 20 discovered, to take a complaint outside an establishment you have to know your way around the services and know 'what the next steps would be'. You have to know who you *can* and who you *should* go to. Ruth doesn't seem to have that local knowledge. We can only guess that she might be relatively new in the post and/or not have received proper induction training which would set out as a matter of course what channels to work through in the event of child protection concerns. So what you see in this clip is the result of her naivety and certainly not an example of good practice.

You will see that she and Mark (who is acting as her sounding board) are working on the basis of a number of misconceptions; see if you can jot them down as you watch the scene.

Comment   1   Ruth assumes that not being 'official' is important: she confuses the official nature of a report with the idea of Draconian action, perhaps influenced by the tabloid press who tend to sensationalise cases with talk of dawn raids accompanied by lurid details. She is expressing the same fear voiced by Bernice in Unit 19, that any action taken by social services would be more punitive than supportive. Mark echoes this by saying that social services would automatically create a 'mess'.

2   She seeks Nicola's help informally, outside the usual channels of communication within the framework of a local social services department, as if Nicola would or could act as a 'lone ranger' in

relation to child protection issues. She says to Mark that Nicola is a 'professional', as if this would enable and allow her to seek out further information and reach an appropriate decision without recourse to anyone else. (You will learn more about what it means to be a professional in Block 7.) She assumes that Nicola is a free agent and could act outside official procedures when in fact she would be bound to log such a request for help and certain to make any further enquiries through appropriate channels. It might be, for example, that Adam and his family are already known to social services; their GP might have parallel concerns; maybe a member of Adam's household is known to the police. So while Nicola as an individual could act as a better informed sounding board than Mark, she would soon have to start acting within her professional *role* not simply on the basis of her own expertise or personal knowledge.

2.4 Clarifying responsibilities

The legal position is that Ruth has a duty to report child protection concerns to her manager, and if he does not act on them, to social services directly. Under child protection procedures, all social services departments will consult in this kind of situation and it will be their decision when or whether to take action. So when Mark said to Ruth, 'it can't be down to you', he was quite right.

All agencies and professionals should:

- be alert to potential indicators of abuse or neglect

- be alert to the risks which individual abusers, or potential abusers, may pose to children

- share and help to analyse information so that an informed assessment can be made of the child's needs and circumstances

- contribute to whatever actions are needed to safeguard the child and promote his or her welfare

- regularly review the outcomes for the child against specific shared objectives, and

- work co-operatively with parents unless this is inconsistent with the need to ensure the child's safety.

(DofH, HO, DfEE, 1999, p. 11)

Activity 12   **Overstepping the mark**

Allow about 5 minutes   View scene 10(i) in which Ruth questions Adam, first through play and then directly, about more bruises.

What do you think of Ruth's actions in the light of the guidelines listed above? Did her actions fall within these guidelines, or go beyond them?

Comment   In this kind of structure Ruth's role is to be alert, pass on her concerns and contribute to whatever actions are necessary to safeguard the child and that is all. Her manager, Tom, is responsible for bringing any concerns regarding the children at the after-school club to the *official* notice of the local social services department via a formal report (not a phone call to Ruth's friend).

Ruth did discharge her main responsibility which was to be alert to the risk of abuse and to pass on her concerns. This she did by telling Tom that she was worried about Adam, but since he did not take her concerns seriously she was left 'holding the baby'. So Ruth also needed a reserve, a back-up, who would pass these concerns on to the local social services department and initiate a preliminary check on existing information and perhaps a low-level intervention such as a brief chat with Adam's mother. It is Ruth's lack of knowledge about how to access this level of support which leads her to take matters into her own hands.

Activity 13   Clarifying your own role

Allow about 30 minutes   If you are employed in a care setting it is worth considering at this stage where *you* fit in. Look at the box 'Job Aid 2' opposite and fill in the names of the people in your service or setting who would carry out these responsibilities. Ask if necessary.

Of course the most important thing is to be clear about the extent of your own responsibility, but you might also want to know who, in your area, allocates or investigates different kinds of cases, and who in the social services department has overall responsibility for child or adult protection.

If you want to expand this activity into one for your portfolio, obtain a copy of your local child or adult protection policy. Read it and note down the arrangements in your agency or local area in relation to either children or vulnerable adults. See if you can put names to roles, even if you have to do some detective work. This directory could then be annotated and put into your portfolio – it shows that you have a sound knowledge of the frameworks for addressing abuse in your local area.

Job Aid 2 – Responding to abuse in your area

When concerns arise about abuse of children or vulnerable adults, who in your agency/area is responsible for:

- **alerting:** that is, passing on a concern to a senior person either inside or, if necessary, outside the 'alerter's' own establishment or agency.

  ....

  Add details if there is a special form you should use or a special number to call:

  ....

- **reporting**: that is, making an official record of the alert and triggering action under the procedures.

  First person to contact:

  ....

  Reserve, in case they do not take it seriously or are implicated in the abuse:

  ....

- **allocating the case**: who will decide what level of response is appropriate and which agency is best placed to lead the investigation?

  ....

- **investigating and assessment**: who will co-ordinate the gathering of information and the conduct of interviews, consulting other appropriate agencies to establish matters of fact and deciding how best to protect the child or vulnerable adult?

  ....

- **calling a case conference**: what are the 'rules' about conducting a case conference to decide what to do next and who else needs to know to keep this person safe and protect others who might be at risk? There may be guidelines in your local policy setting out when, as well as by whom, this should be convened and about who should attend.

  Who calls the conference? ....

  ....

  Within what time scale? ....

  ....

  Who should attend? ....

  ....

- **monitoring**: who needs to contribute to the collection of information about abuse cases in your area? You may need to fill in particular forms, enter particular codes on to the computer and/or produce figures which will be collated into an annual report.

  What information should I record? ....

  ....

  Is there a special form or computer code? ....

  ....

  Is there a regular report produced on abuse in our area?...

  ....

You have now outlined the roles of the different people involved in responding to concerns about abuse. Passing on concerns through official channels is not designed to elicit a drastic or punitive response but one in which a balanced and holistic assessment is made, concerning a particular individual, family or establishment. If prior concerns have been raised these will be revisited and if evidence is needed it will be gathered using agreed procedures and safeguards. Making investigations alone in a 'Miss Marples' kind of way may make it more difficult to act appropriately later, for example through court proceedings, and it may jeopardise the possibility of taking action to keep someone safe or to restrict a perpetrator's access to vulnerable individuals.

2.5 Finishing the story

You have now completed the video activities. Like a Victorian novel I have spared you the worst excesses of the case, but here is the gist as it unfolded through the sequence of EastEnders episodes. Ruth's friend the social worker comes along and warns Ruth about overstepping the mark. She agrees to get involved herself 'unofficially' but then goes and talks to Adam's school, which is an extraordinary breach of confidentiality. Soon there is an irate Mrs Woods and an even more anxious Ruth, and eventually, in one of those 'making everything up over a cup of tea' scenes, which happen in soaps but unfortunately not in real life, Ruth and Mrs Woods become bosom pals!

 So what lay behind it all? If you view scene 10(j) you will find out.

So there you have it! Adam wasn't being abused but he did need help. A multidisciplinary assessment under 'official' child protection procedures might have arrived at the same conclusion with a lot fewer risks to all concerned. As it is, everyone in Walford has got to know about Adam's situation except social services. Ruth should be in deep trouble for overstepping the mark and breaching confidentiality. As for Mark, who shouldn't have been involved at all, he turned out to be the most sensible person in Walford and if I were in charge of Walford social services I think I just might headhunt him!

Ruth ends by saying that there are never any easy answers. You might well have some sympathy with her, but although the answers are rarely clear-cut, in this unit we have mapped out some clear channels for communication which Ruth has not accessed. You at least now know the importance of following agreed procedures when dealing with difficult behaviour, risk and potential abuse.

Having explored the Ruth and Adam situation so closely, it would be worth taking a quick look back at how Dev Sharma coped with assessing the risk to Arthur Durrant, following the 'knife incident' (Unit 4, pp. 202–206). You will see that he too was required to 'work in partnership' to assess risk and plan responses. Knowing what you do now, how well do you think he handled the situation? What else might he have done?

Section 3
Conclusion

In this unit you have explored the skills of managing boundaries and risk. You have seen that this involves being clear about your own and other people's roles and responsibilities, and working within agreed guidelines when you are relating to someone in a professional capacity. You have practised working within one framework for assessing difficult behaviour. When risk *is* identified, keeping accurate records and knowing your way around the system are both critical competences. Knowing who to share your concerns with and appreciating the limits of your role and expertise are also important.

Often services only get one chance to step in when an individual is being abused. Delicate judgments have to be made about when to confront the situation and about whether support or sanctions are most appropriate to the goal of protecting individuals and acting against exploiters or abusers. Good practice has evolved to ensure that no *one* person has to bear these responsibilities alone, but rather that clear and informed decisions are made together.

Managing risk is an unavoidable part of care work. This unit has allowed you to practise your skills and test your judgments, with all the luxury of hindsight and make-believe to shield you from the consequences of getting it wrong. In real life the only protection for vulnerable individuals and those who care for them comes in the form of shared working, agreed procedures and careful decision making.

This block has introduced you to these issues in relation to children and adults in families and residential care. You have learnt how to define abuse and to set a threshold beyond which you will intervene, using only formal channels of communication and decision making. You have also seen how intervention of this kind can support, as well as protect, individuals and families who are under pressure from personal and sexual violence and exploitation.

If you are keeping a K100 portfolio, your work from Unit 21 can be added now.

If you are building a VQ related portfolio, this is a good time to look at *Getting a Vocational Qualification*.

Section 4
Study skills

4.1 Reading graphs

You have already done enough work on number skills in Block 5 so, rather than give you more work here, we suggest you go back over the study skills boxes on reading tables and graphs in Unit 19 (on pp. 84–5 and pp. 89–90) and make sure you understand them. Part C of TMA 05 is based on Figure 2 of Offprint 25.

4.2 More thoughts about the exam

Now we return to the theme running through all the later skills units – preparing for the K100 exam.

Voices of experience

To begin you will listen to four people who have already taken Open University exams. You will hear what their feelings are about exams and how they try to get the best out of themselves at exam time.

Activity 14

Allow about 20 minutes

Coping with exams

First read the Media Notes so that you know who you will be listening to. Then write these headings down the side of a sheet of paper:

1   Feelings about exams
2   Ways of coping with anxiety
3   When to start revision
4   Strategies for revision
5   Tips.

You can make notes under these headings as you listen.

Then listen to side 1 of Audio Cassette 6.

When you have finished, note down any more points you think might be useful to remember. Then, under each of the five headings, summarise your conclusions from the discussion.

Comment

Here are some of the ideas you may have jotted down.

1   It helps to look the exam ogre straight in the eye. Then you know that this is what you are up against – this is as bad as it gets. So on the cassette each person was asked to think of their worst exam experiences. For all of them exams tend to be something of an ordeal. But all felt they had learnt to come to terms with the pressures by taking control of the revision process.

2   Like most people, these students felt pretty wound up over the final weeks and days and especially on exam day. However, they found they were able to settle down once the exam started. Some mentioned taking deep breaths at the start and reading the paper very carefully to get themselves focused. In her first exam Gwyneth

got into a flap, knocking over her drink, but her second exam she said she quite 'enjoyed'.

3   These students all started their revision at least a month before the exam. Three started in August. (It's worth pointing out, though, that all three were studying 30-point courses, whereas K100 is twice that size and continues three weeks into September.) Perhaps Jenny's experience of starting her D103 revision in September is a more realistic guide. You should be starting K100 Unit 28 mid-way through September (a short unit designed to help with your revision). That seems a reasonable target date to be swinging into a full-scale attack on revision. You might begin some preliminary sorting out and dipping back into things before then, but don't let worries about the exam spoil the last part of the course for you. With all the key points boxes, K100 is a fairly straightforward course to revise. You should be able to complete a pretty thorough review in two or three weeks.

4   As you heard in the discussion, revision is not just a dreary plod through the course a second time. It should be much more active and creative than that. One very strong message which comes through is the importance of organisation and planning. After the interview each of the four was asked to write down their three top tips for revision. Of the 12 tips, eight related to organisation and planning.

5   Towards the end of the discussion Julie offered some general tips: don't panic, enjoy the course, but don't leave everything to the last minute, and set about your revision in a planned, methodical way – then you'll start to feel more comfortable and confident. Here are some of the tips the others wrote down after the discussion.
   • Go through past exam papers and look at questions. Look at course material related to the questions. Decide on your strengths and weaknesses and work on the weaknesses.
   • Go through your notes and make new notes.
   • Brainstorm the main titles of the course and do a 'mind map' – it will be a useful guide.

Study skills: Making yourself look ahead

Has listening to the discussion helped to put the K100 exam into perspective? Has it made the exam seem more 'real' and in a sense 'ordinary' – something that will just happen one day and then be over and part of your past, not a vague and mysterious threat looming in the distance? The clearest message that comes from what these students said is the importance of thinking ahead well before the exam – not leaving things to the last minute, when it is too late to get yourself properly organised. As Gwyneth, who got into such difficulties first time, wrote, 'Don't cram – always make sure you have enough time for everything.'

Exam anxiety

Yet however 'rational' and organised you manage to be about the exam, you are likely to experience some anxiety. As you read in Section 1 of Chapter 7 of *The Good Study Guide*, exams put you under pressure. This has both good and bad effects. Stress supplies the energy and motivation to push you to peak performances and bring out your true ability. But if stress isn't controlled and channelled it can also lead to a build-up of anxiety, to a point where it begins to have bad effects both on your exam performance and on you.

Bad effects of anxiety

It's important to look at the common effects of anxiety, so that you can recognise them and work out ways of overcoming them.

Avoidance: putting off thinking about the exam. 'Avoidance' is a common psychological response to uncomfortable situations. You find ways of absorbing your mind with other things (which normally scarcely interest you at all). Deep down you know that putting off facing up to the challenge is making the situation worse. But the worse the situation gets, the greater your incentive to avoid thinking about it. You become ever more creative at finding other 'very important' things to attend to – it's a vicious circle. Then you end up, two days before the exam, facing reality at last but in a complete panic and with no hope of doing yourself justice.

Difficulty with concentration: getting into a state of agitation such that you can't stay focused on anything. You stop frequently to worry about how little time is left and how much you still have to cover; you blame yourself for what you haven't done; you dither and switch from one thing to another, so that you never dwell for long enough to really fix anything in your mind – in short, you spend a lot of time not achieving very much.

Distorted perception and poor judgment: getting the exam out of proportion, so that it seems a life or death struggle; failing to recognise how much you have learnt during the year; feeling that you must cover every last bit of the course, instead of playing to your strengths; thinking you should memorise long lists of facts; hoping that putting most of your time into one really good answer will offset other weaker answers; thinking the exam will be designed to catch you out, instead of recognising that it is just about what you've read in the course. In other words you get blown off course by all those myths you read about in Chapter 7 of *The Good Study Guide*.

Distress: then there is the miserable feeling itself; doubting that all your investment in K100 is worth while; wishing you were a different person; losing sleep; being a gloomy burden to those around you.

Loss of function: not being able to do things that you normally do perfectly easily. (Recently, an acquaintance failed her driving test. The first thing she was asked to do was reverse round a corner and she completely forgot what to do, although she had never had trouble with the manoeuvre before.) You can read more about this in Section 5.2, 'Changes to your mental powers', in Chapter 7 of *The Good Study Guide*. Even though you don't yet need to plan your final couple of days before the exam, read Sections 5.2 to 5.5 now. They will give you a sense of why it is so helpful to start preparing early – and how you can organise your work to take advantage of the effects that anxiety is likely to have on you.

These, then, are some of the ways anxiety can undermine your work towards the exam. What is more, anxiety has a tendency to feed off itself, as Figure 1 shows.

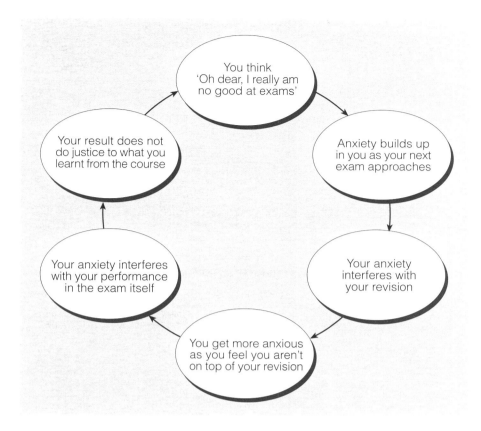

Figure 1
The vicious circle of anxiety

Obviously, you want to break out of this vicious circle if you can, or better still avoid getting into it. But how?

Keeping anxiety under control

Planning and organisation. The main way our four students tackled anxiety was by starting preparations early, before tensions had begun to build up. They then kept themselves busy with carefully organised preparations until the exam. This helps to reduce anxiety through:

- redirecting nervous energy into productive channels

- reassuring you that your prospects of success are improving hour by hour, as you revise

- giving a feeling of being in control of anxiety rather than driven by it.

Avoiding avoidance. It is important to work out ways of cutting through your own avoidance strategies. One way is to set yourself short, undemanding tasks to start with (like sorting out your course materials). Jenny said she found listening again to some of the audio cassettes a non-taxing way of 'getting into it'. Once you get yourself started on *any* exam-relevant task, you begin to break the cycle of avoidance – preventing the build-up of a deep-seated sense of not being able to cope.

Talking yourself down. Another line of attack is to keep reminding yourself what the real priorities of life are so that you maintain a sense of proportion. Of course exams are important, but they are not the most important things in life. In any case, taking them too seriously is counter-productive. You end up doing badly because you are so concerned to do well. Keep glancing back at the early parts of Chapter 7 of *The Good Study Guide*, if it helps.

Talking to other people. Probably the best way of getting exams in proportion is talking to other people, especially when you are studying in isolation most of the time. It's easy to think you are the only person who is having difficulties. Julie says she runs up a huge phone bill just before exams, talking to a friend. Other people find meeting fellow students at tutorials reassuring. Sometimes family members can help. If you have tried all these and still feel anxious, have a talk with your tutor.

Relaxation techniques. There are many ways of relaxing yourself when you are stressed: going for walks, playing sports, evenings out with friends, yoga, listening to relaxation cassettes. One very useful technique is to sit still and upright, and breathe deeply for a minute or two. You need to find out what works for you. It is worth getting a leaflet from your doctor, or browsing along the shelves of a bookshop or library, to give yourself some new ideas to try out.

Medical help. Some people find that none of these approaches is enough in itself. If you are in any doubt as to whether you can stay on top of your exam nerves, consult your doctor. Don't just suffer in isolation. After putting so many hours of work into the course, you don't want to run the risk of letting yourself down in the exam. Make sure you get the help you need.

Study skills: Beating exam anxiety

Most of us feel anxious before exams. So it is important to:

- be aware of effects that anxiety can have on you as you prepare for and take the exam

- work out ways of overcoming anxiety.

Anxiety can have a variety of effects, which people cope with in different ways. But in essence it comes down to:

- facing up to the exam

- getting clear in your mind *what* you need to do and *how* you will go about it

- talking to other people

- getting working (instead of worrying).

Don't let anxiety get you down. As you read in Unit 17, this is your course. You have paid for the exam. Get what *you* need from it. Don't let it get the upper hand. Use the tension to get the best out of yourself.

So what can you begin to do now, nearly three months away from the exam? I suggest that one thing is to take a close look at the specimen exam paper and another is to begin to sketch out a revision timetable.

Reviewing the specimen exam paper

You will have received a specimen exam paper.

Activity 15   **The specimen exam paper**

Allow about 20 minutes   Read carefully through your specimen exam paper, including all the instructions.

(a)   *Structure of the paper.* Notice that the exam is in three parts.

   (i)   What does this mean in terms of how you spend your time in the exam?

   (ii)   What does it suggest in terms of what you need to revise?

(b)   Do the questions look familiar? Can you see what kind of answers are needed?

(c)   Read questions 1 to 5 carefully. Underline key words. (Use pencil so that you can change your mind later.)

(d)   How does looking at the questions make you feel?

Comment   (a)   Structure of the exam paper

   (i)   You have to answer three questions in three hours. All questions are worth the same number of marks. So you should spend roughly an hour on each of your three questions.

   (ii)   You have to choose one question from each of the three parts of the paper. The questions in Part I are from Blocks 1, 2 and 3 of the course. The questions in Part II are from Blocks 4, 5 and 6. The questions in Part III are either directly from Block 7 or are about the course as a whole. **This means that you don't need to revise the whole course in detail for the exam.** You *must* revise Block 7, but you could get away with revising just one block out of the first three and one from the next three. However, that would leave you without any choice. So, just in case there is a question which does not suit you, it is safer to have a 'back-up' block for each of Parts I and II. In other words a reasonable revision strategy is to **focus your revision on Block 7, plus two blocks out of the first three, and two blocks out of the next three.**

(b)   The general form of the questions ought to look pretty familiar. They are very similar to the questions asked in the TMAs. Obviously you can't write anything like such a long answer when you only have an hour. But the basic principles are the same, so you should approach your answers in the same way you approach TMAs.

(c)   You haven't done your studies for questions 6 to 9 yet, but questions 1 to 5 ought to have rung a few bells for you as you did your underlining. Was it obvious to you that question 1 was on Block 1, question 2 on Block 2, and so on? Don't worry if you can't think of all that you might want to put into your answers. The main point is to reassure yourself that you can actually make sense of the questions and that you can see how the questions link to the blocks. Once you start to revise, the key ideas in the blocks will start to come back to you.

(d)   Did you find the first sight of the exam paper a bit nerve-wracking? Lots of people say they do. A very common first reaction is to think you can't make any sense of the questions at all. But as you underline key words you begin to see that the questions are more or less what you would expect. As you work on the paper during your revision, and develop plans for tackling it, the general structure and format will become a lot more familiar and less daunting.

A three-part paper

The idea behind having three parts to the exam is quite straightforward. Parts I and II give you an incentive to consolidate your understanding, both of the early blocks of the course and of the later blocks. But we also wanted to give you a chance to show how your wider understanding of care has developed during the year, so Part III gives you that opportunity. At the same time Part III is the only assessment for Block 7. (There is no TMA for Block 7, to avoid putting additional pressures on you in the last stages of the course.) This works out well because Block 7 takes a broad view of care issues and aims to bring the course together. One of the Part III questions will link to Unit 26 and another to Unit 27. The third question will be a more general one on a broad issue running through the course. Unit 28 gives you help in looking at the course this way.

You can write very good answers in Parts I and II simply by focusing on the block that corresponds to the question number. If it turns out that you are also able to draw on what you have learnt in other blocks, that may make an answer even better. But let this come to you, if it happens. Don't feel you have to strive for cross-block connections. Keep your sights on doing justice to what you know of the particular block. Part III is where you have the chance to write more broadly, bringing together ideas from across the course.

What is a good exam answer?

The basic principles of the exam questions are much the same as for TMAs, although obviously answers are shorter and not as detailed as when you have your books around you. To get a clearer picture of what examiners look for in answers turn now to *The Good Study Guide* and read Section 3 of Chapter 7.

Study skills: Squaring up to the exam paper

As you see, there is no great mystery about the exam paper. You just write three answers of the kind that you have been writing all through the course, but shorter. The links between the questions and the course are quite clear and you have plenty of choice over what parts of the course to write about. Perhaps you felt a bit reluctant as you began exploring the specimen paper, but now you have had a good look you can see that it's pretty straightforward.

Drawing up a rough time plan

For now, all that remains is to begin to think about when you will start your revision. The students on the cassette were very clear about the advantages of doing this. Here are some of the 'key tips' they wrote down:

* time management – give yourself plenty of time
* decide when you are going to start revision and what time you can set aside for it
* plan revision before you start
* do a timetable of how/when/where you should be, so that you can make sure you have covered all the areas of the course.

You don't need to do a detailed plan yet, just a general sketch of the overall timescale and when you think you will get your best opportunities for revision. More detailed planning will be discussed in Unit 28.

Activity 16

Allow about 15 minutes

Planning your revision

Draw a chart showing the next 12 weeks or so up to the exam (a 12 x 7 grid, with days along one edge and weeks along the other) or use a calendar or diary. Write in holidays and any other major disruptions you anticipate. Put the units you have not read yet in the weeks you hope to study them. Fill in TMAs and tutorials and the date of the exam. Now sketch in where you think your main chunks of exam preparation time will come.

Looking at what you have marked as preparation time and thinking about how much time you normally manage to set aside for studying per week, estimate how many hours overall you hope to be able to find for revision.

Comment

Obviously, the amount of time you can find for revision depends on your circumstances. There is no absolute requirement. You make the best use you can of the time you have available. The point of making an estimate now is so that you can begin to think of revision in realistic terms. It's no good hoping that you will somehow find time to re-read the whole course in detail. Once you can see roughly what time you have, you can divide it up between blocks and between different kinds of revision activity. Then you won't just start plodding through from Unit 1 and find that you've only reached half-way through the course when the exam is upon you. Your time is too precious to use haphazardly – you need to allocate it strategically.

4.3 Writing skills: argument and evidence

Now we return to your essay-writing skills to look at one of the trickiest aspects of writing at degree level: developing an argument and drawing on evidence. The reason you write essays for K100 is to help you make the ideas and information you have been studying part of your own mental apparatus – not just something you have read about, but something you can use for yourself. You do this by weaving them together in an argument, written in a way that is convincing to a reader.

Study skills: Learning by arguing

'Speaking' your own thoughts (based on ideas you have been reading about) in the form of written sentences which lead logically from one to the next is perhaps the deepest form of learning on this kind of course. That is why your tutor gives attention to whether your arguments make sense and are backed up by evidence. It is a way of helping you to get to the heart of learning the course. To remind yourself what is meant by 'a coherent argument', quickly re-read Sections 3.4 and 3.5 of Chapter 5 of *The Good Study Guide*.

Grasping the general idea of what 'arguing a case' means is one thing. Being able to do it well is another. It involves developing a range of subtle insights and skills. These are explored in Chapter 6 of *The Good Study Guide*.

Activity 17   **Developing a convincing argument**

Allow about 1 hour   (a)   Write 'Developing a convincing argument' at the head of a sheet of
          paper. Then read Section 5 of Chapter 6 of *The Good Study Guide*.
                   As you read, write the sub-headings, sub-sub-headings and the key
                   points (in brief) down the left-hand side of the sheet.

              (b)   You have written five essays for K100 (including TMA 07), and had
                   comments back from your tutor. Have you looked back over them
                   recently to see how your writing has developed and whether there
                   are any patterns and themes in the comments your tutor has made?
                   Find your essays now and look through the comments written on
                   them. Have your sheet of paper beside you and check whether any
                   of the comments relate to the sub-headings. Where they do, write the
                   TMA number against the heading, along with a brief note of the
                   comment. Also, check whether your tutor's points make sense to you
                   in the light of what you have just read in *The Good Study Guide*.

              (c)   When you have finished, look back over your page of notes and
                   review your progress in writing convincing arguments. Make a quick
                   note of anything to look out for when writing TMA 05.

Comment   How much you were able to write on your page depends, of course, on
            how your essay writing is developing and on your tutor's way of
            commenting. But whether you found a lot of links or just a few, this kind of
            'reflective' exercise is very useful. It is always worth setting your own
            experience alongside the advice offered in *The Good Study Guide*. In this
            case it may have helped to draw together a range of points made by your
            tutor over several months. Or it may have shown that you are doing well
            with your arguments and that you should just carry on developing along
            the same lines.

End of block assignment

> Now you have another chance to develop your skills of arguing as
> you write TMA 05. Your review of your previous essays should
> help here.

> **Study skills: Study diary**
>
> Just a reminder to bring your study diary up to date, to help you
> think ahead to Block 6.

Section 5
Linking K100 studies to professional training

Healthcare connections

Boundaries

Marie, the new healthcare assistant had to cross deeply-rooted social boundaries when giving intimate care. Similarly Lawler (Reader Chapter 26) describes the 'social vacuum' in which nurses work. By breaching the normal boundaries, healthcare workers make both their patients and themselves vulnerable; new boundaries must quickly be established. Workers need written guidelines and training to support them in establishing appropriate boundaries and to guide them when they encounter disturbing situations (Offprint 24).

Protection and control

Developing codes of good practice for managing challenging behaviour (Rosalie) and protecting people who lack the skills to protect themselves (Tony) highlights the need for healthcare workers to strike a balance between control and protection of vulnerable people and respecting their rights.

Abuse

Healthcare workers must be able to recognise potentially abusive situations and be alert to signs of abuse, so they can take appropriate steps to stop it. They must also be aware of their own potential to abuse when they work with vulnerable patients. Unit 19 discusses the ambiguities of the term abuse and suggests how the seriousness of a potentially abusive act or abusive relationship could be judged. It also identifies different forms of abuse.

Power and vulnerability

Unit 20 uses the case study of Jenny, Geoff and Abby to explore perceptions and the reality of women's mental health after childbirth, and problems that can arise through the power of healthcare workers to place diagnostic labels on people. It is important that care workers of all kinds recognise the vulnerability of service users, particularly when their mental state is in question. The unit discusses various diagnostic tools and standards, which help prevent arbitrary diagnoses and highlight the importance of evidence-based practice (see the boxes on pp. 134 and 135). Healthcare interventions show ways community psychiatric nurses, health visitors and other members of the multiprofessional team need to work together and in partnership with patients within holistic and medical model approaches to support women and their families.

Knowing when and how to intervene

Like other care workers, such as Ruth (Unit 21), healthcare workers have to manage risks, respect boundaries and work within their competences. When they suspect abuse they need to know the right channels to gain support from management and colleagues. They also need to make careful observations and keep systematic records (e.g. abc chart) – key skills which healthcare workers use as part of their daily routine.

Social work connections

Intimate care

Social workers working in residential settings often have to break the taboos of normal social relationships by being involved in such tasks as intimate care. The case study of Marie in Unit 18 re-emphasises the importance of professional boundaries and the need for good training and supervision.

Managing challenging behaviour

Social workers also often work with challenging behaviour. Whether working with adolescents or people with learning difficulties, social workers must make fine judgments between protecting a person (or people around the person) and violating that person's human rights. While residential social workers are directly involved in these decisions, field social workers and care managers often become involved as advocates on behalf of vulnerable service users, ensuring that they do not suffer mistreatment.

Definitions of abuse

'Drawing the line' as to what constitutes abuse can be a difficult decision. In the Unit 19 discussion of the Children Act 1989 we see how social workers working with children have to decide whether a child is suffering 'significant harm'. Such harm can take various forms including physical, sexual, emotional and neglect (and with adults financial exploitation).

Child protection

This area of social work activity receives a lot of public attention. Unit 19 highlights society's ambivalence towards the rights of children through exploring the debate over smacking. Social workers have to make complex decisions in this area, taking into account differing attitudes towards parenting, including those based on cultural difference. Unit 19 examines the *Messages from Research* which sought to move the focus of child protection assessments away from incidents to a more holistic perspective on children's needs. This thinking is reflected in the *Framework for the Assessment of Children in Need and their Families.*

Inter-agency work

The case study of Jenny, Geoff and Abby in Unit 20 begins by showing how activating professional support is not always easy. (In this case a member of the extended family had to intervene.) But then it illustrates well how social workers work within a network of professionals to support people at vulnerable points in their lives. You saw how the Department of Health guidance *Working Together to Safeguard Children* (1999) places requirements on all agencies including social services. The case shows the shift in thinking about how decisions are made as to whether a child needs protection. Although Abby was in a vulnerable position, rather than simply implement child protection procedures, a more appropriate response was achieved through the assistance of professionals from different agencies, such as the health visitor.

Rights and responsibilities

Social workers assessing whether a service user is suffering abuse must be prepared to hear their voices (including children's). However they must also recognise the rights of others. The example of Ruth from EastEnders captures the dilemmas that can arise: how through her concern for Adam she developed a prejudiced attitude towards Adam's family. The social worker, in particular, had no right to carry out secret checks. Infringing someone's right to confidentiality is a serious breach of ethical responsibilities.

Evidence-based practice

Unit 20 looks at the concept of evidence-based practice. This is now a very influential idea across the public services and is at the heart of many of the reforms within social work. However you saw that when professionals discuss competing ideas about interventions in the case of someone with mental illhealth, what is considered valid evidence may be contested. Through the establishment of the *Social Care Institute of Excellence,* different forms of evidence will continue to be part of the debate about the future of social work.

Children and young people: connections
Boundaries

The Unit 18 discussion of boundaries of intimacy and how to establish professional distance is very relevant to anyone providing care to children and young people. Personal care is often needed, which gives rise to difficult dilemmas for workers and those they care for.

Advocacy

Unit 18 also discusses advocacy in the context of care for a young man (Tony) considered to be at risk of harming himself. It explores the kinds of issues involved when decisions are made about when and how to intervene in the life of a young person.

Professional discourses

Another Unit 18 case study involves Rosalie, a young person with learning difficulties living in a residential unit. You saw how differing interpretations of her behaviour were embedded in the language carers used when talking about her – and how competing 'professional discourses' develop, each with their own language for describing and explaining people, situations and issues. Anyone working with children and young people needs a knowledge of multidisciplinary working and of the differences between discourses developed within different care disciplines.

Challenging behaviour

Rosalie's case also led to discussion about working with challenging behaviour; the need for clear codes of practice and detailed guidance on how to respond to particularly challenging issues; and the need for working environments which allow staff to express their views and concerns.

Institutional abuse

Unit 18 also introduced the case of the pindown scandal in Staffordshire to examine the evolution and sustaining of restrictive and punitive measures, leading to institutional abuse of children and young people.

Safeguarding children

In Unit 19 you explored the meaning and implications of the term 'abuse' through the complex debate associated with smacking. Safeguarding children was further explored in Unit 21, through the 'Ruth and Adam' video activities, looking at when and how to intervene. Clear roles and responsibilities are essential when child abuse is suspected, as are the development of skilled judgment, the managing of professional boundaries and the managing of risk. These have all been highlighted as features of failure in safeguarding systems in successive child abuse inquiries.

References

Craft, A. and Brown, H. (1994) 'Personal relationships and sexuality: the staff role' in Craft, A. (ed.) *Practice Issues in Sexuality and Learning Disabilities*, Routledge, London, pp. 1–22.

Department of Health, Home Office, Department for Education and Employment (1999), *Working Together to Safeguard Children*, The Stationery Office, London.

Felce, D. and McBrien, J. (1991) *Challenging Behaviour and Severe Learning Difficulties*, First Draft Publications, BILD, Kidderminster.

The Training Organisation for the Personal Social Services (TOPSS) (1999) *A summary of the S/NVQ awards in Care, Caring for Children and Young People, Diagnostic and Therapeutic Support and Promoting Independence*, TOPSS.

Acknowledgements

Grateful acknowledgement is made to the following sources for permission to reproduce material in this unit:

Illustrations

Pp. 191, 198 and 200: BBC.